The Hall Ball

The Hall Ball

*One Fan's Journey
to Unite Cooperstown Immortals
with a Single Baseball*

RALPH CARHART

Foreword by John Thorn

McFarland & Company, Inc., Publishers
Jefferson, North Carolina

LIBRARY OF CONGRESS CATALOGUING-IN-PUBLICATION DATA

Names: Carhart, Ralph, 1972– author.
Title: The Hall ball : one fan's journey to unite Cooperstown
immortals with a single baseball / Ralph Carhart.
Description: Jefferson, NC : McFarland & Company, Inc.,
Publishers, 2020. | Includes index.
Identifiers: LCCN 2020012184 | ISBN 9781476679648 (paperback : acid free paper) ∞
ISBN 9781476637938 (ebook)
Subjects: LCSH: Baseball—United States. | Baseball players—United States. |
National Baseball Hall of Fame and Museum. | Crowdsourcing—United
States. | Carhart, Ralph, 1972– —Travel—United States.
Classification: LCC GV863.A1 C367 2020 | DDC 796.3570973—dc23
LC record available at https://lccn.loc.gov/2020012184
BRITISH LIBRARY CATALOGUING DATA ARE AVAILABLE

ISBN (print) 978-1-4766-7964-8
ISBN (ebook) 978-1-4766-3793-8

Front cover images © 2020 Shutterstock

Printed in the United States of America

*McFarland & Company, Inc., Publishers
Box 611, Jefferson, North Carolina 28640
www.mcfarlandpub.com*

To Anna.
There are many people
who helped me along this path,
but you are the only one
to whom this project belongs
as much as it does to me.
You found the pieces
and stood by me
as I put them together.

And to Bob.
I never would have even started
if it weren't for you.
Thanks, Pop.

Table of Contents

***Between pages 98 and 99 are 8 color plates
containing 16 photographs***

Acknowledgments

It would be logistically impossible to complete a journey such as this on my own. Along the way, I received multiple kinds of support from many people, and I would be remiss not to thank them for what they have done. As The Hall Ball developed, it became a crowd-sourced artifact, an early wish I had for the project. Each of the people named below had a role in making it possible and, in my mind, are co-creators of the project.

The following individuals assisted by providing me access to the living players: Brian Coppola with JP Sports and Rock Solid Promotions; Mollie Ann Bracigliano, Jared Salvato, and Reggie Halloway with MAB Celebrity Services; Brendan Herlihy, Eric Levy, George De Jesus, and Justin Petrie with Steiner Sports; Sean Morgan and Lauren Graziano with Fanatics Authentic. A special thank you to Bobby Brett who, besides connecting me with his brother, also provided me with great seats to a memorable Spring Training game. Thank you to two sympathetic groundskeepers who gave me on-field access to stage a pair of symbolic photos: Quentin Hasak at Doubleday Field in Cooperstown and Brandon Koehnke, head groundskeeper for the Cleveland Indians at Progressive Field. Gratitude to Coach Adam Leavitt of the Cal Lutheran Kingsmen, who kindly opened the gates to Sparky Anderson Field for us, despite being on his way to a game. I also want to give a nod to Joe Pelc with the Illinois Office of Mines and Minerals. It was he who dug up the old maps and helped me locate the mine shaft that served as the location for the photo of Al Barlick.

The Hall Ball started to come to the public consciousness with the creation of the website. The site's existence will always owe a debt to EJ Garr and Lisa Iannucci, with Sportspalooza Radio. EJ and Lisa heard me give a pitch about the ball on a local radio broadcast and became the project's first benefactors, setting up the site and having me as a guest on their show multiple times. I also wish to thank the following people who helped me write some of the over–300 original player biographies that appear on the site: Alan Bard, Brian Beebe, Arthur Boodaghian, EJ Garr, Jeff Greenberg, Tony Milito, Marty & Tisha Peronto, Michael Rinehart, Jr., Steve Rosenberg, and Steve Smith.

A few years into the project, I set up a gofundme to try and defray some of the staggering costs of attempting such a feat. The following individuals contributed economic assistance to help make my financial burden a little less painful: Marjorie Adams, Dan Adamsky, Julia & Ralph Carhart (thanks Mom and Dad!), Randy Cooper, Bill Cornell, Dennis Degenhardt, George Dougherty, Douglas Filomena, Alana Jacoby, Joe Jelden, Beth LaValle, Dakin Lecakes, Daniel Lipton, Sophia McGee, Amelia J. Michael, Laurie & Bob Peterson, Steve Rosenberg, Elizabeth Rothman, Brian Sattinger, John Sawicki, Mel Schmittroth, John Thorn, Marlene Vogelsang, and John Wakelin. An extra special thanks to Peg Samuels, whose very generous donation paid for the rental car for the entire time we were in Hawaii.

I also received support in the guise of a place for an itinerant traveler to lay his head without having to always pay for hotels. The following people allowed me to spend at least one night in their home while I made my way across the country: Rebecca Ash, the Brennans (Meredith, David, Jack and Abigail), Joe Blodgett & Joey Kotfica, Elizabeth Rothman, and Robert Tholkes.

The following people accompanied me on my travels, with some of them even assisting in a little harmless breaking and entering: Rebecca Ash, Meredith Brennan, Reynaldo Cruz Diaz, Martín Dihigo, Jr., Casey Drane, Jeff Greenberg, Sam Hershman, Jess Hoffman, Ken Kerbs, Corey Kilgannon, Jeremy Krock, Dakin Lecakes, Amelia J. Michael, Bob Peterson, Yasel Porto, Jeremy Rishe, Steve Rosenberg, Phil Ross, Mel Schmittroth, Orion Schmittroth, Xavier Schmittroth, Ismael Sene, Brook Silva-Braga, Loren Studley, Robert Tholkes, and Bryan Thomas. An extra shout-out to all the Cubabalistas, especially Clem Paredes, Kit and Pepito Krieger, and Larry Phillips. Without them the trip to Cruces, and the chance to visit the grave of Martín Dihigo with his charming son by my side, would not have been possible.

I must give deepest thanks to Tony Milito. His passion for The Hall Ball rivaled my own. He donated money, wrote bios for the website, and was my most vocal Facebook cheerleader. It was he who wrote the initial letter that brought the project to the attention of the *New York Times*. It cannot be overstated just how influential the *Times* article was with regard to me finishing the project. Tony also took the photographs of Bill Mazeroski and Red Schoendienst, traveling on his own dime both times.

A handful of the photos were taken by others, and I wish to give them a special thanks for their integral role in the completion of the project, as well as agreeing to allow their images to appear in this book. Besides Tony, I also want to thank Mark and Jackson Bell for the photo of Henry Aaron, Sean Morgan for the picture of Mike Schmidt, and Justin Petrie for taking the shot of Trevor Hoffman.

The A. Bartlett Giamatti Research Center at the Baseball Hall of Fame is a historian's dream, holding a mammoth collection of documentation dating back over the life of the game. It takes a special combination of librarian and baseball trivia whiz to work behind the desk there, and their capable team served me well. Led by the indefatigable Jim Gates, and assisted by Cassidy Lent, Hanna Soltys, and Emily Perdue, they spent a week bringing me folder after folder as I prepared this text. Their patience with my barrage of requests will be forever remembered.

Regarding sources, I feel a need to highlight three websites in particular. The first is Protoball.org. I speak of Protoball more in the book, but their database of pre-professional games was my definitive source for finding the earliest contests that have been recorded for each state. Because the information at Protoball is input by users, similar to Wikipedia, it admittedly has the potential for error. However, some of the leading historians of the 19th-century game have contributed, including Larry McCray (founder of the site), Peter Morris, Bruce Allardice, Richard Hershberger, and Craig Waff. They have input thousands of early games from across the country, and while it is always possible that one of them will find an earlier example of game play, I feel confident in what they have found so far.

I also wish to give a nod to Baseball-Reference.com and the SABR Bioproject. B-R is considered by many to be the definitive source for player statistics, as well as team statistical histories, including the nicknames for clubs that changed so frequently during baseball's early days. I also used B-R to find out about minor league franchises, where players went to college, where they were born and, using the site's clever "Oracle" feature, how different players were connected.

The Bioproject, which can be found at sabr.org/bioproject, is another crowdsourced enterprise. Hundreds of members of the Society for American Baseball Research have teamed together to attempt to write short biographies of every person who has ever played, managed, owned, umpired, scouted for, coached, or otherwise been involved in professional baseball. I have contributed a few biographies myself, and I can say that after the initial research is done by the authors, each story is thoroughly fact-checked by SABR's top-notch editors. This collective effort has been invaluable to me.

I must also remember Gary Ashwill and his people at the Negro League Database, hosted by Seamheads.com, which contains the largest online collection of Negro League stats. Because coverage of Negro League games was often limited to the nation's black newspapers, there is much less documentation available. Gary and his small team of dedicated researchers have done an incredible job of compiling what currently stands as the most comprehensive resource for students of this field.

The two-volume masterwork by Peter Morris entitled *A Game of Inches: The Stories Behind the Innovations That Shaped Baseball*, was invaluable to me in fact-checking the myths that are littered throughout the history of the game. The books are, in my opinion, required reading for any fan of baseball and a necessary part of any researcher's collection. Chances are, if I mention someone being the "first" to do something in the game's history, that fact was verified by the thorough research of Morris.

Without the research and passion of fellow grave hunter and baseball fanatic Stew Thornley, the hundreds of hours I spent wandering around cemeteries likely would have been closer to thousands. His website, which provides GPS coordinates and photographs that served as profoundly helpful visual markers on my hunt, can be found at stewthornley.net/halloffamegraves.html.

A warm thanks needs to go to John Thorn. Not only did he kindly agree to take time out of his busy schedule to write the foreword to this book, but his encouragement throughout the project was a beacon during those times when I was filled with doubt. It is easy to see

The Hall Ball as the Quixotic quest of a fool, and I felt that way more than once. John's continued support reminded me that often passion is confused for madness and that he, at least, understood that difference.

There is nothing more humbling to an author (and former English major) than submitting their book to an editor. Fortunately, I was lucky enough to have the first two people to read and give me feedback on the book be two individuals who love me dearly. Without the tireless work of Kate Nachman and Amelia J. Michael, it is doubtful McFarland would have ever even given this manuscript the time of day. They coalesced half-finished thoughts, helped me winnow down useless text, made sure my tenses were right, and tamed my comma addiction. In short, they took the work you are holding and made it readable. Amelia has also served as my business partner on The Hall Ball for almost three years. Not only did she assist me as we shopped this book around to publishers, but her social media advice was invaluable when the *Times* article brought the ball into public notice. They both know that I will never be able to repay them for all they have done.

Finally, I thank my family, including my wife Anna and my children, Finn and Violet. They have all sacrificed on this journey. They lost time with their husband and father while he traveled. They saw their family vacations dictated by where a dead ballplayer was buried. They gave me the space and time to write this book. Most importantly, they never once stopped believing in me. When I would lament the foolishness of the exercise (usually around the time the credit cards came due), it was Anna who held my hand and reminded me that we wouldn't let something like a price tag interfere with chasing our dreams. She has never once voiced a single word of regret over the project, and she has done nothing but show me the kind of support that a person dreams about when they pick a life partner. She is, to put it mildly, the perfect wife.

Foreword

by John Thorn

"A stone can tell the story of a man," the author notes gravely, having visited the final resting places of so many historical figures. And so can the absence of a stone, as with the long unmarked burial site of baseball pioneer James Whyte Davis, at Brooklyn's Green-Wood Cemetery, a veritable city of the dead for early baseball.

What inspired Ralph Carhart to think about this amazing project was a celebrated Green-Wood shrine, the ornate memorial marking Henry Chadwick's grave, where baseballs are to this day left behind by unknown admirers, more than a century after the Hall of Fame writer's death. The stone may tell *his* story, but it is the ball that tells ours.

The game we love is about the bat, but mostly it's about the ball, that ancient symbol of life's journey from birth to death and over again, without beginning or end. Containing endless circles within circles, the ball is about a dangerous voyage, mirrored on the baseball field where a hero's quest for glory begins at home hoping, after overcoming perils between the safe bays of the open seas, to return home ... and then venture out again. The destination matters but it is the journey that is paramount.

That's what baseball is about, I say, though of course it is so much beyond, supplying legends of demigods and epic feats, and a landscape of free-floating memory that connects us with others who love the game, and even with our former or future selves—recalling for the old what it meant to be young, and

shining a light for children on what it may mean to grow up.

So if that's what baseball is about, what is this strangely moving book about? It's about baseball, sure, and it's about those men who played it so well that their likenesses are enshrined on plaques at the Baseball Hall of Fame in Cooperstown. And it's about parks—not only stadiums where baseball was played but also the parks where its departed worthies reside. The author loves cemeteries as if they were parks, which of course they were when baseball began: rural reposes—*rus in urbe*—in the bustling cities of industrial America, places for contemplation and connection, where the dead might be revered and the children might play.

But what about the many living Hall of Famers who **posed with** The Hall Ball, their playing days long behind them yet still a vital part of who they are, not merely who they had been? Like their counterparts under the sod, they are eternally players in The Great Game, even if this is seldom or never a conscious thought.

Players. That standard baseball term, on which we seldom reflect, derives from the theater, that simulacrum of real life to which Ralph Carhart has devoted his professional life. Practitioners of the baseball arts were thus named because they were regarded as entertainers, and they endured all the scorn and suspicion that upstanding members of society would heap on those who played for a living.

Baseball and theater are his two loves,

the author declares, apart from family; but they are truly one. Baseball is theater with an unscripted outcome ... unlike the drama crafted by the playwright, or life itself, where the ending is known.

I think that I have had my own strange, seemingly obsessive "Hall Ball experience," and many of you who will read and love this book will have had it too. The quest described here may at first seem like flagpole sitting—*why do it? because no one else has thought to*—but at the end I completely understood it: all those who care deeply about some one *thing*—beyond how they might feel about some one or more persons—will understand it, too. The love of an idea can be a passionate if lonely feeling, but a lucky few of us do get to share that unrequited love in print.

John Thorn is the official historian of Major League Baseball. He has written The Hidden Game of Baseball *(with Pete Palmer),* Baseball in the Garden of Eden, *and, since 1974, many other books.*

Introduction

The pages that follow are the story of *The Hall Ball*, my quest to photograph the same baseball with every member of the Hall of Fame. I have also attempted, in a microcosmic way, to make this book be about the story of baseball. Over 19,000 men have played major league baseball. Tens of thousands more people have played in the Negro Leagues, in the All-American Girls Professional Baseball League, in the minor leagues, in foreign leagues, in independent leagues, on semi-pro teams, and on sandlots since the rules for the game were codified 160 years ago. To examine the complete history of baseball in a single volume would be impossible, so for the most part I have chosen the very narrow lens of the Hall of Fame.

I have also attempted to give some background that goes beyond just the 322 men and one woman (as of 2018) who are members of the Hall. I visited 34 states, one U.S. Territory and one foreign nation over the course of the project. I became fascinated, with each new location, with the role that baseball played in the small towns and giant cities that I witnessed on my quest. The story of the development of baseball in those cities and towns became as interesting to me as the stories of the men who played it.

This fascination is reflected in the way I have structured many of the chapters dedicated to the various states I visited. Readers should know that each state chapter explores the first *currently* verifiable examples of when baseball was played in that area. Baseball research continues every day, and it is possible that by the time this book goes to print, someone will have discovered an earlier example of the first game played in Washington, Hawaii, or any of the other locations I visited. The dates used in this book were the most current knowledge as of the fall of 2018.

Each state chapter also spends some time noting which locations have major league franchises and which ones used to have them, but lost them in the ever-evolving world of baseball geography. When a state does not or never has had a major league team, I mention some of the more notable minor league teams that have played there. I also sometimes look at significant hometown players who never made it to the Hall who are from the states I visited.

There are other chapters sprinkled throughout the book that aren't about the individual states. Some are dedicated to the living players. I spend less time looking at the historical accomplishments of those gentleman and instead tell the story of my interaction with them. One chapter is about a series of symbolic photos I took to represent the members of the Hall of Fame who chose to be cremated or who are otherwise not accessible. There are also separate chapters dedicated to the stories of the graves of Sol White and Cristóbal Torriente. Once you read them, you will understand why they, perhaps more so than any other graves in the project, had a profound effect on me.

I believe you will find that this book is not much like any other baseball book you have encountered. I hope that is the case. I created *The Hall Ball* because I wanted to do something unique. I believe I have done that and that this book reflects my efforts. Now, enough explanation. It's time to get started. Enjoy my journey. I know I did.

Prologue

For Christmas of 2009, my father-in-law, Bob Peterson, gave my wife Anna and me a self-made book he had been compiling for some time. It was a history of his family line, on his mother's side, that went back to the 1400s. Among other revelations, it proved how Anna is a first cousin (14× removed) of William Shakespeare. Those who know me know that my sacred trinity consists of the three "Bs": Baseball, the Beatles, and the Bard. I had married into literary royalty.

My curiosity whetted, I began to dig into my own family history, and before I knew it I was embroiled in a full-blown obsession. I spent countless hours poring over documents and photos, trying to find out as much as I could about family centuries dead. This meant, as any genealogist could tell you, spending an inordinate amount of time in cemeteries.

As a child, cemeteries simultaneously fascinated and terrified me. As an adult, I had spent little time in them until the spring of 2010. As soon as the thaw began, I was taking every available opportunity to visit the graves of my ancestors, both recent and ancient. A rubbing of the stone of my Great (×8) Aunt Mary Carhart now hangs in my living room, her death date of 1737 clear and easy to read.

I grew to truly love cemeteries. They are quiet and green, and rarely are there any other people there to interfere with my enjoyment of them. Cemeteries are a place of introspection and they often seem like a private park, just for me. The art of gravestones has evolved over the years, and the artist and historian within me appreciates the beauty of a well-designed monument, as well as the depth of information that can be gathered from one. Every time I discover the grave of someone to whom I am connected, a thrill shoots through me. Each relative is a treasure, waiting to be discovered.

Which brings me to our family vacation that summer. Having spent months researching my family, who were more local to our native New York City, we decided to spend a few weeks looking into Anna's kin. In addition to Shakespeare, Anna is a direct descendent of William Bradford, the original Governor of the Plymouth Colony. The descendants of the Bradfords left Plymouth and spread throughout New England, and we spent 14 days tracking them down. With one small side-trip.

Two years earlier we had been in Cooperstown, New York, during the Major League Baseball All-Star break, and we were fortunate enough to catch the game at the Baseball Hall of Fame and Museum. Every year the Hall sponsors an All-Star Gala. They show the game in their Grandstand Theatre while they give away hot dogs, sodas and snacks. There's trivia, contests, and games in between innings. The Midsummer Classic had begun to lose some of its luster for me in recent years, and this opportunity to spend a little extra time in the Hall, after hours, had helped to recapture the magic. We had a blast that first time and decided in 2010 to divert from our genealogical road trip to try and catch lightning in a bottle again.

The night before the game, we were early for our dinner reservations and Anna suggested we check out the local cemetery. Neither one of us was aware of any family from that area, but it had become habit. The closest was Lakewood Cemetery, on the southeastern coast of Otsego Lake. Lakewood is built into a steep hill that seems to wind up into eternity. The most notable name to be associated with the cemetery is the writer, James Fenimore Cooper. Interestingly, the giant monument honoring the native son, whose own ancestors gave the town its name, is a cenotaph, an empty tomb erected to honor an individual who is buried elsewhere. Cooper is actually buried in Christ Churchyard, about two blocks from the Hall of Fame at the heart of town.

Lakewood is also the final resting place of Emmett Littleton "Ash" Ashford, the first African American to umpire a Major League Baseball game. He accomplished that feat in 1966, almost 20 years after Jackie Robinson erased the color line for players. Fifteen years before that, in 1951, he became the first black umpire in organized baseball. His was a life of breaking barriers. Ashford went on to a mildly successful acting career, appearing in the television show *The Jacksons*, a variety show hosted by the singer Michael Jackson and his multitude of siblings. He also appeared in the comedic film about life in the Negro Leagues, *The Bingo Long Traveling All-Stars & Motor Kings*. He died in Marina Del Ray, California, but felt so connected to the town that has become the spiritual home of baseball, that his wife sent his ashes to the Hall, where they were eventually interred in this jewel of a cemetery.

Anna and I wandered through the seemingly endless rows of this fascinating collection of New Yorkers, looking for familial names that we had trained our eyes to find. Instead of Carhart or Peterson, however, Anna found Doubleday. Abner Doubleday.

At first we believed we had found the mythical "inventor" of baseball. We quickly realized that this Abner died in 1812, making it impossible for him to be the Civil War hero who was wrongfully credited as the progenitor of the game. This Abner was, instead, the grandfather of the famous one. We searched for a while, looking for "our" Abner, but with no luck. I later learned he was buried at Arlington National Cemetery, but in the end it didn't matter that he wasn't there. The door had been opened. I had seen the name of baseball's Odin written in stone, in the town that the game had adopted as its birthplace. One obsession was about to give way to another.

The next night we arrived at the Hall early so we could enjoy the museum before the All-Star Game started. The seed of the idea that was planted the evening before bloomed into the foundation of a quest as I walked through the Hall's famous Plaque Gallery. It had never occurred to me before then how much the visually striking plaques resembled tiny tombstones. Of course, I was looking at them with a different set of eyes than I ever had previously.

Abner Doubleday, grandfather of "our" Abner.

I looked at row upon row of the greatest, most influential individuals to touch the game over its history and decided then and there that I was going to visit the graves of each and every one of them. My love of baseball and my newfound love of cemeteries had fused into a single quest. I was going to absorb the history of the game in a whole new way, one Hall of Famer at a time.

As soon as we returned home from vacation, I began my research, and Google quickly introduced me to Stew Thornley. It turned out that Stew seemed to have the same love for cemeteries, and baseball, and had already gone on a similar journey. He had created a website, complete with photographs and rough GPS coordinates, of all of the Hall of Famer graves to that point.

This was good news for me. It meant that I had all the location information I needed to get started. Plus, the photos made it easier to find the graves themselves once I actually got to the cemeteries. It was also frustrating. I had thought my idea was original, and to know that it had already been done was discouraging. I had worked in theater for 25 years and had always desired for my art to be unique. I was already beginning to think of the endeavor as an artistic one, though the actual manifestation of that art remained vague in my mind. Still, I needed to own this idea in some way and began to think of variations that could make it mine.

While I was contemplating that dilemma, I was able to get a healthy head start on the whole thing simply by luck of location. My first stop was right over the Verrazano Bridge, in Brooklyn, at perhaps the most famous cemetery in all of New York City. Green-Wood is well-known both for its size and beauty. Some of its more famous residents include Leonard Bernstein, Samuel Morse, "Boss" Tweed (who was once a partial investor in a baseball club) and Charles Ebbets, owner of the Brooklyn Dodgers. There is even a book titled *Baseball's Legends of Brooklyn's Green-Wood Cemetery*, written by Peter J. Nash, formerly known as Prime Minister Pete Nice of the rap trio 3rd Bass. There are over 200 former major leaguers buried there (along with 51 Carharts).

There is only one Hall of Famer, though, but he's one of my favorites. Henry Chadwick is the only member of the Hall whose election was primarily based on his work as a writer. There is, of course, the J. G. Taylor Spink Award that is given annually to a baseball scribe, but contrary to popular misconception, a Spink recipient is not a Hall of Famer. Chadwick is in the Hall, itself. As someone who appreciates the artistic inspiration that comes from baseball, I have always had a soft spot in my heart for the British-born writer.

At the impressive main gates, gothic spires that reach to the sky, maps of the massive cemetery were available which clearly marked the location of Chadwick. Minutes after my arrival, I was standing at my first Hall of Fame grave. It is one of the most celebratory graves I have ever seen. The sight of three baseballs, left behind like religious offerings, made my smile wider. I considered them briefly and, in one of those moments of perfect clarity, I realized a way I could make my tour of the graves different from Stew's.

I wasn't going to make the trip on my own. I was going to bring a baseball with me, a special baseball that I was going to photograph at each of the sites. I was going to create my own artifact. And I knew just the ball I wanted to use.

On the trip to Cooperstown when we found Grandpa Abner, Anna and I had gone to Doubleday Field to watch a game. Doubleday is a small ballpark located on a piece of land that was once a farmer's pasture. The field had been used for baseball for decades when, in 1939, the year the Hall opened, the current steel, concrete and brick structure was constructed as a WPA project. The result remains a centerpiece of the village today.

When you watch a game at Doubleday, you feel like you've traveled in time. It is small and unfettered by modern ballpark conveniences. The electric scoreboard is the kind my high school used in the 1980s, with a series of incandescent light bulbs forming the numerals.

The park doesn't even have any lighting. All games at Doubleday Field are day games.

On this particular day, Anna and I were sitting in the back row of the grandstand, giving us a view of Willow Brook, the small stream that runs next to the park. Anna noticed a baseball sitting in the water and went down to fish it out. This was the ball I wanted for the project. After all, this ball had come from Cooperstown, giving it a Hall of Fame pedigree. Of course, between having spent an unknown amount of time in the water which smudged the green manufacturer logo, this was not a ball that one might expect for a "major league" project. Made by Diamond, the ball was from their NFHS line, and intended for use in high school games. But to me, these defects lent to the character.

The only problem was that I couldn't find it. I could have sworn it was somewhere in the car, but after pulling out all of our camping gear (still sitting in our trunk in antici-pation of another upcoming trip), I gave up and grabbed another ball that was sitting in the back seat. It was in even worse shape, brown and scuffed from a game of catch that took place on concrete. I took a Sharpie out of the glove compartment, briefly considered how I was going to mark the ball to make it clear that each photograph was of the same one, and quickly scribbled "The Hall Ball." It wasn't profound, but there it was.

I placed the ball on one of the more interesting features of Chadwick's grave, took my photo, and set off on the next stop of the tour. By the time the day was over, I had succeeded in reaching only six of the nine graves I had set out to see. I was also thoroughly frustrated by the fact that the time I *had* spent was wasted because it wasn't the ball I really wanted to use. By twilight, I had decided I was going to need to revisit everywhere I had gone that day, this time with the proper ball.

The gothic spires of Green-Wood Cemetery.

The original Hall Ball, even more battered than the final one.

I also still felt the need to differentiate my quest in another way from Stew's, besides the ball. Despite my standing at the feet of some of the biggest names in the history of the game that day, inspiration had not come. A few days later, as I was finishing the packing for the camping trip, I found the ball. It had been in the trunk the whole time, buried in the large canvas duffel that also contained our sleeping bags and the poles for our tent. I knew I was right in choosing this ball as soon as I placed my fingers upon it. With the same lightning clarity that came at Chadwick's grave, when I touched the ball I had an epiphany.

Why stop with taking the ball to the graves of the dead Hall of Famers? Why not also bring it to the living ones? And there it was. My quest in full. This ball was going to be either at the graves, or in the hands, of every member of the Hall of Fame. It would unite the rich history of the game in a way that would be unique, bringing Alexander Cart-

wright, the first-born member of the Hall, together with heroes who wouldn't even be crowned at the time the adventure began.

Almost simultaneously I realized that if I, an artist, made such a treasure, I would not want it to languish on the shelves of my office. I want people to see my work. I don't direct a play so that the actors can entertain me at home. Like all artists, I want an audience. There was no better place for such a creation to be seen than the Hall of Fame. I would donate the ball to the Hall, to their permanent collection. There it could be seen by at least a quarter-million people annually. I had grandiose thoughts of the Hall continuing the tradition after I gave it to them, taking photographs of the new inductees every year, making it a true artifact that would outlive me.

I was certainly putting the cart before the horse. I had no realistic concept of how long it would take me to do all of the travel, nor how I was going to get access to the living players. But this was a day of inspiration, not logistics.

I had no idea at the time just how far that inspiration would take me.

The Hall Ball.

Where Our Story
(and the Game) Began
◆ NEW YORK ◆

Baseball historian John Zinn refers to New York City as the "incubator of baseball," an appropriate metaphor because, despite its pastoral mythology, the game as we know it was nursed from its fragile beginnings to its ultimate cultural status on the cobblestone streets of Gotham. Quickly enough the burgeoning city forced the game to spread to neighboring Hoboken, across the Hudson River in New Jersey, where there was more room and less opportunity for a stray foul ball to break expensive windows.

The most famous, though not first, of the early New York squads that helped establish the game was the Knickerbocker Base Ball Club, founded in October 1845. They were preceded by the New York Base Ball Club (also known as the Gothams or the Washingtons) and the Magnolias, an obscure team whose history was only recently brought to light. One-hundred seventy years later, baseball is played across the globe. There are professional leagues in 16 countries, including Japan, Dominican Republic, Venezuela, Italy, and Netherlands. Still, the home address of Major League Baseball, the reigning heir of the first professional league formed in 1871, is 1271 6th Avenue, New York, New York.

According to the Pre-pro Database of Protoball.org, a web-based project dedicated to chronicling all the teams that existed before baseball became a professional enterprise, over 1,010 baseball clubs called New York

State home before that seminal date. The brain child of researcher Larry McCray, Protoball is an invaluable resource to anyone studying the game in its infancy, back when the rules were still being written, the schedules were flexible, and teams were born and died with the lifespan of a housefly.

Since the foundation of the first major league, the National Association, there have been 21 teams based out of New York that were considered "major." Even casual fans can name the Yankees and Mets, as well as the Giants and Dodgers before they famously went west to seek their fortunes. The list also includes the Atlantics, Eckfords, Gladiators, Tip-Tops, and Ward's Wonders (all five of Brooklyn), three different incarnations of Buffalo Bisons (more on them later), an additional Giants (part of the 1890 Players' League), an additional Metropolitans (an American Association squad that played from 1883 to 1887), two New York Mutuals (one of which had Tammany Hall kingpin William M. "Boss" Tweed as an investor), the Rochester Broncos, two different Syracuse Stars, and two clubs from Troy, the Trojans and Haymakers.

With such a history, it is perhaps no surprise that there are 14 Hall of Famers buried in the Greater New York City area alone, including the five boroughs, Long Island, and Westchester County. That number goes up when you add in metropolitan New Jersey. As I was beginning this crazy adventure, it was a nice boost to morale to know that I could get so many photos without having to go very far. If I lived in North Dakota, hundreds of miles away from even a single Hall of Famer, it is unlikely I would have started this project in the first place.

The journey began *very* close to home for me. Fifteen minutes to be exact, give or take traffic. Staten Island has always been the red-headed stepchild of the five boroughs, and its role in baseball history is admittedly the smallest when compared to its brothers. Only a handful of pre-professional teams played there, most notably the Quicksteps. The American Association Mets called the St. George Cricket Grounds (where, in 1884, lawn tennis was first introduced to the United States) home in 1886 and 1887. One hundred and twelve years later, the Yankees placed their short-season A-ball minor league franchise on the neglected island. Other than a smattering of major leaguers who called Staten Island home, including "Shot Heard Round the World" hero Bobby Thomson, this represents the greater sum total of Richmond County's contributions to the game.

Sol White
Frederick Douglass Memorial Park, Staten Island

Staten Island does serve as the final resting place for a single Hall of Famer, despite the fact that he likely never set foot on the island when he was alive. King Solomon "Sol" White was black baseball's first historian, as well as an incredible infielder and successful team executive. He began his professional career in 1886, long enough ago that the famous "color line" did not yet exist, allowing him to play alongside whites, briefly. After his baseball days were over, he retired to Harlem, where he eked out a living as a writer. When White died in 1955 at Central Islip State Hospital in Long Island, he was penniless and had no family around to claim him. The state paid to have his body buried at Frederick Douglass Memorial Park, an African American cemetery established in 1935 by a group of Harlem undertakers.

The unmarked grave of Sol White.

I was saddened to discover that White was in an unmarked, communal grave. The cemetery itself was suffering under severe financial constraints. The crumbling brick wall at the main gate could never be confused with the spires of Green-Wood. It seemed a depressing way to begin the journey. On that sunny August day, it was impossible for me to predict the impact White's grave would have on me and just how closely I would become linked to the quest to bring him and his family their due.

Henry Chadwick
Green-Wood Cemetery, Brooklyn

Henry Chadwick's grave in Green-Wood is one of the most impressive and, dare I say, fun of any member of the Hall. Adorned with a catcher's mask on one side, a mitt on the other, with both of them mounted on a pair of crossed bats, the monolithic stone itself is only the beginning.

Chadwick's delightful grave plot.

A plaque on the obelisk of Henry Chadwick, naming him the "Father of Base Ball."

The four corners of his plot are marked by bases, featuring the perfect detail of stone straps to tie them down, a convention of Chadwick's time. Because the plot is rectangular and not diamond-shaped, it unintentionally looks similar to the field used in the Massachusetts Game, an alternate version of baseball that, during the game's infancy, vied for popularity with the New York Game we now play. The obelisk itself, which names Chadwick the "Father of Base Ball," is not far from where a Massachusetts striker would stand.

Wee Willie Keeler and Mickey Welch
Calvary Cemetery, Long Island City

Wee Willie Keeler and Mickey Welch are buried in prestigious Calvary Cemetery in Queens. Frequently used by filmmakers, Calvary served as the location for Don Corleone's funeral in *The Godfather*. Massive, there are over three million souls buried at Calvary, making it the largest cemetery, by interments, in the nation. If Calvary were a city, it would have the third-highest population in America, trailing only Los Angeles and New York City itself. While not carrying as much cachet as Green-Wood, it is still a pretty fancy place to be buried.

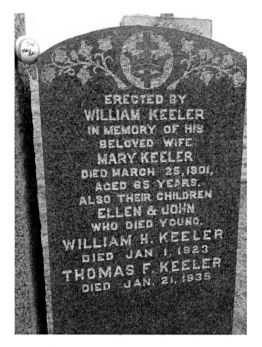

A bachelor, Wee Willie Keeler is buried in the same plot as his parents and siblings.

The entirety of Welch's career took place in the 19th century, while Keeler's straddled the gap into the modern era. They were both on the roster of the 1892 New York Giants. It was Keeler's first season and Welch's final. The elder gentleman appeared in only one game that year, surrendering nine runs in a single five-inning appearance before deciding to hang up his spikes after winning 307 games in 13 seasons. Keeler batted .341 lifetime, including a hefty .424 in 1897. He is best known for summing up the secret to successful hitting by proclaiming, "keep your eye clear and hit 'em where they ain't," to *Brooklyn Eagle* sportswriter Abe Yager. It took another five years after I took their pictures for me to discover that there is possibly a third Hall of Famer buried in Calvary, a fact unknown to the world at that point. More on him later.

Babe Ruth
Gates of Heaven Cemetery, Hawthorne

Mickey Welch's stone contains his birth name, Walsh.

Babe Ruth's massive stone.

The ball rests near the Babe's little-used given name.

Lou Gehrig, Ed Barrow and Jacob Ruppert
Kensico Cemetery, Valhalla

The tale of the graves of Babe Ruth and Lou Gehrig is an early favorite from the project. The two legends are buried in separate cemeteries that share a border, making them virtually indistinguishable if looked at on a map. Gates of Heaven, where Ruth is buried, was in fact once a part of Kensico, where Gehrig lies. Ruth's grave is gigantic, nearing nine feet tall and about eight feet wide, standing atop a steep hill overlooking the bulk of the cemetery below. Large and ostentatious, is it inscribed with a quote about Ruth's inspiration to America's youth, originally spoken by Cardinal Spellman, former archbishop of New York, who performed Ruth's funeral service. It features a raised image of Christ and a little boy in a baseball uniform. There was no way to properly photograph the entirety of it so that the identifying writing on The Hall Ball could be seen. It is completely befitting of the man.

Gehrig's, meanwhile, is roughly four feet tall and about four and a half feet wide, with a simple copper door installed in the center which protects the ashes of the Iron Horse and his wife, Eleanor. The stone's modesty is all the more noticeable in the context of Ruth's grandiosity. While Ruth bathed in the adoration from a worshipful public, Gehrig used to map out the best routes to enter and leave Yankee Stadium without having to interact with people (until Eleanor convinced him of his responsibility to the fans). Their graves, a study in contrasts, are a perfect summation of the two men, and their relationship, in a tidy nut-shell.

Ed Barrow and Jacob Ruppert, two of the greatest architects of the Yankees dynasty, are also buried near Gehrig in Kensico. Barrow's family crypt is within sight of Gehrig's grave, and Ruppert's massive mausoleum isn't all that far away from either of them. Kensico also holds Paul Krichell, the scout who discovered Gehrig and was a Yankees birddog for almost 40 years; Joe Reichler, an Associated Press scribe who covered the Yanks; and Robert Merrill, the Metropolitan Opera baritone who sang "The Star-Spangled Banner" for special events at Yankee Stadium for over 50 years. Plus, barely 20 feet from Ruth at Gates of Heaven is the final resting place of Billy Martin, one of the most famous Bronx Bombers players and managers in history. The concentrated location of these men may make this one of the most sacred spaces in Pinstripes lore.

Behind the copper door are the ashes of Gehrig and his wife, Eleanor.

Family mausoleum of Ed Barrow, architect of ten World Championships.

Ruppert's mausoleum reflects the tremendous wealth of the Yankees owner.

Jackie Robinson
Cypress Hills Cemetery, Brooklyn

When baseball first came to Brooklyn, the borough was an incorporated city of its own, completely independent of Manhattan. It was not until January 1, 1898, that it officially became a part of New York City. The move was controversial at the time because of the pride

Brooklynites took in *not* being from Manhattan. This pride extended to their sport. Because of the relatively open space that King's County provided, at least compared to the City, it played host to many of the dozens of teams that came into existence during the post–Civil War golden age. Clubs like the Eckfords, the Excelsiors, and the Atlantics dominated the early landscape of the sport and often reigned as league champions before the advent of professionalism.

Today, the mythos of Brooklyn and baseball continues to run deep. It is a romance that certainly existed from the game's earliest days, but it reached the level of Greek tragedy when owner Walter O'Malley took the Dodgers all the way across the country to Los Angeles in 1957. This unexpected rending of a passionate fan base from their beloved team has resulted in gallons of ink spilled in lamentation of the loss. Perhaps no figure in the entire history of Brooklyn baseball can claim as much of that ink as Jackie Robinson.

The day before I visited the grave of the man who integrated baseball, a tornado tore through New York City, felling trees and flooding streets. When I arrived at Robinson's grave, downed branches were scattered everywhere, and cemetery workers were putting in overtime to assess the damage. Tucked in a corner, seemingly untouched by the chaos, was Robinson's relatively simple stone. It was ironic that a man who caused and lived such turmoil seemed so removed from the destruction around him.

His marker is engraved with the sentence that has come to be most associated with Robinson and his immeasurable effect on the game: "A life is not important except in the impact it has on other lives." This same sentiment is inscribed across the length of the Jackie Robinson Rotunda at the home of the New York Mets, Citifield, which is designed to resemble the famed entryway to Ebbets Field. Cypress Hills Cemetery, where he is buried, is located partially in Brooklyn and partially in Queens, and it is split down the center by the Jackie Robinson Parkway.

Robinson's understated grave, sheltered from the storm.

Frankie Frisch and Alex Pompez

Woodlawn Cemetery, Bronx

Like Brooklyn, the Bronx was a popular location for early baseball because of the available space. However, the population of the northern-most borough has never been close to that of its more famous brother and, as a result, fewer teams claimed it as their home. The most famous of the early pre-pro squads was the Union Base Ball Club of Morrisania. Hall of Famer George Wright spent some time with the Unions, as did Esteban Bellán, the first Latino ever to play professional baseball.

Woodlawn Cemetery, located near Van Cortlandt Park, was named a National Historic Landmark in 2011. Founded in 1863, it is the burial site of Elizabeth Cady Stanton, Miles Davis, Irving Berlin, and the master architect of much of the layout of New York City, Robert

Moses, just to name a few of its more notable residents. It is also one of the 20 cemeteries that houses the remains of more than one member of the Baseball Hall of Fame.

While today the Bronx is most readily associated with the Yankees, the two Hall of Famers buried there were never a part of baseball's most famous franchise. Frankie Frisch, whose nickname "The Fordham Flash" was earned when he was a track star for the college in the late 1910s, was born in the Bronx. He spent eight years playing across the East River for John McGraw's New York Giants before he was traded to the Cardinals for Rogers Hornsby. He played 11 more years in St. Louis, where he won an MVP Award in 1931 and two World Series.

On the other side of the cemetery lies one of the more controversial figures in baseball history, Alex Pompez. The son of Cuban immigrants, Pompez originally made a name for himself running numbers in Manhattan.

The visit to Frisch's grave happened in the dead of winter.

Alex Pompez's grave is strangely missing his name.

After gangster Dutch Schultz took over his business, ultimately landing Pompez in hot water with New York special prosecutor Thomas Dewey, he briefly went on the lam in Mexico. He was arrested there and extradited back to the United States, where he agreed to testify against Schultz. He ultimately gave up the gangster life and dedicated himself to his legitimate business, running a baseball team. He became one of the most important individuals in Negro League history. As owner of the Cuban Stars and New York Cubans, and later a scout with the San Francisco Giants, he played an integral role in introducing Latin players to American teams. Interestingly, his marker, which was originally purchased by Pompez himself after the death of his sister, does not have his first name inscribed on it.

Ford Frick
Christ Church Columbarium, Bronxville

The day I visited Ford Frick's grave was one of the more unusual ones on the quest. I was accompanied by my hero, William Shakespeare. Jeremy Rishe, an actor friend, had been filming a web series starring a profane, drunk, sexist stuffed doll that looked like the Bard. When Jeremy learned of The Hall Ball, he thought it would be fun to make an episode in which Shakespeare tried to grasp the complexities of baseball, not to mention what would drive a person to go out in the cold, pouring rain (it was a truly unpleasant day) just to take a picture of the grave of a man who had been dead for over 30 years. The episode was never finished, but we had a hell of a time filming it.

Ford Frick's plaque on his niche in the courtyard of Christ Church.

Frick was a sports journalist who also served as Babe Ruth's ghostwriter. He was elevated to National League President in 1934, a position he held until 1951, when he became the third commissioner of baseball. He served until 1965, overseeing the expansion of the major leagues from 16 to 20 teams and the season from 154 to 162 games. For many, his tenure as commissioner has been reduced to a single punctuation mark. When Roger Maris was on track in 1961 to defeat the home run record of his old friend, Ruth, he declared that all single-season records set after the 154th game were to have a "distinctive mark" next to them in the record books, given that he viewed the expanded 162-game season as an aberration. History has come to identify that mark as an asterisk. However, writer Allen Barra points out that not only did Frick never declare which punctuation to use, but publishers, whom he had no authority over, ignored the edict. Not a single one of the 1962 record books contained a mark of any kind differentiating Maris's accomplishment from Ruth's.

John Montgomery Ward
Greenfield Cemetery, Uniondale

John Montgomery Ward was a rarity in baseball, in many ways. During his early career, from 1878 to 1884, he was a premier pitcher for the Providence Grays, leading the league in wins in 1879 with 47. As his pitching skills diminished from overuse, he moved to the infield and specialized in stolen bases, stealing 111 in 1887. A graduate of Columbia Law School, he was an early force in the world of the player labor movement. Ward helped create the short-lived Players' League in 1890 and represented them in court in their fight for labor equality. A complicated man, later in life he used his law degree to support baseball management, arguing in favor of the reserve clause which he had earlier tried to destroy.

Ward died of pneumonia on a hunting trip in Georgia; his body was brought back to Long Island.

His first wife, Helen Dauvray, was a famed stage actress and loved baseball so much that she created the Dauvray Cup, bestowed upon the winner of the 1880s incarnation of the World Series.

Bowie Kuhn
Quogue Cemetery, Quogue

Bowie Kuhn was the fifth Commissioner of Major League Baseball and served from 1969 to 1984. The success of his tenure was seen as mixed. Baseball grew, both at the turnstiles and the cash registers, but it was his reign that brought about perhaps the most volatile period of labor strife in the history of the game.

Kuhn was inducted into the Hall in 2008, just nine months after his death.

Major League Baseball experienced two lockouts and three labor strikes while he held office, including the disastrous 1981 strike which canceled over 35 percent of the season's scheduled games. He was the named defendant in Curt Flood's Supreme Court lawsuit that attempted to end baseball's reserve clause. Kuhn won that case, but it was a short-lived victory. Within five years, free-agency became the law of the land, and the reserve clause, which tied a player to a team indefinitely, was effectively dead.

Dan Brouthers
St. Mary's Cemetery, Wappingers Falls

Dan Brouthers was a well-traveled slugger in the nascent years of the professional game. In the volatile labor world of early baseball, he played for 10 different teams between 1879 and 1904. Despite how often he moved, his skills were always in demand, as he was a frequent league leader in batting average. He retired with a lifetime mark of .342. Hitting for distance in the pre-power age, he was the career leader in home runs from 1887 to 1888 and ultimately retired with 107 round-trippers.

There is a statue of Brouthers in Veteran's Park, not far from the churchyard of St. Mary's.

Johnny Evers
St. Mary's Cemetery, Troy

With the completion of the Erie Canal, Troy became one of the more important industrial cities of the mid–19th century, and its booming population reflected that. Between 1850 and 1880, the city nearly doubled in size, to almost 57,000. Still, it was small for a major league market, which is why the National Association Haymakers (1871–1872) and the National League Trojans (1879–1882) were unable to make a viable go at keeping a franchise there. Despite its brief time as a major league town, numerous future Hall of Famers played for Troy, including Buck Ewing, Roger Connor, Mickey Welch, Tim Keefe, and New York native Dan Brouthers.

Only one of baseball's immortals was ever born there. Part of the famed trio of Chicago Cubs infielders, Johnny Evers is the Hall of Famer most closely buried to the place where I learned to play baseball as a boy in upstate New York.

The family stone of Johnny Evers, which includes his estranged wife.

Despite a successful career in which he played on three World Series champion clubs, his election to the Hall is often thought to owe more to the power of the written word than his statistics. Evers was the middle man in Franklin Pierce Adams's poem "Baseball's Sad Lexicon," more commonly known as "Tinker to Evers to Chance." Nicknamed "the Crab" because of his unpleasant disposition, he and his wife separated after the death of their daughter Helen in 1914, the year Evers won the National League MVP. Catholics, Evers and his wife never divorced, and the whole family is buried under their sizable stone in Troy.

Joe McCarthy
Mount Olivet Cemetery, Tonawanda

Arguably the greatest manager in Yankees history, Joe McCarthy.

Jimmy Collins
Holy Cross Cemetery, Lackawanna

I visited the two cemeteries located near Buffalo accompanied by Hall Ball supporter and old friend from college, Dakin Lecakes. When I knew him, Dakin was a poet. Today, his vocation is a lawyer. He used to split his life between Buffalo and Toronto, but spends far more time on the Canadian side these days. Roughly 10 years since I had previously seen him, his hair was a little whiter and his wrinkles a little more pronounced. Still, the

gleam of the dreamer danced in his eyes, just as when we were younger men. After a necessary lunch of Buffalo wings, he guided me through the area.

Buffalo's three Bisons franchises played an integral role in the development of the game, if only to prove how large a market must be in order for a major league team to be sustainable. The original squad of that name were members of the National League, from 1879 to 1885, and, like Troy, featured an unlikely number of Hall of Famers in their short existence, including Dan Brouthers, Pud Galvin, Jim O'Rourke, Deacon White, and Old Hoss Radbourn. The second Bisons were members of the 1890 Players' League and would add Connie Mack to the roster of notables. The final incarnation (which also went by Blues or Buffeds) struggled through the two seasons of the Federal League in 1914 and 1915 before the death knell of major league baseball in Buffalo finally sounded. Today, the Toronto Blue Jays have their Triple-A affiliate located there, a two-hour drive from Rogers Centre. With a nod to history, they are also known as the Bisons.

Though he was financially devastated by the Great Depression, Collins's stone is substantial.

Jimmy Collins was born and died in the area, but it was in Boston where he built his career. First playing for the National League Beaneaters (Braves) before joining the American League Americans (Red Sox) in 1901, Collins spent 12 of his 14 big league seasons in the city that has grown to be the mortal enemy of most New York fans. That animosity did not yet exist in Collins's day, primarily because New York had yet to field a team as successful as the dynastic Boston squads. Collins won two pennants with the Beaneaters and played third base for the victorious Americans in the first World Series in 1903, when he also served as the team's manager.

Joe McCarthy spent his childhood in Philadelphia, but after attending Niagara College made Buffalo his home. He had an unprecedented run as the manager of the Yankees, winning seven World Series and 2,125 games over his career. In 1914 and 1915, before his managing days, McCarthy played for the independent International League incarnation of yet another team named the Buffalo Bisons, which were in direct competition with the Federal League squad for fans. The old adage about needing a scorecard to know the players was doubly true in Buffalo during the game's developmental days. Just keeping track of the Bisons alone could lead to a vaudeville routine that Abbott and Costello would admire.

Springtime Home
◆ FLORIDA ◆

Florida joined the Union in 1845, just seven months before the Knickerbockers approved their charter. Once one factors in the delay that the growth of baseball universally suffered as a result of the Civil War, it becomes obvious why the state was a little late in joining the party that was baseball-mania. The first two amateur clubs in Florida, one in Jacksonville and one in Tallahassee, weren't established until February 1867. It took another 126 years before they nabbed their first major league team, the Florida (now Miami) Marlins. Five years later, the Marlins were joined by the Tampa Bay Devil Rays, now simplified to just the Rays.

Despite its late entry into the majors, Florida has a rich baseball history that owes some debt to the Philadelphia Phillies. In 1889, when newspapers still referred to the club as the Quakers, the Philadelphia squad decided to stage their Spring Training exercises in Jacksonville. Spring Training was still a relatively new concept, first established in 1884 by the Minneapolis Millers of the minor Northwestern League, who held theirs in still-chilly St. Louis. The Quakers were the first to experiment with training in the warmth of the Florida sun. It took a few decades for the Sunshine State to become a regular spring destination for clubs, but by the 1920s it had firmly established its role as *the* place where the new season was reborn. Today, 15 of the 30 major league clubs are part of Florida's Grapefruit League.

Heine Manush
Sarasota Memorial Park, Sarasota

An already planned family vacation brought us to Port Charlotte just after taking Sol White's photo to begin the project. Anna and I spent an afternoon dodging rain showers to collect the first four Florida pictures. The first was of Heine Manush, an excellent hitter who spent time with six different clubs in his 17-year career. He surpassed .300 in 12 seasons and lead the league in batting with a .378 mark in 1926. Born in Alabama, Manush spent the final years of his life in Florida so he could pursue his other passion, golf, without having to wait for spring. In typical Florida fashion, Manush's grave was covered in fire ants and necessitated the removal of my shoes to clear myself of one of nature's tiniest monsters.

A colony of fire ants was hidden in the mulch around Manush's grave.

Wilhelm's grave denotes his Purple Heart, earned at the Battle of the Bulge.

Hoyt Wilhelm
Palms Memorial Park, Sarasota

Few could have predicted that when Hoyt Wilhelm finally made it to the big leagues in 1952, at the wizened age of 29, his major league career still had two decades to go. In his rookie season with the New York Giants, he appeared in a league-leading 71 games and fashioned an NL-best 2.43 ERA. Using his ubiquitous but effective knuckleball, he pitched in the majors until the nearly unfathomable age of 49. Wilhelm can be considered the link between the progenitors of the role of reliever, men like Firpo Marberry and Johnny Murphy, and the more modern incarnation. He was the career leader in saves (a statistic that wasn't official until 1969) from 1964 to 1979, with 228, and had a no-hitter against the Yankees in 1958. When he retired, he held the record for games by a pitcher, a crown he wrested from Cy Young.

Bill McKechnie and Paul Waner
Manasota Memorial Cemetery, Bradenton

Paul Waner and his first manager, Bill McKechnie, became the first two Hall of Famers I visited who were considerate enough to be buried in the same cemetery. Despite leading the Pirates to a World Series victory in 1925, McKechnie was gone after 1926, Waner's first year, and the two greats only crossed paths again as National League opponents. Waner was one of the greatest hitting forces of the 1920s and '30s. He led the league in batting three times, including a .380 mark in 1927 that helped secure the sophomore slugger his lone MVP Award.

McKechnie was an influential enough presence in Bradenton that the minor-league stadium located there since 1923 was renamed to honor him after his Hall of Fame election in 1962. Seven years later, it became the Spring Training home of the Pirates and remains so today. Three miles away from the park, the two former Bucs are spending eternity buried 100 yards from each other.

The rain that dappled Bill McKechnie's grave…

…became a downpour before we could get to Waner's, making us wait in the car for it to subside.

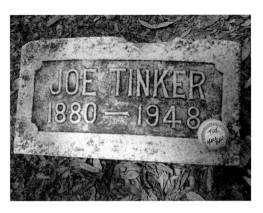

Tinker's original footstone; later a larger headstone was installed, featuring a replica of his Hall of Fame plaque.

Joe Tinker

Greenwood Cemetery, Orlando

Joe Tinker spent 14 of his 15 major league seasons playing for Chicago, both with the Cubs and the Federal League Whales/Chi-Feds. A native of Kansas, he moved to Florida in 1920 after his playing days were over in order to aid his wife's poor health. In the years that followed, he became a prominent businessman in the Orlando area. As with McKechnie, the local ballpark was named after the Hall of Famer. Despite being named to the U.S. National Register of Historic Places in 2004, the grandstand of Tinker Field, and its extant buildings, were demolished in 2015 in order to make room for Citrus Bowl Stadium. Tinker is buried less than 10 minutes away from the former stadium in Greenwood Cemetery, which is also the final resting place of Tinker's teammate on the Whales, Mickey Doolin.

Al López

Garden of Memories Cemetery, Tampa

Al López was the son of Spanish immigrants who came to Florida via Cuba in 1906. He was, at one point, the longest-lived member of the Hall of Fame, dying in 2005 at the age of 97 years, two months and 10 days. That record has since been surpassed by Bobby Doerr.

Al López was baseball's oldest Hall of Famer when he died.

When López became manager of the Cleveland Indians in 1951, it marked the first time that a Tampa native was tapped as the full-time skipper of a major league team. López won only two pennants in his career but that was mainly due to poor timing. Splitting his managerial tenure between the Indians and the Chicago White Sox, he finished second to the dynastic Yankees squads of the 1950s and '60s nine times over his 17-year managing career.

*   *   *

When Miami finally brought Florida into the major league fold in 1993, the fledgling Marlins suffered the typical growing pains of an expansion franchise. Finishing sixth in the seven-team National League East, they were 33 games behind the eventual division champs, the Philadelphia Phillies. However, fans did not need to wait long for a champion. Despite never having won their division, thanks to the advent of the Wild Card, the Marlins won two World Series in their first 11 years of existence. That equals or surpasses the number of crowns won by 15 of the other 29 franchises currently in the majors.

Jimmie Foxx

Flagler Memorial Park, Miami

Miami also houses the remains of three Hall of Famers, with another three within an hour and a half drive. The first one I visited was one of the most powerful sluggers in the history of the game, Jimmie Foxx. Nicknamed both "Double X" and "Beast," Foxx cut an imposing figure at the plate. In a 20-year career primarily split between the Philadelphia Athletics and the Boston Red Sox, he led the league in home runs four times, including a 1932 campaign that saw him threaten the record of the Babe, when he swatted 58. The following year he won the Triple Crown and his second of three MVP Awards. When he retired after the 1945 season, his lifetime home run total of 534 ranked second only to Ruth. Oddly, both Foxx and his beloved wife, Dorothy, died from asphyxiation less than a year apart.

The grave of Jimmie Foxx still receives flowers.

Max Carey
Woodlawn Park North Cemetery, Miami

With a 20-year career that evenly split the Deadball Era and the Roaring Twenties, Max Carey was never a home run threat, but woe to the pitcher who allowed him to get on base. He led the league in stolen bases 10 times and finished with a lifetime total of 738 swipes, still enough to rank him as ninth all-time, nearly 90 years after he played his final game. Born in Indiana, he moved to Florida in his later years, and in his Hall of Fame induction speech in 1961 he made an impassioned plea for MLB to consider his adoptive home for a franchise.

Carey's wife, Aurelia, is buried by his side, though her death year of 1985 has never been filled-in on their stone.

He and Foxx both served as the managers of the Fort Wayne Daisies of the All-American Girls Professional Baseball League, Carey from 1950 to 1951 and Foxx in 1952. The two were friends, and when Foxx died in 1967, Carey served as one of his pallbearers.

Bill Klem
Graceland Memorial Park, Coral Gables

Over the course of a 45-year career in umpiring, Bill Klem became one of the most ubiquitous names in all of baseball. During the first half of the 20th century, if something important happened on a National League diamond, chances are Bill Klem was there. He appeared in 18 World Series and was on the field for five no-hitters. Considered by many to be the greatest arbiter of the game, he is credited on his Hall of Fame plaque with the introduction of hand signals, although this is apocryphal. Hand signals preceded Klem's career by at least two decades. He holds the career record for ejections, a number aided by his automatic hook when someone referred to him by the hated nickname of "Catfish."

The first game Klem ever umpired featured the barnstorming black team, the New York Cuban Giants, which admittedly fielded few actual Cubans in its long history. Today, Klem is buried in Coral Gables, minutes from Miami's famed Little Havana community.

Klem's weathered marker.

His grave is within sight of Graceland Memorial Park's Mausoleo Cubano, which houses the remains of over 100 members of Miami's Cuban community.

Ed Walsh
Forest Lawn North, Pompano Beach

Forty-five minutes north of Miami, in Pompano Beach, is the grave of arguably the greatest spitballer ever to soak a pill, Ed Walsh. While he played 14 seasons in the majors, all but one of those with the Chicago White Sox, the bulk of his statistics were earned over a seven-year stretch between 1906 and 1912. In that span he led the league in innings pitched four times, including a now-unfathomable 464 in 1908, when he also won 40 games. The overuse of his arm led to the abbreviation of his career, and he appeared in only 33 games over the last five years he played.

Walsh's grave, oxidized by Florida's sea air.

In his heyday, using the now-outlawed spitter, Walsh was dominance incarnate. He still ranks first in lifetime ERA with a 1.82 mark and second in WHIP, a modern metric that represents Walks and Hits divided by Innings Pitched, with a 0.9996. The only modern-day pitcher to even come close to that kind of mastery is Mariano Rivera, with a career WHIP of 1.000. Rivera's lifetime ERA of 2.20 is more than one-third of a run higher.

Billy Herman and Gary Carter
Riverside Memorial Park, Tequesta

Prior to World War II, Billy Herman was one of the top-hitting second basemen in the game. He batted better than .300 in seven of his first nine seasons.

The batter on Herman's plaque is a lefty, but Billy himself batted right-handed.

I should not have needed to visit the grave of Gary Carter.

He led the league with 227 hits in 1935, including 57 doubles, and was a 10-time All Star. Herman even tried his hand at managing, first for a single season with the Pirates in 1947 and then, 17 years later, two seasons with the Boston Red Sox, but he never had the success that he did as a player. In between those two stints, he worked as a coach for the Brooklyn Dodgers and the Milwaukee Braves. Herman died of cancer in 1992 at the age of 83.

Cancer also claimed the life of the Hall of Famer whose grave is barely 50 steps from Herman's, although Gary Carter was considerably younger when he died at the age of 57. In a 19-year career spent primarily with the Montreal Expos, Carter was an 11-time All-Star whose exuberance earned him the nickname, "Kid." A reliable hitter with a lifetime batting average of .262 and 324 home runs, Carter's contributions could not be measured by offensive statistics alone. Many credit his trade to the New York Mets in 1985 as being the final piece of the puzzle that led that franchise to a championship the following year. It was his hit with two outs in the tenth inning of Game 6 of the 1986 World Series that initiated the rally that eventually ended with Mookie Wilson's dribbler rolling between the legs of Bill Buckner. When he died from a brain tumor in 2012, nine years after his election to the Hall, both Montreal and New York mourned.

I once had a chance to photograph Carter with the ball while he was still alive. This was not long after I had begun the project, so I had not yet approached any of the living members nor, more importantly, any of the baseball card show promoters about access. Still uncertain about how I was going to reach those who were alive without paying more money than I was willing to commit to a single photograph, I left the card show with the thought that Carter was young enough that there would certainly be a second chance. There never was. Walking away without that image is my greatest project-related regret.

Dazzy Vance
Stage Stand Cemetery, Homosassa Springs

Sources disagree as to how Charles Arthur "Dazzy" Vance earned his memorable moniker. Some say it was for the dazzling fastball that he threw as a teenager. Vance himself once claimed it was his grandfather who fixed the boy with the name because of the youth's fascination with a cowboy entertainer who mispronounced the word "daisy" when he saw something he liked, as in, "ain't that a dazzy." No matter the real story, few players had a more unlikely start to a Hall of Fame career. Brief appearances in the majors in 1915 and 1918 were unimpressive. When he won his first game during the 1922 season with the Brooklyn Dodgers, as a 30-year-old, no one could have guessed that he had another 196 victories to come over the next 14 seasons. He led the league in strikeouts for seven straight years and took home an MVP Award in 1924, when he also won the pitching Triple Crown.

The cemetery where Vance is buried, Stage Stand in Homosassa Springs, also had an unlikely beginning. The "stand" was a stopping place for mail runs in the early 1800s. One day, when the local Harrell family did not come out to pick up their mail, it was discovered that they were murdered in the night, ostensibly by Native Americans.

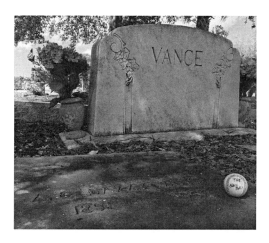

There is some debate as to whether Vance's given name was Charles Arthur or, as his stone indicates, Arthur Charles.

The neighbors buried the family near the stand and, ultimately, decided to keep the location as a cemetery. In the days before a small band of pioneers would have the resources or the inclination to properly carve a marker, graves were denoted by large slabs of unmarked rock. Many of the original slab markers remain there to this day.

Ray Dandridge
Fountainhead Memorial, Palm Bay

Ray Dandridge is the lone Negro Leaguer buried in Florida. If he had been born just a few years later, the contact-hitting third baseman for the Detroit Stars, Newark Eagles, and New York Cubans would have had a chance to leave his mark in the majors. By the time integration occurred, he was in his mid–30s and too old in baseball years to be "starting" a career. After eight seasons in the Mexican League, Dandridge did break into the minor league American Association in 1949 with the help of Alex Pompez. He rewarded the scout's faith with a torrid .362 average that season. In the five years he played in the organized minors, he batted .312.

Just 45 minutes from Cape Canaveral, the mausoleum at Fountainhead Memorial where Dandridge and his wife are interred features a beautiful stained glass window depicting a rocket lifting off into space and an astronaut holding an American flag.

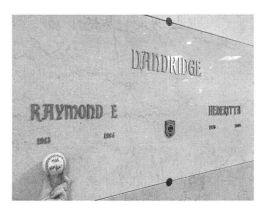

Dandridge's mausoleum niche has a small plaque denoting his membership in the Hall.

It reads "We came in peace for all mankind," part of the text on the plaque left behind on the Moon by the Apollo 11 astronauts in July 1969.

Bill Terry
Evergreen Cemetery, Jacksonville

Bill Terry was a stalwart at first base for the New York Giants from 1923 to 1936. From 1927 until the end of his career, the eagle-eyed Terry never hit below .310. His crowning season was his 1930 campaign, when his 254 hits resulted in a .401 batting average. To this day it remains the last .400 season in the National League. He followed his playing days with a successful managerial career, steering the Giants to three pennants and the World Championship in 1933, his first full season at the helm. Player-manager Terry hit .273 in that Series and had a home run in the fourth inning of Game 6 to open the scoring in an eventual 2–1 Giants victory.

Buried in Jacksonville, Bill Terry became a successful local businessman outside of baseball.

Nap Lajoie
Daytona Memorial Park, Daytona Beach

When Nap Lajoie became the manager of the Cleveland Naps in 1905, the club had already adopted his name as their own two years previously.

Lajoie's grave highlights some of his career accomplishments.

One of the most beloved players in Cleveland history as soon as he walked through the stadium doors, he originally made his considerable mark in Philadelphia in 1896. He hit better than .300 in 17 out of the 21 years he played, including a blistering .426 in 1901 with the Athletics, when he helped legitimize the newly formed American League. He is often mentioned in the same breath as Ty Cobb, who by 1907 had seized Lajoie's crown as the league's best hitter. Their famous 1910 batting race was the only time they would finish with the top two marks in the same year.

Lajoie is buried in vacation mecca Daytona Beach, home to the Daytona Tortugas, a class-A advanced affiliate of the Cincinnati Reds as of 2015, although they were a part of the Cubs organization for the 20 years prior. The Tortugas play at Jackie Robinson Ballpark, built in 1914 and originally known as City Island Ball Park. The name change is a nod to the fact that when Robinson arrived in Florida for Spring Training as a member of the Montreal Royals in 1946, Daytona Beach was the only city in the state that would allow the Dodgers to field an integrated team. Today, a statue of Robinson stands near the front entrance of the stadium to commemorate the city's important role in the story of baseball's finest hour.

The Playground
◆ NEW JERSEY ◆

If New York City was the incubator of the game, New Jersey was its playground. Although the legendary Knickerbockers briefly played in Madison Square Park in Manhattan, they moved across the river to Elysian Fields in Hoboken almost immediately. Already a popular location for Manhattanites to escape from the city, the park began hosting games of ball at least as early as November 2, 1843, when the little-known Magnolias Base Ball Club played a match "precisely at one o'clock" followed by a celebratory "chowder at 4 o'clock." Many of the most important games from the nascent days of the 1840s and 1850s were played on this hallowed ground, and four future Hall of Famers called it home: Alexander Cartwright, George & Harry Wright, and Henry Chadwick.

Its proximity to both New York City and Philadelphia makes it difficult for New Jersey to claim enough of an audience to field a major league team. They did try, twice. The Elizabeth Resolutes were a part of the 1873 National Association season, but after a miserable year in which they won only two games and lost 21, they disbanded. The Federal League offered one more opportunity for the state, when the Newark Pepper joined the league in 1915. Originally the Indianapolis Hoosiers, the club won the Federal League championship in 1914. Despite their success in the Midwest, executives saw more dollars to be made near New York and shifted the team to the East Coast. The Pepper finished a respectable 80–72 and featured not only future Hall of Famer Edd Roush, but the second half of their season was managed by Bill McKechnie, his first opportunity ever to steer a team. The Federal League collapsed at the end of 1915, and New Jersey has never hosted another major league team since.

Mule Suttles
Glendale Cemetery, Bloomfield

In later years, New Jersey was an important home for Negro League baseball. Three of the four Hall of Famers buried in New Jersey earned their glory playing black ball. Home to the Newark Eagles from 1936 to 1948, some of the greatest names in black baseball played for owner Effa Manley, including Ray Dandridge, Leon Day, Willie Wells, and Mule Suttles. Suttles, who earned his nickname because of the brute strength he used to propel balls over the fence, remained in Newark when he retired as a player in 1944 after nine seasons on the Eagles.

Mule Suttles's grave, featuring a portrait of the powerful hitter.

Suttles was so strong, he once hit a ball out of Estadio Tropical in Havana, a distance of roughly 600 feet. Today, he is buried in Bloomfield. His grave went unmarked for 40 years until his election to the Hall of Fame in 2006.

Frank Grant

East Ridgelawn Cemetery, Clifton

Frank Grant starred on the diamond long before the Negro Leagues even existed. Like Sol White, Grant played in the 1880s, which allowed him to be one of the select few African Americans to make an appearance in professional baseball before the color line was drawn with such rigidity. Considered by many to be the greatest black ballplayer of the 19th century, Grant was similar to White in another way. He became the second player on the quest who had no marker. I was only a few graves into the journey, but a disturbing trend was beginning to emerge.

Frank Grant; another black ballplayer, another unmarked grave.

Pop Lloyd

Atlantic City Cemetery, Pleasantville

A premiere shortstop during his playing days, Pop Lloyd was called the black Honus Wagner. Despite that legendary comparison,

perhaps his greatest impact came after he finished his time on the field and brought what he had learned about the game to the children of Atlantic City. He was such a leader in the community that the Little League field was named in Lloyd's honor in 1949, at a time when it was still illegal for blacks to join whites on the city's famous beaches. In truth, the naming of the field was an attempt by State Senator Hap Farley to curry the black vote. It was a ploy among many by the astute politician that must have had some success, as Farley had a 30-year career in New Jersey politics, even becoming the de facto head of the Republican Party in Atlantic City. Despite the somewhat dubious reasons for the naming, the honor remains well-deserved. Generations of African American children in South Jersey learned the game from Pop Lloyd.

The stone is original from his death but the additional marker was placed in 1997 by the Committee to Restore Pop Lloyd Stadium, a group that achieved its founding purpose in 1995.

The original and updated stones of Pop Lloyd.

Goose Goslin
Baptist Cemetery, Salem

Goose Goslin was a multi-faceted slugger who could hit for power and average, with enough speed to twice lead the league in triples. He led the league in RBIs in 1924 with 129, while leading the Washington Senators to their first World Championship. Goslin batted .344 in the Series and had three home runs and seven RBIs, cementing the 23-year-old's status as a Washington hero. He led the league in hitting in 1928, batting .379 to edge out Heine Manush's .378. Two seasons later, in June 1930, Goslin was traded to the St. Louis Browns for Manush and pitcher General Crowder. Goslin and Manush, who actually played together in 1933 when Goslin briefly returned to Wash-ington, were seemingly linked in history. Both elected to the Hall by the Veterans Committees of the mid-to-late 1960s, they died only three days apart in May 1971.

Goslin's nondescript grave in his hometown of Salem.

A Tale of Two Cities
(and the Places In-Between)
◆ PENNSYLVANIA ◆

With two of the most important cities in the history of baseball serving as bookends, Pennsylvania really is a keystone in the game's story. Not only have they contributed a wealth of talented players to the sport's rosters, but Philadelphia and Pittsburgh have also served very different roles in the development of baseball. Most starkly, that difference can be seen in their legacies regarding race. Pittsburgh served as an epicenter of the Negro Leagues, while Philadelphia would eventually pass a resolution in 2016, apologizing to Jackie Robinson for the treatment he received from the city when he joined the Dodgers.

The Philadelphia area is a relatively concentrated one for Hall of Famer graves, which is appropriate when one considers the historic role the city had in the game. As early as 1761, the Charitable School, Academy and College of Philadelphia had posted an edict banning ball play, though they certainly were not referring to baseball as we know it. In the 1850s, it became one of the first cities after New York to organize the game enough to see the regular play of scheduled contests. Interestingly, the popularity of baseball in Philadelphia was likely hampered by the tremendous success of cricket in the city, a fascination that lasted until nearly the end of the 19th century.

For the first 55 years of the 20th century, Philadelphia hosted two Major League Baseball teams, the Athletics and the Phillies, the latter of which were also known in their infancy as the Quakers. The Athletics moved to Kansas City in 1955, but the Phillies have remained. The story of the Phils is one that is riddled with futility, but they did have one of the most dominant runs in their history recently, from 2007 to 2011.

George Davis
Fernwood Cemetery, Fernwood

Five of the six Hall of Famers buried in Philadelphia and its suburbs made their mark before the so-called Golden Age of the 1950s. George Davis played for three different teams, but had his finest years from 1893 to 1901 with the New York Giants. In that time, he never hit below .300. He was elected by the Veterans Committee in 1998, 58 years after his death, and sports an informative stone installed by the now-defunct George Davis chapter of the Society for American Baseball Research (SABR), which represented northeastern New York, where he was born. The marker was placed soon after his induction to the Hall. Davis died in a mental asylum due to the effects of syphilis, and his wife did not mark his grave at the time. His fate was unknown until 1968, more than a quarter-century after he died, and was only uncovered by the detective work of Hall of Fame historian Lee Allen.

Davis's belatedly installed stone.

Harry Wright
West Laurel Hills Cemetery,
Bala Cynwyd

Henry Wright was one of a small handful of individuals in the Hall whose initial contributions to the game came before the major leagues were even conceived. He was a regular on the Elysian Fields of Hoboken, playing for the Knickerbockers and the Gothams. He was the founder and manager of the famed 1869 Cincinnati Red Stockings, who went 57–0 in the first year a "professional" designation was applied to NA clubs. After the Cincinnati club folded in 1870, Wright served as the skipper of the National Association Boston Red Stockings from 1871 to 1875, joining them when they moved to the National League in 1876. He also managed the Providence Grays and, in 1884, took over the Philadelphia club, where he steered the cornerstone franchise for the next 10 years.

The pedestal of Wright's grave, naming him "The Father of Baseball."

Made of bronze, Wright's statue was sculpted by Edmond Thomas Quinn.

His marker is a monument and features a giant pedestal adorned with a life-size statue of the man. It was erected using money collected on April 13, 1896, "Harry Wright Day," throughout the National League. All gate receipts that day went to a fund to honor the founder whose role in the development of the game rightfully earned him the moniker of "The Father of Baseball," a title he shares with several other men. From the size and grandeur of his statue, it's clear the promotion was a success.

Richie Ashburn

Gladwyne Methodist Church Cemetery, Gladwyne

The lone local Golden Era player is Richie Ashburn, whose career spanned 1948–1962. Ashburn was a beloved member of the Philadelphia Phillies for over 45 years, first as a player and then as a broadcaster following his retirement.

Ashburn's stone sadly notes the death of his daughter and grandson, both of whom predeceased him.

He was a reliable presence in Philadelphia, rarely missing a game or a pitch. After his rookie year, he failed to appear in fewer than 20 games over the course of his remaining 11 years on the Phillies. He averaged only 38 strikeouts per season during his career and twice led the league in hitting. As a broadcaster, his dry wit made him a favorite to listeners at home, who enjoyed hearing him beside the sonorous voice of Harry Kalas for over two decades. Ashburn died in his hotel room in New York City in September 1997, not long after calling a game against the Mets, the team he spent his final season as a player with in 1962.

Louis Santop

Philadelphia National Cemetery, Philadelphia

Louis Santop, the great Negro Leagues catcher, became the first player I visited on the quest who was buried in a National Cemetery. Santop was a power hitter with a confidence that bordered on arrogance. His antics and strength earned him the nickname "The Black Babe Ruth," before the tag was affixed to Josh Gibson. Sadly, the end of his career was marred by an error in the 1924 Colored World Series. Playing for the Hilldale Daisies, he dropped a late-inning pop-up that ultimately led to a Kansas City Monarchs victory. Santop never recovered from the public humiliation unleashed upon him by his manager, Frank Warfield, and he was out of baseball two years later.

Santop's standard, government-issued white stone, which equalizes military men in death no matter their rank in life, is starting to "sugar," a grave hunter's term for the crumbling that happens to some marble graves over time. It also sports his full name, Lewis Santop Loftin, which does not appear on his Hall of Fame plaque. There is some confusion about his moniker, beyond the alternate spellings of his first name. Depending on the source, the two final names are sometimes swapped, appearing as Louis Loftin Santop, including on the Hall of Fame's website.

The "sugaring" stone of Louis Santop.

The elongated grave of Connie Mack.

Connie Mack
Holy Sepulchre Cemetery, Cheltenham

Connie Mack, the longest-tenured manager in baseball history, is buried in an above-ground crypt. Setting the standard for mediocre players who went on to heralded managing careers, no skipper has won (or lost) more games than Mack. Simultaneously tight-fisted and generous, the stately gentleman who always appeared in the dugout in a jacket and tie was one of baseball's most complicated men.

It is therefore interesting that his grave is relatively understated. It is uncertain whether the great length of his crypt is due to his famous height (he was 6'1" in an age when that was uncommon in the sport) or whether it was to accommodate the entirety of his birth name, McGillicuddy. Born in East Brookfield, Massachusetts, he fittingly chose to be buried in Philadelphia. He led the Athletics for 50 years, winning nine pennants and five World Series. For the first half of the 20th century, Mr. Mack was Philadelphia baseball.

Chief Bender
Hillside Cemetery, Roslyn

Charles Albert "Chief" Bender spent the bulk of his illustrious career pitching for Mack on the Athletics and was an integral part of the A's glory days. He helped lead them to five pennants and three World Series titles between 1905–1914, en route to a career 2.46 ERA and 212 victories. His skills fading, he left the game after the 1917 season and spent a year contributing to the war effort, working in the Philadelphia shipyards. After managing for a few years in the minors, Bender returned to the big leagues as a coach for the Chicago White Sox.

In 1925, eight years after Bender last pitched in a major league game, White Sox manager Eddie Collins put the 41-year-old in for one final inning. Bender surrendered a two-run home run to Roy Carlyle in the 6–3 loss to the Red Sox. After the game, Bender told reporters that he was in better shape than "two-thirds of the men in the American League," and he hoped that his inning signaled a possible full-time return. That hope did not come to pass.

Bender's Native American heritage made him a rarity in the game, even then, and led to his unfortunate nickname. However, the name's usage on his stone proves that by the end Bender, who was elected to the Hall the year prior to his death, had accepted that in the annals of baseball history, he would forever be "Chief."

The inclusion of his nickname on the stone of "Chief" Bender is telling.

Nestor Chylak
Saint Cyril and Methodius Church Cemetery, Peckville

Nestor Chylak was one of the most respected umpires of the post-war era. Looking for work after World War II, where he fought in the Battle of the Bulge, Chylak started umpiring college and minor league games. He called his first major league game in 1954. A model of consistency, he had a 24-year career in which he called three American League Championship Series, six All-Star Games, and five World Series. He was known not just for his steady judgment, but also for his ability to listen to the objections of managers and players without escalating the situation.

Chylak's stone notes his service in World War II.

Chylak was the crew chief during the unfortunate "10-Cent Beer Night" promotion staged by the Cleveland Indians in 1974. The eventual drunken brawl that occurred led him to declare the game a forfeit.

Bucky Harris
St. Peter's Lutheran Church, Hughestown

With a managerial career that began at the young age of 27, Bucky Harris spent 29 seasons as a major league skipper. His first chance to lead came as the player-manager of the 1924 Washington Senators, his first of three separate tenures leading the ball club in the nation's capital. He immediately guided his team to a World Series Championship, the first and only in Washington history. After he left the Senators following the 1928 season, he had brief stops managing the Detroit Tigers, Boston Red Sox, and Philadelphia Phillies, as well as another eight-year stint with the Senators, before he joined the New York Yankees in 1947. He won his second World Series that year, but after a third-place finish in 1948, he was out of job and back with the Senators again in 1950. He spent two final seasons leading the Tigers in 1955 and 1956 before retiring at the age of 59. His 2,158 managerial wins ranks seventh all-time. While Harris was mostly a mediocre hitter, he began his career as a specialist at being hit by pitches, leading the league three seasons in a row from 1920 to 1922.

"Boy manager," Bucky Harris.

Jennings's stone was updated after his induction into the Hall.

Hugh Jennings

St. Catharine's Cemetery, Moscow

Like Bucky Harris, Hughie Jennings was an expert at getting hit by a pitch, leading the league for five straight years from 1894 to 1898. Part of the rough and tumble National League Baltimore Orioles team that featured John McGraw and were led by Ned Hanlon, they excelled at getting on base by any means necessary. His career total of 287 HBP remains the highest in baseball history, two more than modern leader Craig Biggio. Jennings managed the Detroit Tigers for 14 years, from 1907 to 1920, winning three pennants. His .543 winning percentage ranks 19th all-time.

Christy Mathewson

Lewisburg Cemetery, Lewisburg

Three hours west of Philadelphia is the town of Lewisburg, home of Bucknell University. Forty-three attendees of Bucknell appear in the baseball-reference database of major league players, but only Christy Mathewson is in the Hall of Fame. Mathewson, for his part, seemed rather fond of his alma mater as he chose to be buried in its backyard. Within walking distance of Christy Mathewson Memorial football

stadium, as well as Depew baseball field, Mathewson's grave highlights his military service and does not mention baseball. He is the only member of the Hall to die as a direct result of serving in the armed forces, his lungs seared by poison gas during a training exercise in World War I.

The only Bucknell alum to appear in more major league games than Mathewson was Mickey Doolin, who appeared in 1,728 of them between 1905–1918, primarily for the Phillies. Doolin was a freshman in 1899, the same year Christy Mathewson entered college, making the two likely teammates. Mickey played for the Bucknell Bisons until 1904. By 1901, Mathewson's school days were done. He dropped out and instead proceeded to win 373 regular-season baseball games, with a lifetime ERA of 2.13 and a WHIP of 1.058. He was one of the five selected to be a founding member of the Hall in 1936, along with Ty Cobb, Babe Ruth, Honus Wagner and Walter Johnson. Almost 100 years after his death, Mathewson is still cited as one of the greatest pitchers of all time.

* * *

Perhaps no other place, with the exception of Kansas City, can claim as close a connection to Negro Leagues history as Pittsburgh. Home to both the Pittsburgh Crawfords and the Homestead Grays (who in later years split their playing time between Pittsburgh and Washington, D.C.), the city was a capital of black baseball for many years. Between 1933–1948, either the Crawfords or the Grays were division champions 12 times. Legendary players such as Cool Papa Bell, Oscar Charleston, Josh Gibson, Judy Johnson, Buck Leonard, Satchel Paige, and Smokey Joe Williams all spent time playing in Pittsburgh. Today, the Heinz History Center, located just a mile from the Pirates' home PNC Park, honors that tradition by dedicating a portion of their Western Pennsylvania Sports Museum to the city's connection to its Negro Leagues past.

The lack of a foundation for the stone of Cum Posey will make its survival subject to extreme weather.

Cum Posey
Homestead Cemetery, Homestead

Homestead Cemetery is on the other side of the Monongahela River, after one has crossed Homestead Grays Bridge. The bridge itself is decorated with fluttering banners which feature images of some of the biggest talents ever to play for the club. Buried in the cemetery, appropriately, is Cumberland Willis Posey. Originally a pitcher for the Grays, Posey became the team owner in 1920. He built them into a perennial powerhouse, winning nine pennants between 1937–1945. He also, with the help of his co-owner, Rufus "Sonnyman" Jackson, left the team solvent enough to outlive Posey himself by five years. He missed the integration of the major leagues by 13 months, dying from lung cancer in March 1946.

Josh Gibson
Allegheny Cemetery, Pittsburgh

The greatest slugger ever to play for Posey, Josh Gibson, is buried 30 minutes away in Allegheny Cemetery, adjacent to the eponymous river. Gibson starred for the Grays *and* the Crawfords. His fame is eclipsed by only Satchel Paige's in the annals of black baseball. While Mule Suttles hit more verified home runs than Gibson, only Mark McGwire has

ever hit them at as furious a pace. Gibson hit a home run every 10.6 at bats, McGwire every 10.61. Ruth trails them both at 11.76.

The story of Gibson's stone is a sadly familiar one. Buried in an unmarked grave for 30 years, Gibson's simple marker was installed due to the efforts of his former teammate, Ted Page (and some financial assistance from Willie Stargell and Bowie Kuhn) in the late 1970s. When Page himself died, murdered with a baseball bat in 1984, there was no one to raise funds for him. His ashes remained in a community vault at Allegheny Cemetery until 2013, when an organization known as the Negro Leagues Baseball Grave Marker Project came to the rescue. There'll be much more about the NLBGMP later in the book.

Gibson's grave site is one of the few I altered for the photo. Normally I do not touch any of the mementos that people leave behind because I think of them as part of the story. However, in this case I set aside a rain-soaked, poorly laminated picture of Manny Sanguillen and a leaping Steve Blass, celebrating the Pirates' 1971 World Series victory. It had turned to mostly decomposed pulp and was just ugly.

The remaining Hall of Fame graves in the Pittsburgh area are predictably all connected to the Pirates. Originally named the Alleghenys, the Pirates were founded in 1882 and remain one of baseball's most storied franchises.

The simple, long-overdue stone of the Negro Leagues' greatest slugger, Josh Gibson.

They appeared in the first World Series, losing to Boston five games to three. They have been in six more Fall Classics since then and have won five of them, all save the 1927 Series, which they lost to the famed Yankees' Murderers' Row. Two other major league teams have called Pittsburgh home, the Players' League Burghers of 1890 and the Federal League Rebels, who played in 1914 and 1915.

Pud Galvin
Calvary Cemetery, Pittsburgh

James Francis "Pud" Galvin was born on Christmas Day in 1856. After a brief debut with the National Association St. Louis Brown Stockings in 1875, he disappeared off the major league map until 1879. After his return, he spent seven seasons dominating National League hitters as part of the Buffalo Bisons, twice winning 46 games. He brought his star power to Pittsburgh in 1885, when he joined the Alleghenys. He pitched there until 1892, winning 138 games between two Pittsburgh franchises, including a single season with the Burghers. His death just 10 years later was an untimely one, leaving a wife and six children in poverty. When I first visited the cemetery, the small family stone that marks the plot was solid enough, but the stone that specified Pud's location was cracked and severely compromised, bearing only his name and no other information. That would change by the time The Hall Ball was complete, in no small part due to my efforts. Yet another story for later in the book.

The great crack running down the length of Galvin's stone assures it will not last.

Wagner's ground-flush stone was a challenge to find.

Honus Wagner
Jefferson Memorial Park, Pleasant Hills

Eight years after Galvin retired, Honus Wagner played his first game for the Pirates. Between that final year of the 19th century and Wagner's last season of 1917, Pittsburgh fans were treated to some of the greatest baseball excellence from any era. Bill James ranks Wagner as the second-greatest player of all time in his "New Historical Baseball Abstract," trailing only Ruth. Nearly 100 years after Wagner played his final game, he still ranks in the career top 10 in hits, doubles and triples. His grave marker is flush to the ground, in a style that was popular at the time of his death. It turned out to be one of the most difficult for me to find, as there were no visual clues in the field of low-lying stones (or Stew Thornley's photo) to aid me. Anna and I scoured the field for nearly an hour before we finally located him.

Barney Dreyfuss
West View Cemetery, Pittsburgh

Wagner was brought to Pittsburgh by Barney Dreyfuss. Born in Freiburg, Germany, Dreyfuss was the embodiment of the American dream. At 19 he immigrated, working as a bookkeeper. Just three years later, in 1888, he was a partial investor in the National League Louisville Colonels.

After the overheated hunt to find Wagner, Dreyfuss's shady grave was a respite.

A faded cap adorned the grave of Pie Traynor.

When the Colonels folded in 1899, Dreyfuss, now the sole owner, purchased a portion of the Pirates and brought many of his star players with him, including Deacon Phillippe, Rube Waddell, and Wagner. He steered the team to four World Series before he died in 1932. The Dreyfuss family plot is substantial, but not ostentatious. Barney's stone is quite simple for an owner who was so influential during his time. Compared to the mausoleums of contemporaries like Charles Comiskey and Clark Griffith, Dreyfuss's ivy-covered and shady grave seems downright modest.

Pie Traynor
Homewood Cemetery, Pittsburgh

The last great Pirate buried in the area is Pie Traynor, who made his debut with the club just three years after Wagner retired. That means that from Galvin's first appearance with the Alleghenys in 1885 until Traynor's final game in 1937, a period of 52 years, in only 11 of those years did one of these three men not grace a Pittsburgh roster. Traynor retired with a lifetime batting average of .320. Perhaps his most memorable season came in 1925, when he starred in the World Series, hitting .346 with a home run and four RBIs en route to leading the Pirates to a seven-game victory over the Senators. Traynor is buried in Homewood Cemetery, as are three generations of Heinz family scions and Josh Gibson, Jr., who had a brief Negro Leagues career of his own before a broken ankle ended his playing days.

Nellie Fox
St. Thomas Cemetery, St. Thomas

In a 19-year career, the bulk of which was spent with the Chicago White Sox, Nellie Fox was a 12-time All-Star who hit better than .300 six times. Despite hitting only two home runs for the 1959 season (in a career in which he would slug only 35 total), and hitting a solid but not earth-shattering .306, Fox took home MVP honors that year while leading the Sox to their lone World Series appearance during his tenure. Known for the distinctive way he choked up on the bat, Fox was an effective contact hitter and an on-field dynamo. Manning second base in 2,295 of the 2,303 games he appeared in, Fox won three of the first four Gold Gloves awarded to the position.

The statistically informative stone of Nellie Fox.

Because his offensive stats were weak compared to most Hall of Famers, it was a long road for Fox to gain entry to Cooperstown. He was not elected until 22 years after his death. Once he was, his family clearly wanted to make sure that it was known to posterity, as his gravestone was altered to include the date of his induction, August 3, 1997. Although he spent most of his adult life in Chicago, it was telling of the man that he would forever call the town of his birth, St. Thomas, home.

Eddie Plank
Evergreen Cemetery, Gettysburg

Another hometown hero was the pride of Gettysburg, Eddie Plank. Arriving in the majors the same time as the American League, Plank was a stalwart for the Athletics from 1901 to 1914, winning 20 or more games seven times with the A's. He won another 21 in 1915, at the age of 39, with the St. Louis Terriers of the Federal League. By the end of his 17-year career, he notched 326 victories, currently 13th all-time. Always considered a trifle odd, Plank talked to himself on the mound and went through an elaborate ritual before throwing each pitch. It was said that hitters would often swing at bad pitches simply because they wanted to get things moving.

Plank is buried in Evergreen Cemetery in Gettysburg. On the day of my visit, the two planters that flank his grave were filled with baseballs.

Born just 12 years and two months after the battle that has forever marked this little town, it is certain that Plank was raised on the tales of the heroic deeds done over those three days in July 1863. It is also certain that at some point he paid homage at Soldiers' National Cemetery, which was consecrated in November of that year as a way of managing the volume of the dead from the battle. Soldiers' shares a border with Evergreen. Thus, "Gettysburg" Eddie's eternal rest is taking place just a few hundred yards from the spot where Abraham Lincoln inspired a nation.

Herb Pennock
Union Hill Cemetery, Kennett Square

Herb Pennock already had some success with the Boston Red Sox before he joined the Yankees in 1923, but as with so many others, it was in pinstripes where he really blossomed. Pennock was another of Red Sox owner Harry Frazee's ill-conceived deals, though not as egregious as the selling of the Babe. The left-hander had won 60 games in seven seasons in Boston. By the time he left the Bronx in 1933, he had won 162 more. He had a record of 5–0 in World Series games, including the 1926 contest in which he won two games as a starter. In Game 7 of that Series, he also made a three-inning relief appearance.

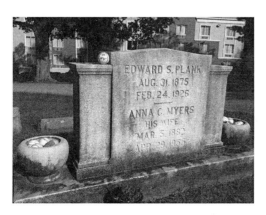

Eddie Plank's well-visited grave.

Pennock's wife, Esther, outlived him by four decades.

Pennock had pitched a complete-game, 10-inning, 3–2 victory three days before, and he held the Cardinals scoreless during his three innings of emergency work, scattering three hits. Unfortunately for him, Grover Cleveland Alexander was simultaneously having the crowning moment of his storied career, also joining the game in relief after defeating the Yankees just the day before in his own complete-game masterpiece. After striking out Tony Lazzeri to end a bases-loaded threat in the seventh inning, Alexander held the Yankees hitless for two more innings and secured the Cardinals' first world championship. Pennock's own heroic effort has largely been forgotten to history.

The Land of Our Irish Founders
◆ MASSACHUSETTS ◆

Kids have been playing ball on Boston Common since at least 1834, when Robin Carver's *The Book of Sports* featured an engraving of boys playing an unidentified ball game in what is now the oldest city park in the United States. By the mid–19th century, boys (and men) played what was known as the Massachusetts Game on the historic site. A variation of baseball that eventually succumbed to the better marketing of the New York Game, official Major League Baseball Historian John Thorn has noted that the Massachusetts Game "was in many ways the superior version, for both players and spectators." Today, few know of this obscure variant. Among its many differences from the game we know was that it took place on a square playing area instead of a diamond, with the striker standing between the first and final bases. It also allowed a baserunner to use the whole field and not be contained to pre-determined paths when trying to advance to the next base.

By the time of the founding of the National Association, the New York Game had won the war for the hearts and minds of the public. After the dissolution of his Cincinnati Red Stockings in 1870, Harry Wright founded a team of the same name in Boston for the 1871 season, and the city has remained an important presence in Major League Baseball ever since. When the NA folded, Wright's Red Stockings shifted to the National League and played under multiple names, including the Beaneaters, Doves, Rustlers, Bees and, ultimately, Braves. They remained in Boston until 1953, when they moved to Milwaukee, shaking up the major league baseball map for the first time since the Federal League in 1914.

By far the most popular team in Boston history is, of course, the Red Sox originally known as the Americans. Despite boasting some of the brightest stars in baseball history, the Red Sox famously went 86 years between championships, earning them a cult following. Between the highly dramatic fashion in which the Red Sox lost some of their more heartbreaking games and the sheer quantity of scribes who are based in Boston, tens of thousands of pages of text have been written about those years of futility. That all changed in 2004, when on a night that featured a lunar eclipse, the Red Sox became champions of baseball. They have won three more World Series since, in 2007, 2013 and 2018, and are perennial post-season contenders.

During the 1850s, half a century before the Red Sox became founding members of the American League, as the two different versions of the game still battled for supremacy, the city of Boston saw a huge influx of Irish immigrants. Many left the Emerald Isle, suffering from what history has come to call the Great Famine, despite the fact that the country was producing and shipping roughly 40 shiploads of food a day to their English colonial masters. Fleeing the potato blight that was robbing the Irish of what little food they were allowed to keep, they washed up on the shores of Massachusetts. Once there, they had an immediate impact on the blossoming American game.

At the time of this writing, nine Hall of Famers are buried within the general vicinity of Boston. Of those nine, five were first-generation Americans whose parents emigrated from Ireland. In addition, serving as a testament to Boston's role in establishing the early game, only one of those nine began his career in the 20th century.

He was a shooting star, burning hot and bright for 15 years of exceptional professional play, with a lifetime .307 batting average, before fizzling out of the game at the age of 35 due to the effects of hard living and alcohol. He died a year later in 1894, from a case of pneumonia that was exacerbated by his lifestyle. It was reported that over 7,000 people attended his funeral. Despite this, his grave is modest and crumbling. Without intervention, it will likely not survive into the next century.

King Kelly
Mount Hope Cemetery, Mattapan

Buried in sprawling Mount Hope Cemetery is the man who is considered by many to be the quintessential 19th century Irish ballplayer, Mike "King" Kelly. A character who was larger than life, Kelly inspired not only a legion of fans, but also was responsible for one of the first musical odes dedicated to a ballplayer, "Slide Kelly Slide." Tales of the devilish Kelly, both clever and talented, could fill volumes.

Tommy McCarthy and Hugh Duffy
Mount Calvary Cemetery, Roslindale

The other four locals whose parents left Ireland are Tim Keefe, Hugh Duffy, Tommy McCarthy, and John Clarkson. Each of them made his major league debut in the 1880s and, other than Keefe, each spent multiple seasons playing on one of the professional squads that called Boston home. Playing a single season for the American Association Boston Reds in 1891, followed by nine more on the Beaneaters, Duffy had the longest Boston tenure of the four. A keen hitter, he ended his career with a lifetime batting average of .326, which included an 1884 season that saw him hit an unparalleled .440. That staggering number stands as a single-season record to this day and will never be beaten.

King Kelly's grave belies how admired he was at the time of his death.

Holder of the single season batting average record, Hugh Duffy.

Another victim of the bottle, John Clarkson.

McCarthy is credited by some as being responsible for the infield fly rule.

Buried in the same cemetery as Duffy, McCarthy made his debut with the 1884 Union Association Boston Reds before moving over to the Beaneaters the following season. He played alongside Duffy from 1892 to 1895, and the two were known as the "Heavenly Twins" of the Boston outfield. McCarthy was a successful base stealer, pacing the circuit in 1890 with 83. Despite this, his election to the Hall remains one of the more controversial, as his brief 13-year career featured only a small handful of exceptional seasons.

Tim Keefe and John Clarkson
Cambridge Cemetery, Cambridge

Clarkson was also a member of the 1892 Beaneaters (as was Kelly), although his time playing with McCarthy and Duffy was brief. By mid-season, he was released by Boston and signed on with the Cleveland Spiders. Clarkson won 328 games in his career, including a mind-boggling 53 in 1885, as well as another 49 in 1889, when he won the pitching Triple Crown, striking out 284 batters with a 2.73 ERA.

Keefe's stone pays homage to two relations of his who died in the Civil War.

Sadly, he spent the final years of his life in psychiatric hospitals, a victim of "mental disorders" that included depression and paranoia, both of which were worsened by his alcoholism. He was just 47 when he died.

Keefe, the final verifiable Irishman, is buried at Cambridge Cemetery in a plot not far from Clarkson. Keefe never played for a Boston squad but was instead a darling of New York. In a career that began with the upstate Troy Trojans in 1880, he played for the American Association New York Metropolitans, the National League New York Giants, and the Players' League New York Giants before finishing in Philadelphia, playing three seasons for the Phillies. He retired in 1894 with a lifetime 342 wins and 2.63 ERA. From 1883 through 1888, he was one of the most successful and durable arms in the game, twice leading the league in wins, ERA, and innings pitched.

Connolly is buried in the same plot as just some of his seven children.

Selee is the lone Hall of Famer born in New Hampshire.

Tom Connolly
St. Patrick's Cemetery, Natick

Umpire Tom Connolly was born in England and is credited with bringing about integrity and gravitas to the role of arbiter. A founding umpire of the American League, he remained on the field until 1931. He served as AL Umpire in Chief until 1954, a judicious presence in the game for over half a century. He was elected to the Hall in 1953, the same year as Bill Klem, making them the first two umpires to receive the honor. Connolly, who was 83 at the time, was too ill to attend his induction, but he lived another eight years, continuing to follow the game he helped legitimize.

Frank Selee
Wyoming Cemetery, Melrose

Frank Selee gained his fame as the manager of the Beaneaters from 1890 to 1901. In those 12 seasons, he steered his charges to five pennants. He spent four more years in Chicago with the Cubs, retiring after the 1905 campaign with a lifetime winning percentage of .598, third highest all-time for a manager with more than 10 seasons experience. Selee had an incredible eye for talent and was responsible for putting together the Cubs' famed infield of Joe Tinker, Johnny Evers, and Frank Chance. After a battle with pleurisy in 1902, Selee's lungs remained forever compromised, and in 1909 he died at the age of 49.

George Wright
Holyhood Cemetery, Brookline

When George Wright was a boy, his British-born father introduced him to cricket. When the elder Wright's Manhattan cricket club moved to Elysian Fields in Hoboken, George and his older brother, Harry, grew to learn and love the game of baseball, which was becoming the more popular sport at the Manhattan-adjacent sanctuary.

While not as grandiose as his brother's, George Wright's stone is substantial.

While Harry was the business pioneer, George was the one with amazing talent on the field. The highest-paid player on the famous 1869 Cincinnati Red Stockings, George dominated at the plate that year, hitting .633 in 57 games. Just two years later, the Wright brothers were founders of the Boston Red Stockings of the newly formed National Association, along with teammate Al Spalding. George hit .413 his first year and never below .329 in his five years with the dominant Boston squad. With the creation of the National League in 1876, Wright joined the second iteration of the Boston Red Stockings, where he played until 1881. He played one final season with the 1882 Providence Grays before leaving baseball and returning to cricket. He retired with a lifetime batting average of .301 in league play. Wright lived until 1937, long enough to see himself elected to the newly formed Hall of Fame. His post-playing legacy included serving as a member of the 1906–07 Mills Commission, which labeled Abner Doubleday the creator of baseball.

Eddie Collins
Linwood Cemetery, Weston

The final Boston-area Hall of Fame grave belongs to Eddie Collins, who certainly has a name that bespeaks of an Irish heritage, even if current research can only trace his father's family back two, America-based, generations prior. His mother was old–New England stock, pre-dating the Revolution. Of this pioneering group of Bostonian burials, Collins is the lone member to debut in the 20th century, in 1906. He spent 25 seasons playing for the Philadelphia Athletics and the Chicago White Sox. Through skill and longevity, his lifetime statistics rank him as one of the greatest to play the game, and may mark him as the single-most under-appreciated player in the Hall. As of the completion of the 2018 season, he was still 13th in lifetime WAR (a modern metric representing the number of wins he provided over a replacement player) and career on-base percentage. He was also

11th in hits, 12th in triples, eighth in stolen bases, and first in sacrifice hits.

No one has ever played more games at second base than Collins. With a career that is perfectly divided between the Deadball Era of Cobb and the power age of Ruth, his lifetime stats serve as an excellent barometer for the two epochs of the game. He is arguably the greatest player the person sitting next to you at the ballpark has likely never heard of.

While not as well-known as other Hall of Famers, Collins remains popular enough that the groundskeepers I asked for help immediately knew where to find him.

Candy Cummings
Aspen Grove Cemetery, Ware

Candy Cummings is in the Baseball Hall of Fame not so much for what he statistically accomplished, but for being credited as the inventor of one of the most important tools in a pitcher's arsenal, the curveball. According to Cummings himself, as a teenage boy he became fascinated at the way he could get clamshells to bend through the air when he threw them, leading him to study the physics involved in throwing a baseball.

The family plot of Candy Cummings.

The plaque later affixed to Burkett's grave gives special attention to his local resume.

After six seasons playing for two teams in Brooklyn, he joined the National Association in 1872 as a member of the New York Mutuals. He played for four more teams over the next five seasons, winning 140 games in that span. He was finished by 1877, when teams solved his now widely-used signature pitch. While his claims of creating the curveball have ensured his fame, some historians argue that others besides Cummings could claim credit, including Phonney Martin, Fred McSweeny and, perhaps most notably, Fred Goldsmith.

Jesse Burkett
St. John's Cemetery, Worcester

Jesse Burkett was an amazing control hitter who mastered the art of fouling off the ball until he got the pitch he wanted. Debuting with the New York Giants in 1890, he originally split playing responsibilities between the pitching mound and the outfield. His move to the Cleveland Spiders the following year ended his pitching career, but he had a breakout season in 1893, batting .348. It was the first of 10 straight .300 seasons, including two seasons, 1895 and 1896, when he hit over .400. He led the League in batting three times in his career and had six campaigns of 200+ hits. He played his final season in 1905 for the Boston Americans, near the adopted hometown he loved, Worcester, MA.

Burkett is one of two Hall of Famers whose unpleasant disposition resulted in the nickname "The Crab." The other is Johnny Evers.

Rabbit Maranville
St. Michael's Cemetery, Springfield

Rabbit at rest, the military stone of Maranville.

Jack Chesbro
Howland Cemetery, Conway

Rabbit Maranville and Jack Chesbro are both buried in western Massachusetts. Maranville's Hall of Fame credentials have been called into question since the day he was elected. In a career that spanned 1912–1935, he was a lifetime .268 hitter with a total of 28 home runs.

There is no more singular marker than that of Jack Chesbro.

The 19th century speedster, Billy Hamilton.

One cannot even look to his 291 stolen bases as evidence of some sort of offensive excellence. However, by the weight of more modern metrics, he had a lifetime dWAR of 30.8, meaning that over the course of his career, he won nearly 31 games for his team based on defense alone. That mark stands as seventh-highest all-time. His numbers very closely resemble those of his modern equivalent, Ozzie Smith, the all-time leader in dWAR with 43.4.

Chesbro's election is perhaps even more suspect, combining a relatively short career of 11 years along with an even shorter period of sustained excellence. He did, however, have a season for the ages in 1904, playing for the New York Highlanders (Yankees). He won 41 games, accounting for 45 percent of the team's victories. He also led the league with 48 complete games and a ridiculous 454⅔ innings pitched. Today he is buried under a stone that can only be called unique. The giant boulder that stands as his marker is a marvelously symbolic testament to a man whose pitching arm, if only for a short while, was as durable as they come.

Billy Hamilton

Eastwood Cemetery, Lancaster

Billy Hamilton made an inauspicious debut with the American Association Kansas City Cowboys in 1888, batting .264 in 35 games.

It was the last time he would hit below .300 until his final season in 1901. Hamilton had incredible speed, leading the league in steals five times and runs four times. He was the all-time leader in stolen bases for 80 years, until Lou Brock broke his record in 1978. His lifetime average of .344 is tied for seventh all-time, alongside Ted Williams. Hamilton is one of only three players in the history of baseball to have more runs scored than games played. His single-season record of 198 runs is now 124 years old and will likely never be broken. The closest any 20th century player has ever come to challenging that record was Babe Ruth, who scored 177 in 1921.

Joe Cronin

St. Francis Xavier Cemetery, Centerville

Located in the mid-cape Barnstable section of Cape Cod, Centerville has all of the charm you would expect for its ideal locale, but few of the crowds. While it does contain two trademark bay beaches, Covell and Craigville, it is more residential and less commercial than the sunburned Outer Cape. At its modest St. Francis Xavier Cemetery lies Joe Cronin. Cronin was a wunderkind, taking the reigns as player-manager of the Washington Senators at the tender age of 26. He found immediate success, winning the 1933 pennant. Traded to the Boston Red Sox following the 1934 season, he had a 13-year run as their skipper.

Despite his varied and impressive resume, there is no mention of the game on Joe Cronin's grave.

It was in 1946, with the help of returning war-veteran hero Ted Williams, that he finally led the Sox to their first World Series since Babe Ruth helped beat the Cubs in 1918. He took over as general manager of the club in 1947 and was named President of the American League in 1959. He held that position until 1973 before finally retiring. Considering the breadth of his accomplishments, his story is one of the lesser-told these days, and it's unfortunate. His legacy is considerable.

Buried just a short distance away are the only other two "famous" members of St. Francis, and one of them had a very lasting impact on sport indeed. Sargent and Eunice Mary Shriver (née Kennedy) are located in a relatively modest plot, especially considering that she was the sister of the President of the United States and a tremendously powerful woman in her own right. Among her numerous other accomplishments (she graduated from Stanford and won the Presidential Medal of Freedom, as well as the Civitan International World Citizenship Award), she is most famously remembered as the founder of the Special Olympics. Since the first International Special Olympics Summer Games in July 1968, her pioneering organization has grown to hold 50,000 competitions annually. Shriver's vision changed the world's ideas about sporting competition for those with intellectual and physical disabilities, and that has inspired countless lives.

Day Trip
◆ CONNECTICUT ◆

Neatly situated between New York and Massachusetts, it was inevitable that Connecticut would see baseball come quickly. The earliest known record of a game in the state took place in New Haven, July 4, 1858, a tilt between the "Worst Thirteen" and the "Best Eight," in an intra-squad match of a club whose name remains a mystery. Later that year, the Mazeppa "Marrieds" played a match against the "Singles," on Thanksgiving Day in Stamford. Thanksgiving, now associated with football, was a common date for the final baseball game of the year in those antediluvian days. That year, the bachelors won their holiday contest by the modest score of 84–31.

Professionally, the Hartford Dark Blues played in the NA from 1874 to 1875 and then shifted over to the NL for the 1876 season. By 1877, the team was taking the train down to Brooklyn for home games because there was more money to be made in the city. The Blues disbanded after that lone year of nomadic play, and Connecticut has never been a major league state since. In 2016, Hartford acquired a double-A minor league affiliate of the Rockies, which they nicknamed the Yard Goats. Delays with the construction of their new stadium gave them a nomadic year of their own, with their entire initial season played on the road.

Jim O'Rourke
St. Michael's Cemetery, Stratford

O'Rourke is buried in a family plot that includes his parents and children.

Roger Connor
Old St. Joseph's Cemetery, Waterbury

Because of its small size, as well as the relatively limited number of Hall of Famers buried there, Connecticut marked the first time I conquered an entire state in a single day. Along with co-worker and fellow baseball fan

Jeff Greenberg, I played hooky and left work early, spending the day taking a stroll through some of the more antiquated names in baseball history. Jim O'Rourke and Roger Connor made their mark prior to the 20th century. O'Rourke was an outfielder, catcher, and first baseman who had a lifetime batting average of .310. Connor was the greatest home run hitter in the history of the game before Babe Ruth.

The two men played together from 1885 to 1892, mostly with the National League New York Giants, although they both defected to the Players' League team of the same name in 1890. When the league folded at the end of the season, they both returned to the NL incarnation, O'Rourke for two more seasons and Connor for one before going off to Philadelphia in 1892, where the 34-year-old led the league in doubles. Like George Davis, Connor was another 19th-century legend who was largely forgotten and lay in an unmarked grave until 2001, when the Waterbury Monuments Committee installed the one pictured in this book's color insert.

immortality are very different. Weiss was one of the builders of the great Yankees squads, first as their farm director from 1936 to 1943, and then as general manager from 1948 to 1960. He later was an original architect of their cross-town rival New York Mets. During his tenure, the Yankees won 17 pennants and 13 World Series. His was a life spent in baseball, and his claim to the Hall is legitimate.

Bulkeley is in the Hall due more to fate than his role in the game. Although the true father of the National League was Chicago magnate William Hulbert, the owners were wary about the perception of handing the reigns of presidential power over to Hulbert, whose Chicago background and vested interest in the league made him a target for critics. Instead, they tapped Bulkeley, a prosperous banker who owned the Hartford Dark Blues. Bulkeley wasn't really a baseball man, and he only served in the role for a single season before Hulbert took over.

George Weiss
Evergreen Cemetery, New Haven

George Weiss died one year after his election to the Hall.

Morgan Bulkeley
Cedar Hill Cemetery, Hartford

George Weiss and Morgan Bulkeley were both baseball executives, but their claims to

I had to jump to place the ball on the small ledge located halfway up the marker of Morgan Bulkeley.

Bulkeley's other "contribution" to the sport was to serve as a member of the Mills Commission, which in 1907 incorrectly named Abner Doubleday the inventor of baseball. His selection to the Hall occurred because when American League Founder Ban Johnson was rightfully elected in 1937, the Centennial Committee that chose him thought it only fair that both leagues were represented by their first presidents. It took another 58 years for Hulbert to get his due. When the inevitable debate occurs between baseball nerds about who doesn't belong in the Hall of Fame, Bulkeley is my go-to answer.

The Birth of the Big Leagues
◆ ILLINOIS ◆

The first recorded game of baseball played in Chicago by two different teams took place on July 7, 1858, between the Union Baseball Club and the Plowboys Club of Downer's Grove. The Plowboys won that day, and it seems as though Chicagoans have been torn amongst themselves ever since. It is the only city to have had two major league baseball franchises every year since 1901. They even had a third, briefly, from 1914 to 1915 when the Whales represented Carl Sandburg's "City of Big Shoulders." Unfortunately, their shoulders weren't big enough to sustain the weight of three teams. The Whales, along with the rest of the Federal League, disbanded after two seasons, despite Whales owner Charles Weeghman having built a new stadium for his club. Weeghman bought the Cubs the following January and quickly moved the team from their West Side Grounds to his eponymous park. The Cubs still call it home today, though by the name of a different magnate, William Wrigley.

The Cubs are beloved in Chicago, winning the World Series in 2016 after a 108-year run of failure that makes the Red Sox's 86-year drought seem like a long weekend. Across town, the White Sox had their own string of hopelessness. After eight players conspired to throw the 1919 World Series, they *also* had to wait 86 years to atone for their sins in the eyes of the baseball gods. They finally took home the Commissioner's Trophy in 2005, the year after the Red Sox broke their own curse.

National League creator William Hulbert worked with Albert Spalding from his home in Chicago to create the framework of the National League in late 1875. It was also in Chicago's Great Northern Hotel where the owners of the minor Western league gathered in 1899 to, among other business, officially change their organization's name to the American League. Like Hulbert, AL President Ban Johnson ran his league from Chicago for many years. When the office of the Commissioner was created in 1920, the man chosen to fill the position was another Chicagoan. The city can rightfully claim that it is the birthplace of the NL, the AL, and the office of the Commissioner.

Chicago is a baseball town, and it is fitting that nine Hall of Famers were born there, more than any other city but New York's combined five boroughs. As of this writing, 13 are buried there. Luckily, Anna's family is from Chicago (her Mom is a South Side Sox fan), and we visit frequently. There were a lot of graves to go see.

Freddie Lindstrom and Gabby Hartnett
All Saints Cemetery, Des Plaines

Freddie Lindstrom and Gabby Hartnett are both buried in All Saints Cemetery in Des Plaines. Their careers were concurrent, in the 1920s and '30s, but they played together for only a single season, on the Cubs. Hartnett, born in Rhode Island, spent 19 years behind the plate for the Cubbies and was adopted by the city.

Lindstrom shares a birthdate (November 21) with fellow Hall of Famers Stan Musial and Ken Griffey Jr., as well as your humble author.

The English major in me wonders why the ellipses are placed after Gabby Hartnett's Hall mention.

Lindstrom only got to play for his native town in 1935 as his career was winding down. Lindstrom's grave bears no evidence of his baseball past. Hartnett's has a modest line, engraved below the family name but above the names of himself and his wife, Martha, reading "Entered Baseball Hall of Fame 1955." The visit to these two graves marks the only time I was accompanied on a Hall Ball trip by my

father-in-law. Bob died not long after I finished *The Hall Ball*. I hope he understood how his genealogy bug, which introduced me to the greater purpose and possibilities of cemeteries, inadvertently made this odyssey possible.

William Hulbert
Graceland Cemetery, Chicago

William Hulbert has a splendid grave marker, a large baseball engraved with the charter cities of the National League on its surface. As mentioned, he was denied his rightful place in the Hall because of bad luck. It took the Veterans Committee 107 years after he died to rectify the matter. The National Association, predecessor to the National League, sported top-tier talent but was destined for failure because it lacked a visionary of Hulbert's magnitude to create something that had never previously existed. SABR historian David Bohmer refers to him as the "Father of Professional Sports Leagues," a claim that would be difficult to debate.

Part of the charm of Hulbert's stone is the nod to franchises that are long since defunct.

When one considers the amount of revenue generated by the collective professional sports in America, it could be argued that when it comes to pure dollars and cents, there has been no greater founder than Hulbert.

Will Harridge
Memorial Park Cemetery, Skokie

Will Harridge never played baseball and didn't have much interest in the sport as a young man. It was a twist of fate that led to American League President Ban Johnson hiring Harridge as his personal secretary in 1911, the beginning of a 47-year career in the major leagues. His role evolved into secretary for the whole league, a position he kept until 1931, when he became the third president of the American League. As president, he was instrumental in the creation of the All-Star Game, oversaw the relocation of the St. Louis Browns and Philadelphia Athletics, voided the contract of 3'7" tall Eddie Gaedel, and ruled the league with a professionalism and lack of bluster that the owners never experienced under Johnson. Despite having the second-highest office in Major League Baseball, Harridge never had a formal written contract during his 28 years as AL president. The photo you see is the second version taken. The first one, shot on a late, cloudy afternoon, was so dark you could barely read Harridge's name. It wasn't until my second visit, when I was hoping to somehow capture a little more sunlight in the secluded corner of the mausoleum at Memorial Park in Skokie, that I discovered that his family's niche had a light switch connected to an overhead fixture.

Ray Schalk
Evergreen Cemetery, Evergreen Park

Joining the Chicago White Sox in 1912, Ray Schalk was the backstop for the South Siders for 17 years. Although he never excelled at the plate, he was a reliable defensive team leader.

Schalk's family felt his greatest role was as a father.

He led the league in games caught seven times, putouts nine times, and still holds the career record for double plays turned by a catcher. He also led in caught stealing percentage three times, including an incredible 71.8 percent in 1925. He helped his White Sox defeat the New York Giants in the 1917 World Series and was one of the players who remained clean of the stain of the Black Sox scandal two years later. Schalk is credited as one of the first catchers to back up corner infielders, though the practice had loosely been in place for nearly a decade when he joined the White Sox. He has the lowest batting average of any position player in the Hall of Fame, with a lifetime mark of .253.

Cap Anson and Kenesaw Mountain Landis
Oak Woods Cemetery, Chicago

Adrian Constantine "Cap" Anson and Kenesaw Mountain Landis are not names that your average contemporary baseball fan would immediately think of when tested about the Hall of Fame, but they were both giants in their times. Anson made his debut the same year as the first professional league, in 1871, as a member of the Rockford Forest Citys of the National Association. In 1876, the year the National League was created, he joined that circuit's Chicago White Stockings who, after a few name changes, became the modern-day Cubs.

He played the rest of his almost unfathomable *27-year* career with the Pale Hose and upon his retirement owned virtually every record in baseball, including being the first player to record 3,000 hits. All have since been surpassed.

Landis was baseball's first commissioner, a man who brought a sense of integrity to one of baseball's darkest hours—the scandal of the 1919 World Series. His hiring was a direct response, and he was effective.

Anson's massive grave bespeaks his immense fame at the time of his death.

The unique, asymmetrical stone of Landis looks like it was pulled from the mountain he was named after.

He abolished rowdyism and squelched gambling, and his stern authority helped turn the ballpark into a place where one could feel safe to bring a family, a part of the game's modern identity that barely existed at the time. Some say Babe Ruth saved baseball after the Black Sox. Landis deserves perhaps as much credit.

The careers of both Landis and Anson were marred by their unfortunate attitudes on race. Landis famously enforced the unwritten color barrier that kept blacks out of major league baseball. Branch Rickey had to wait for Landis to die to implement his plan for integration. Anson, for his part, was a participant in the enforcement of the original color line back in 1887. His initial refusal, on August 10, 1883, to play an exhibition game against the Toledo Blue Stockings because they featured a black catcher named Moses Fleetwood Walker, was only one of many voices rising against integrated ball. But his was a powerful voice. Anson's grave marker is made of angles and clean lines. Landis's looks like a miniature representation of his namesake. Both are cared for by the staff at Oak Woods, who are almost exclusively African American.

Charles Comiskey and Hank O'Day
Calvary Catholic Cemetery, Evanston

This round of photos was taken nine months after the first visit to Chicago, with the exception of Hank O'Day, who wasn't elected until 2013 and necessitated visiting Calvary a second time. O'Day, the tenth umpire elected to the Hall, is buried in the same Catholic cemetery as Charles Comiskey, an important name in the history of baseball and a legend in the Windy City. Playing for St. Louis, Cincinnati and, for the lone year of the 1890 Players' League, Chicago, Comiskey was a solid, if not outstanding first baseman. It was his later role as executive and owner that defined his legacy.

The door to the Gothic mausoleum of Charles Comiskey.

The grave of Rube Foster, as substantial looking as the man himself.

O'Day also played and managed in the majors, as well as umpiring for nearly thirty years.

Comiskey built one of the most successful charter franchises of the American League. His name graced the park the White Sox called home for 90 years, before corporate naming rights finally dethroned him in 2003. Sadly, his legacy will be forever connected to the 1919 scandal. His body lies in a family mausoleum, the design of which is very befitting of a man nicknamed "The Old Roman."

Like Comiskey, Foster began as a player. Unlike his white counterpart, Foster likely could have been elected to the Hall on his statistics alone. Foster was a brilliant pitcher and a leader. He played for, managed, and owned the Chicago American Giants starting in 1910. In 1920 he founded the Negro National League, the first of its kind in terms of organized scheduling and post-season play. Like so many tales from the Negro Leagues, his ends tragically, this time with madness and an early death. Where this story differs from Sol White, Frank Grant, and Pete Hill, is that 3,000 people attended Foster's funeral. His gravesite bears a solid, large monolith that looks eternal and was a perfect choice for this giant of a man.

Rube Foster

Lincoln Cemetery, Blue Island

Another owner lies buried about an hour south of Comiskey, in the misleadingly named city of Blue Island. Andrew "Rube" Foster is a name that should be as well-known as Comiskey's, in Chicago and beyond.

Pete Hill

Holy Sepulchre Catholic Cemetery, Alsip

Pete Hill, meanwhile, is another matter entirely. Amongst his many travels, Hill starred for White's Philadelphia Giants from 1904 to 1907 as well as Foster's American Giants from

1911 to 1918. He left a legacy of speed and power. When The Hall Ball began in 2010, Stew Thornley and the Hall of Fame believed that Pete Hill was the lone member for whom we did not know a burial location. Unbeknownst to me, researcher Jeremy Krock was hard at work trying to solve this mystery.

Krock is the founder of a group called the Negro Leagues Baseball Grave Marker Project, which itself is a subset of the Negro Leagues Committee of SABR. The name of the NLBGMP is self-explanatory, and as of this writing they have installed stones at 30 previously unmarked grave sites. Jeremy himself, an anesthesiologist, is one of the warmest, most unassuming people you could meet.

Jeremy ultimately learned that Hill had been buried at Holy Sepulchre Catholic Cemetery in the Chicago suburb of Alsip, despite dying in Buffalo, New York, in 1951. Hill's son, Kenneth, had lived in Chicago at the time and had his father's body shipped out to be buried by his church. Once again there was no stone. I asked Jeremy if the NLBGMP was going to install something, and he told me that he wasn't certain, as the surviving family had voiced an interest in handling it themselves.

The photo of the patch of grass under which Hill lies was officially number 100 in the project. As someone who appreciates numbers (as all baseball fans must, to a certain extent) there was a tragic symbolism to this.

Numbers 1 (Sol White) and 100 belong to two Negro Leagues greats, teammates in fact, for whom time and circumstance had robbed them of their due. While there was little that could be done about the lost decades, thanks to Jeremy the circumstances were about to change.

Lou Boudreau
Pleasant Hill Cemetery, Frankfort

One of the most successful player-managers of all time, Boudreau made his major league debut with the Cleveland Indians. He played one game in 1938 and by 1940 was the regular shortstop. In 1942, at the tender age of 24, with only two years of full-time play under his belt, Boudreau became the manager of the Tribe. The team would struggle through the early years of his tenure. When baseball broke the color barrier in 1947, forward-thinking Indians owner Bill Veeck hired Larry Doby and, the following season, Satchel Paige, who both helped to change the Indians' fortunes. Boudreau himself had an unparalleled season in 1948, winning the MVP Award and steering his newly stocked club to the championship, making him the only player-manager in baseball history to accomplish the dual feats. After his playing and managing days were over, Boudreau had a 30-year career calling games for the Chicago Cubs from the broadcast booth.

The unmarked grave of Pete Hill serves as another reminder of the challenges for those who played in the Negro Leagues.

Lou Boudreau was beloved in Chicago as well as Cleveland, where he played for thirteen years.

The government-issued stone of Urban "Red" Faber.

Warren Giles is buried in the same plot as his parents, in Moline, minutes from the Iowa border.

Red Faber
Acacia Park Cemetery, Norridge

Spending his entire 20-year career with the Chicago White Sox, Urban "Red" Faber won 24 games in 1915, just his second season. He went on to win 20+ three more times and twice led the league in ERA. He was brilliant during the Sox's successful 1917 World Series, winning three games and holding the New York Giants to a .213 batting average. The greater portion of his career was marred by injury, and although he played for another 10 years, he never had a sub–3.00 ERA after 1923. He still ranks second on the all-time list for wins by a White Sox pitcher, trailing only Ted Lyons. Faber was a founder of Baseball Anonymous, a charitable organization that focused on helping old ballplayers who were sick or had fallen on hard times.

Warren Giles
Riverside Cemetery, Moline

Warren Giles made his first foray into baseball in 1920, when he unexpectedly became the team president of his local club, the Moline Plowboys of the Three-I League (Illinois, Indiana and Iowa). A community leader, he was invited to attend a meeting about saving the financially strapped baseball team. By the end of the discussion, he had been placed in charge.

Rising quickly through the ranks, by the mid–1920s he was a part of Branch Rickey's Cardinals farm system. Ten years later, he was the President of the Cincinnati Reds, whom he led to a World Championship in 1940. Giles was one of the finalists, along with eventual winner Ford Frick, for the vacant Commissioner's seat when Happy Chandler was removed in 1951. Instead, Giles became President of the National League, a post he held until 1969. During his tenure, he oversaw the moves west of both the Dodgers and Giants, as well as the first wave of expansion. His progressive views about black and Latino players aided the National League in superseding the Junior Circuit. His stance is best summarized by a quote from his *New York Times* obituary: "We are a game of tradition. The right kind of tradition has made baseball what it is, but blindly following tradition may lead into a rut. Baseball must always keep pace with the times." By keeping pace with the times, the National League went 16–5–1 in All-Star Games under his leadership.

Deacon White
Restland Cemetery, Mendota

The very first hit in major league history came on May 4, 1871, when the Cleveland Forest Citys faced the Fort Wayne Kekiongas of the newly established National Association.

White's election to the Hall owes no small amount of credit to the efforts of SABR member Joe Williams.

That seminal hit, a double, came off the bat of Cleveland catcher Deacon White. White was erased from the basepaths when he made the blunder of straying too far off the base after teammate Gene Kimball's pop fly was caught by second baseman Tom Carey, also resulting in major league baseball's first double play. This ignominious beginning gave no indication of the legendary career to follow. White was one of the premier hitters of his day, leading the league in batting average twice and RBIs three times. He played for an impressive 20 years. It was no small feat for a man who spent the first nine years of that primarily as a catcher, in an age when protective equipment for the hazardous position was virtually non-existent. When he joined the Buffalo Bisons in 1881, the 33-year-old White shifted to the infield, where he played for another 10 seasons. In 2010, he was chosen as the second recipient of the SABR Overlooked 19th Century Base Ball Legends award. Three years later, he was elected to the Hall of Fame, 123 years after his final game.

Old Hoss Radbourn
Evergreen Memorial
Cemetery, Bloomington

What Charles "Old Hoss" Radbourn accomplished in his brief, 11-year career is impressive, but what he did in 1884 is unparalleled.

Charles Radbourn's grave features an alternate spelling of his name.

The durable hurler had already thrown over 1,400 innings in his first three seasons with the Providence Grays, including 632⅓ in 1883. In his signature year, he pitched 678⅔ innings, winning 59 games, completing all 73 of his starts and finishing two others just for good measure. All of that was wrapped around mid-season drama that saw him miss a number of games due to arm troubles and contract haggling. Fascinatingly, while Radbourn's 59 wins are a record that will never be broken, his single-season inning total is four outs behind that statistic's standard bearer, Will White, who accomplished his feat in 1879.

The visit to Radbourn's grave was one of the more memorable in the project. I was stalling in the cemetery office, waiting for Jeremy Krock to join me. I had become friends with Jeremy, and Bloomington was the closest Hall of Fame grave to his hometown of Peoria. We had agreed to meet there and have lunch. While waiting, I struck up a conversation with the cemetery administrative assistant, Gaye Nichols, who asked about the project. When I explained to her that the genesis for the whole thing came, in part, from the unexpected discovery of Abner Doubleday's grandfather, she interrupted me to say, "Oh yes, his father's here."

I was flabbergasted. She had to be mistaken. It just couldn't be possible. The National Geological Survey claims there are 109,000 cemeteries in the United States. For me to accidentally stumble upon Doubleday's grandfather was unusual, although somewhat explainable by location. For me to then, four years later, also trip over his father's grave 782 miles away borders on the divine.

She wasn't confused. She showed me the booklet the cemetery had put together highlighting some of the more famous interments, which included Adlai Stevenson and Dorothy Gage, the five-month old infant who inspired the name of L. Frank Baum's *The Wonderful Wizard of Oz* heroine. Graye knew exactly what she was talking about. Sadly, however, she did not have an exact location of the grave, just a general area.

Ulysses Doubleday (1792–1866) was a successful printer, apprenticing in Cooperstown before becoming an editor in Ballston Spa and Auburn, New York. In 1831 he became a member of the United State House of Representatives, an office he held until 1833, and then again from 1835 to 1837. By 1837, he had lost his fortune when the stock market crashed. After that, Doubleday spent time as a merchant and farmer but never recovered his wealth. Upon retirement he moved to Bloomington, and when he died he was either buried without a marker or with one so modest that it has since been swallowed up by the earth.

Capital Heroes
◆ MARYLAND ◆

The famous pre-professional Brooklyn Excelsiors took baseball's first "road trip" in 1860, where they battled the Baltimore club of the same name on September 22. The Baltimore incarnation had been founded in 1858, the first team in the state to play by the New York rules. After local grocer George Beam witnessed a game of the Brooklyn squad while visiting New York, he immediately came home and formed his own Excelsiors. Two years later, on that autumn day in 1860, dominated by the inventor of the fastball, Brooklyn's Jim Creighton, the Baltimores suffered a crushing 51–6 loss. As was the custom of the time, no one really seemed to mind as the celebratory dinner that followed was enjoyed by all.

Four different major league teams were based in Baltimore before the current American League Orioles, who didn't come to town until 1954, when the Browns abandoned St. Louis to the sole possession of the Cardinals. Since then, Baltimore has been the home of some of the greatest names in the history of the sport. Despite an absence of major league representation between 1915–1954, they can still boast 12 playoff appearances, six pennants, and three World Series titles. Sixteen Hall of Famers spent time in an Orioles uniform (technically, Lee MacPhail wore a suit). Three of them spent the entirety of their careers playing in Monument City: Brooks Robinson, Jim Palmer, and of course, Cal Ripken, Jr. Of the seven who are buried in the vicinity, however, only one name would likely spark the memories of the average fan.

Leon Day and Ben Taylor
Arbutus Memorial Park, Arbutus

Both Leon Day and Ben Taylor are buried in Arbutus Memorial Park, located about 20 minutes southwest of the heart of the city. Day pitched during the Golden Era of the Negro Leagues in the 1930s and '40s, and was considered a quintessential big-game pitcher. The greater portion of his career was spent playing for the Newark Eagles, although like most black ballplayers of the time he spent a few years logging innings in Cuba, Mexico, and even Canada. With fellow hurlers Max Manning and Rufus Lewis, Day was integral in the Eagles winning their lone championship in 1946.

Day's stone highlights his decency and the fact that he is also a member of the Puerto Rican Hall of Fame.

65

The freshly polished stone of Ben Taylor.

After leaving the Orioles in 1898, Hanlon managed the Brooklyn Superbas (Dodgers) and Cincinnati Reds.

Taylor's heyday was in the 1910s, before Rube Foster's Negro Leagues even existed, and his playing days continued until 1929. He was one of four brothers to have a successful baseball career. I had trouble finding his grave and needed to ask a groundskeeper for help. The upbeat gentleman not only knew immediately where Taylor was buried, but he quickly ran to his cart and pulled out his cleaning supplies to make sure that Ben looked good for his photo. The shine you see on his marker was not due to rain, but was a result of the polish they use at Arbutus, still drying in the morning sun.

John McGraw, Joe Kelley, Ned Hanlon and Wilbert Robinson

New Cathedral Cemetery, Baltimore

Less than five miles from Camden Yards, home of the Orioles, is New Cathedral Cemetery. Besides being the only cemetery owned by the Archdiocese of Baltimore, it holds the unique distinction of being the location in which the most Hall of Famers are buried.

There are four baseball greats located on its 125 acres, all connected deep in the marrow of Baltimore baseball: Ned Hanlon, Wilbert Robinson, Joe Kelley, and the incomparable John McGraw.

The original Baltimore Orioles were founded in 1882 as part of the American Association, famously known as the Beer and Whiskey League for their willingness to sell adult beverages at games, unlike the stodgy National League. Despite the extra concession sales, the league folded at the end of the 1891 season. The Orioles had been a successful enough franchise, though, that they were absorbed into the expanded National League. It was in this 1892 season that these four men came together.

The manager was "Foxy" Ned Hanlon. He had premiered as a player in 1880 with the NL Cleveland Blues and had a decent 13-year playing career, batting .260 lifetime. Base stealing statistics, which weren't kept until halfway into Hanlon's career in 1886, indicate that he was quick on the basepaths, stealing 329 bags in just six years (though at the time, when a runner advanced by an extra base on a hit, it was considered a steal). He had previously managed with little success in Pittsburgh, with both the Pirates and the Burghers of the Players' League, when he arrived in Baltimore in 1892.

Robinson died just five months after his friend and sometimes nemesis, McGraw.

Catcher Wilbert Robinson joined the club in 1890. A solid backstop, Robinson had never hit above .244 prior to Hanlon's arrival and had finished 1891 batting a horrendous .216. Obviously inspired by his new skipper, he hit over .300 four times in the six years after Hanlon took over the club. Joe Kelley began 1892 with the Pirates, but in September he was traded to Baltimore for George Van Haltren. Beginning in 1893, Kelley hit over .300 13 seasons in a row, including a blistering .393 in 1894. Amazingly, Kelley came in sixth that season in the batting race. Fellow Irishman Hugh Duffy paced the circuit with a historic .440 mark.

The final piece of this wrecking crew was John McGraw. In a 16-year playing career, he

was an on-base machine. He led the league in OBP three times and broke the .500 mark three times, meaning that every other time John McGraw stepped up to bat, he got on base. He was the quintessential example of the hardscrabble player, barreling and brawling on his way to home plate.

Beginning in 1894, the Orioles had a dynastic run. They won three consecutive NL Pennants and finished second twice.

Later in life Kelley became active in local Democratic politics.

McGraw's mausoleum is another grave that was too large to fit in a single picture and still feature the ball.

Their rough and clever style of play earned them few friends but won them a heckuva lot of games.

At the end of the 1898 season, the foursome was broken up as Hanlon and Kelley went to Brooklyn. McGraw and Robinson stuck around in Baltimore for one more year. All three protégés followed in the footsteps of Hanlon and went on to become managers. Kelley had the least success, never finishing higher than third in five seasons. Robinson took over the Brooklyn squad in 1914 and he became such a beloved figure in the borough that for a brief time the press more regularly referred to the club as the Robins. Robinson steered them to the World Series in 1916 and 1920, losing both. He continued to lead the club until 1931, although they finished higher than fourth only once in the ensuing decade.

McGraw became one of the most successful and memorable managers in the history of sport. He took over the New York Giants at the end of the 1902 season and ruled the Polo Grounds for the next 30 years. He is still second in all-time managerial wins, trailing only the eternal Connie Mack, and remains first in the National League. With the recent retirements of Tony La Russa, Bobby Cox and Joe Torre, his place in the record books is safe for at least the next decade.

The bonds the four men formed with the city of Baltimore, and each other, led them all to be buried in the same place. Their graves are all different, with Kelley's being the most modest and McGraw lying in style inside his private family mausoleum. New Cathedral is also the final resting place of John Steadman, member of the National Sportswriters and Sportscasters Hall of Fame. He covered Baltimore for 55 years and even had a brief minor-league baseball career of his own.

Rube Marquard
Baltimore Hebrew Cemetery, Baltimore

Pitcher Rube Marquard won 200 games, including more than 20 games in a season three times, and 19 straight wins in 1912, still a record. He also led the league in wins that season, with an impressive 26 victories.

His period of sustained excellence was brief, however, and many attribute his election to the Hall to his role in Lawrence Ritter's outstanding oral history of the early 20th century entitled *The Glory of Their Times*. Marquard has the dubious distinction of appearing in five separate World Series, 1911–1913 with the Giants, as well as 1916 and 1920 with Brooklyn, and never being a part of a championship team. He is the only Hall of Famer buried in a Jewish cemetery, despite not being a Jew. He and his wife, Jane Hecht Guggenheimer, considered themselves Christians but chose to be buried near her family, who were Jewish.

Marquard's stone originally featured an incorrect birth year.

Walter Johnson
Rockville Union Cemetery, Rockville

When the family and I went to Washington, D.C., for the project, it was the Fourth of July. We watched the fireworks over the Capitol that night, and the next morning I went grave hunting for baseball heroes while Anna and our oldest child, Finn, played at the water park attached to our campground. The campsite itself was named after the husband of the first woman George Washington ever loved, Lake Fairfax. It was an All-American weekend for the Carharts.

The first cemetery I visited was Rockville Union Cemetery, which has the appearance of being in someone's backyard.

The oft-visited grave of Walter Johnson.

A lovely caretaker's home is located at the entrance, and the smallness of the cemetery, combined with its subtle hillside layout, makes the gravestones seem more like a private statuary display. Walter Johnson's grave is tucked under the shade of a cluster of large trees and makes no mention of baseball. However, on the day I was there, it was covered in mementos.

The practice of leaving a token at a grave, traditionally a small stone, dates back to the very real need of placing heavy stones over a burial site to prevent wild animals from disturbing the dead. It has evolved, largely through the Jewish faith, into a practice meant to show that someone who cared had been there. The more secular world of baseball fandom has removed the stone and replaced it with balls. As well as hats, helmets, shoes, photographs, baseball cards, bats (regular and fungo), coins, silly bands, feathers, American flags, ceramic tchotchkes and, in the case of Babe Ruth, a half-smoked cigar placed next to a plastic My Little Pony bowl.

Not every player has tokens left at his grave. Most do not. It is usually cemetery policy to remove those kinds of things regularly to prevent a grave from becoming a dumping ground. The majority of the graves I visited were unadorned, as you can see in the pictures. I left the gravesites as I found them, and I almost never moved any of the mementos left behind. A few times the "gifts" were covering the name on the marker and had to be shifted for the photo, but I always tried to

make sure they still appeared in the shot. One of the lessons I've learned over the life of the project is that these gifts, which range from the mundane to the bizarre, likely say more about the people who left them than they do about the dead themselves.

Johnson's stone was covered in a respectable pile of hats and balls. Not bad for a guy who threw his first major league pitch over a hundred years ago. His numbers, 417 wins, 110 shutouts, a lifetime ERA of 2.17, all earned while pitching for a mostly lousy Washington club, are untouchable, and he truly is one of the immortals. Baseball legends like him are hard to come by anywhere, but especially in Washington. Despite the city first being the home of a major league team in 1884 and maintaining a club of one name or another for 95 out of the next 130 years, only four other Hall of Famers are buried near the District of Columbia.

Sam Rice
Woodside Cemetery, Brinklow

One of those buried near D.C., Jud Wilson, is technically buried in Virginia and will be discussed later. Of the other three, Sam Rice was an Indiana boy who first joined the Senators in 1915 and spent the bulk of his 20-year career playing alongside Johnson. He twice led the league in hits and had more than 200 safeties in six separate seasons.

Rice's gravestone features the initials of his birth name, Edgar Charles.

A reliable defender, as a right fielder Rice remains fifth on the all-time list in assists and third in double plays. After his retirement, he opened a poultry farm and bred racing pigeons.

Joe Williams
Lincoln Memorial Cemetery, Suitland

Smokey Joe Williams was a Negro Leagues flamethrower who once defeated Johnson, as well as Grover Cleveland Alexander and Chief Bender, in exhibition play. In games versus major league competition, Williams was 8–3 with an ERA of 1.74. Part Native-American, Williams was the fastest pitcher in black baseball until Satchel Paige, and he once outranked Paige in a 1952 survey conducted by the *Pittsburgh Courier*. In their only contest facing each other, in 1930, he defeated Paige, 1–0. His speed, combined with a pinpoint precision, made him a force in black baseball for over a quarter-century.

Researcher Ryan Whirty can find no connection between Williams and the two men who share his grave.

Clark Griffith
Fort Lincoln Cemetery, Brentwood

Clark Griffith, a fabulous player in his youth, was first Johnson's manager and eventually Washington team owner. In the years after Griffith gained controlling interest of the team in 1920, there was cause for optimism, as the Senators improved and even appeared in back-to-back World Series in 1924 and 1925.

The vase at the base of Griffith's grave is a gas-powered "eternal flame" that wasn't lit on the day of my visit.

Griffith had a keen eye for inexpensive Latin talent, and he was one of the prime motivators in introducing Latinos into the Majors. Unfortunately, he also was a subtle advocate of the color line, and he ignored the incredible talent of the local Homestead Grays who, by 1940, were splitting playing time between Pittsburgh and more lucrative Washington, D.C. He willingly rented his stadium to them, but he refused to ever consider one of their players for the Senators. The majority of the years Griffith owned the team, they were buried in the second division. This was a fate most Washington teams suffered until the post-season appearances of the Nationals' squads of the 2010s.

Lefty Grove
Frostburg Memorial Park, Frostburg

Few pitchers can claim as immediate an impact as Lefty Grove. He led the league in strikeouts in each of his first seven seasons, an unprecedented run of early dominance.

Arguably baseball's most underrated pitcher, Robert Moses "Lefty" Grove.

That stat pales in comparison, however, to his most impressive feat, winning nine ERA titles over a 17-year career, a record that is likely never to be touched. It could be argued that his 1931 season was the single greatest example of pitching excellence ever. He won 31 games, pitched 27 complete games and four shutouts, struck out 175, had a 1.077 WHIP and 2.06 ERA, each statistic the best in the league. His effort earned him that season's MVP Award. He was the cornerstone of the Philadelphia Athletics dynasty in 1929–1930, winning four World Series games and two Championships for skipper Connie Mack. He retired with a perfectly round 300 wins, a number that was greatly hampered by the fact that his major league career was delayed by years when Jack Dunn, the owner of the International League Baltimore Orioles, refused to sell Grove to the big leagues. In the five years he pitched for the Orioles, he won an additional 108 games.

Home Run Baker

Spring Hill Cemetery, Easton

Like many a baseball nickname, Frank "Home Run" Baker's was born from a single event, as opposed to any sort of long-term evaluation.

The subtle inclusion of baseball equipment in the design on Baker's stone is a nice touch.

After all, while Baker led the American League in home runs in 1911 with 11, his lifetime total to that point was 17 round-trippers. His final tally was only 96, a decent amount for a man who debuted during the Deadball age in 1908, but certainly fewer than many of his less well-known contemporaries, including Gavvy Cravath and Tillie Walker. Even Ty Cobb, who eschewed the home run, had 21 more. But Baker hit his sobriquet-earning blasts on baseball's biggest stage, the 1911 World Series, on consecutive days off of Rube Marquard and Christy Mathewson, two greats who were both Hall of Fame-bound. Leading the Philadelphia A's to the championship, Baker's new name stuck for the remainder of his career—and sticks with him today.

The Most Sacred Ground of All
◆ VIRGINIA ◆

It is unclear when baseball first came to Virginia, but for certain there was a club in Norfolk that played a tragic game in April of 1860. In a match against the Marion Club of Brooklyn, the Sumpter Club of Norfolk was doing well, battling to an 11–11 tie in the seventh inning. That was when a Marion slugger, S. B. English, hammered what was certain to be a home run. Unfortunately, English collapsed within "four feet of home," the victim of a heart attack. He died within minutes of being carried from the field. The Sumpter club was kind enough to award the Marions the run that English never scored, effectively giving them the victory. It was the least they could do.

Very briefly, in 1884, Virginia had a major league team. Originally a part of the Eastern League, the Richmond Virginians joined the American Association when the Washington Statesmen could not complete their season. The Virginians went 12–30 in their abbreviated campaign. By the following year, they had been contracted from the AA and returned to the EL. They folded for good at the end of the 1885 season. The Virginians were the first team in major league baseball to represent one of the former Confederate states, and they were also the last until the Houston Colt .45s were founded in 1962.

Jud Wilson
Arlington National Cemetery, Arlington

Jud Wilson is the lone member of the Hall of Fame buried in the most famous burial ground in all of America, Arlington National Cemetery. Commonly associated with Washington, D.C., its address is technically in Virginia. There are over 140 national cemeteries in the United States. They were first established in 1862, although a handful of the burial sites were already in existence before they were adopted by the Federal government during the early days of the Civil War. Abraham Lincoln served as President during the foundation of approximately the first 30. His most famous speech, the Gettysburg Address, was delivered at the ceremonies commemorating the opening of the one in that pivotally important Pennsylvania town.

Wilson enlisted in June of 1918, just six months before the end of World War I, and served as a Corporal in Company D of the 417 Service Battalion Quartermaster Corp. As was the case with most African American military units in the still segregated Army, Wilson's company never saw combat. When the war ended, Wilson played semi-pro ball in his native Virginia until 1922 when he joined the independent Baltimore Black Sox. He dominated Negro Leagues pitching until 1945, the end of the Second World War, retiring with a documented lifetime average of .351. He was also famous for his violent temper and intimidated even the most hard-nosed of his fellow players.

Wilson's grave, of course, makes no mention of his ballplaying days. There is a strict uniformity to gravestones in a national cemetery, and such frivolities are not allowed. However, by this point in the quest, a very definite pattern had begun to establish itself and one gets the sense that Wilson, like many of his fellow military veteran Hall of Famers, would not have wanted it mentioned even if it had been permitted. Besides Wilson, 12 Hall of Famer graves (Hoyt Wilhelm, Louis Santop, Rabbit Maranville, Christy Mathewson, Nestor Chylak, Red Faber, Oscar Charleston, Willard Brown, Larry MacPhail, Jocko Conlan, Duke Snider, and Bullet Rogan) note the member's military service but do not acknowledge baseball in any way. Some, like Grover Cleveland Alexander and Ted Lyons, mention both.

There are over 20 former professional ball players of lesser stature buried in Arlington, but there really is only one other interment that stands out in in the annals of baseball history. In the words of Donald Honig, Abner Doubleday likely "didn't know a baseball from a kumquat," but the machinations of Albert Goodwill Spalding have intrinsically linked Doubleday's name to the creation myth of the sport. It is his name, inscribed in stone (or more specifically, his grandfather's), that put The Hall Ball in motion, and for that I owe him a debt. Rising to the rank of Major General as the veteran

of numerous Civil War battles, including the very first at Fort Sumter as well as Gettysburg, we all owe him some measure of gratitude. Just not for anything having to do with America's Pastime.

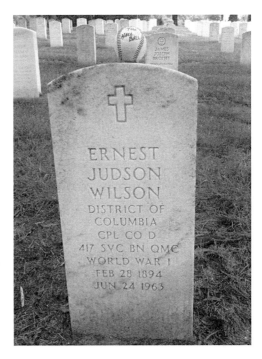

The endless rows of the dead surrounding Jud Wilson are a moving sight.

The Living Members
◆ I ◆

After I decided to add the living member element to the project, I thought it best to first concentrate all my energies on locating and visiting the graves. I knew that at some point I was going to have to figure out how to reach the living guys. Before I got bogged down in the logistics of something that I had no clue how to tackle, however, I thought it best to see how much success I had with the more predictable part of my journey.

By the end of the first year, I had taken enough photos that I knew it was time for me to finally work out these details. But where to start? I had seen players around Cooperstown during Induction Weekend, but it is against my nature just to approach fame in the street. I'm from New York City. You just don't do that here. Famous people live in New York for the anonymity. My career in theater management has often put me in the same room with some of the most famous actors in America, but my particular experiences usually have me meeting them on the day of the event. The nature of theatrical professionalism makes it taboo for me to simply approach them and ask for a photograph. Usually I'm the guy protecting them from picture seekers. There are no pictures around my house of me with Robin Williams or James Earl Jones, although I have worked on events with both of them. I would have to overcome the professionally ingrained trait of camera-shyness if I expected to get anywhere.

I began by meeting with Sue MacKay of the Hall of Fame Acquisitions Committee. When one wishes to donate an artifact to the Hall, it is arranged through this committee. Anxious about revealing the project to a Hall official, I told her my story. I explained that because it was my intention to donate the ball when I was finished, I was hoping they might be able to assist me by putting me in contact with the living members. Ms. MacKay was polite, professional, and encouraging of the project, but she explained that there were very strict codes that the Hall needed to abide by. One of those codes involved the privacy of the members of the Hall. Just as it is inappropriate for me to ask Glenda Jackson for a picture while I'm at work, the same holds true for the employees of the Hall of Fame and Reggie Jackson. But, Ms. MacKay pointed out, I was in Cooperstown and it was Induction Weekend. She suggested I hit the streets and see what I could do on my own.

So I did. Within minutes of stepping out of the Hall and into the bright July sun, I found a large cluster of people standing outside a restaurant on Main St. Once I was able to work my way through the crowd, I discovered what the fuss was all about. Sitting at a table, wearing a bright pink golf shirt and sporting a slightly askew Yankees cap, was one of the most beloved figures in New York history, Yogi Berra.

Yogi was getting 50 dollars for his autograph that day, but I didn't want an autograph, just a picture. Fortunately, he had a small can set up in front of him. For a nominal donation (five bucks was considered standard), Yogi would let you take a photo.

The money from that would then be donated to a local charity. That is how, within 10 minutes of being told that I was on my own for this part of the project, I had my first photograph of a living member of the Hall of Fame.

I had great success that first weekend, getting nine photos in total. I did end up having to pay full price for some of them, including Gaylord Perry and Fergie Jenkins. I knew that I wasn't going to be able to keep up that pace of expense and continue with the project. I needed to save my pennies for trips to Cuba and Hawaii. I couldn't keep forking over yet even more money every time I met one of the (then) 60+ living members. The cost of obtaining the signature of a Hall of Famer could range anywhere from $30 (Perry is pretty ubiquitous and thus relatively inexpensive) to as high as $600, as one woman I met on my travels discovered when she got a jersey signed by Henry Aaron.

I wouldn't even have a signature to show for it when I was finished. I had made a very firm decision when laying out the parameters of the project that I was not going to pursue autographs. There were multiple reasons for this. To begin with, there simply isn't enough room on the ball for every living member to sign it. A ball can hold roughly 30 legible signatures, and I needed twice that. Plus, that would mean that the deceased members would be excluded from that portion, and the original goal was to unite and celebrate all of the members, not just those who could still wield a pen.

Finally, and perhaps most importantly, athlete signatures are a commodity. While most of the newest inductees were paid well enough during their careers that they likely don't *need* to work, that doesn't change the fact that for many of them, the autograph circuit is how they now make a living. Because the intention was for the ball to be donated to the Hall (all artifacts at the Hall have been donated; they do not buy items), I wanted it insulated from the potential taint of being a money-making enterprise. Keeping it autograph-free helped maintain that integrity.

The ubiquitous Gaylord Perry.

As successful as I had been during Induction Weekend, that only happens once a year. I would have to find other means if I was going to complete this in my lifetime. I thought about my experiences meeting ballplayers in the past. Other than the infrequent chance interaction during a pre-game batting practice session, the only time I had ever had a chance to speak with a professional athlete was at a baseball card show, 30 years earlier when I was a teenager handing over my entire allowance for the latest box of Topps. I cracked open the laptop and began looking for baseball card shows in the New York City area.

I discovered JP's Sports and Rock Solid Promotions. They had a show lined up at the Westchester County Center in White Plains, and three Hall of Famers were going to be in attendance. The day of the show, I arrived early, hunted down the promoter, Brian Coppola, and told him about the project. Fortunately, Brian is a collector himself and he immediately appreciated what I was trying to accomplish. He promised me access to the three guys he had that day, and welcomed me back in perpetuity. I cannot overstate what Brian's generosity did for the project.

Since that day, I have met with promoters from MAB Celebrity Services, Steiner Sports, and Fanatics Authentic. Besides Brian, the most enthusiastic aid to the project has been provided by Brendan Herlihy, formerly of Steiner Sports, but each of the above-mentioned companies has lent a hand in acquiring the photographs of the living members. As for the players, some of them were happy to be a part of the project, some were skeptical, and only two ever told me "no" to my face (though I ultimately got both of their photographs anyway). Each time I was able to photograph a living member of the Hall holding the ball, I could feel its mojo getting stronger. I know that sounds absurd, but with the addition of the living players, the ball soon became something that could never be duplicated.

Goose Gossage's mustache remains as impressive as ever.

*   *   *

The first nine were photographed over three days during induction weekend 2011. The fact that Yogi was the very first meant a lot to me. This is not only because he is one of the most beloved athletes ever, but also because of his connection to both New York teams. My father, Ralph Sr., is a Yankees fan and is one of those old-timers who believes that the days of his youth, when Yogi squatted behind the plate to catch a Whitey Ford breaking ball, will never be surpassed by the modern game. I am a Mets fan who is admittedly too young to remember when Manager Berra guided the Amazins to the 1973 World Series. I'm also a romantic, and the fact that '73 was the first World Series played after I was born has never been lost on me. There is little about baseball that Dad and I agree on, but Yogi Berra may be the one great unifier.

The photographs of Goose Gossage, Rollie Fingers, Juan Marichal, and Frank Robinson were the same set-up in front of the restaurant where I had found Berra. Like Yogi, they had a can where you could toss in a few bucks and get the pic. I was particularly awed by Robinson.

"The Dominican Dandy," Juan Marichal.

While he is often overshadowed by that other groundbreaking Hall of Famer who shares his last name, Robinson was the first full-time black manager in the Majors. Ernie Banks technically preceded him, when he managed a single inning in 1973 after Cubs manager Whitey Lockman was ejected in the

11th inning. Banks took the reins for the eventual Cubs victory. Hired by the Cleveland Indians in 1975, Robinson became the first player-manager since El Tappe steered the Cubs for 20 games at the start of the 1962 season. Since Robinson, only Don Kessinger, Joe Torre, and Pete Rose have held the title, one that we will likely never see again. Robinson is the only African American to have ever filled that role.

My fandom also made meeting Ralph Kiner a huge thrill. I never had a chance to see him dominate the National League during one of the most concentrated periods of sustained excellence, when between 1946 and 1952 he led the league in home runs in each of his first seven major league seasons. But between 1984 (when I first aligned myself with the Metropolitans) and 2013, he was a regular fixture in my life. One of the original Mets broadcasters in 1962, along with Bob Murphy and Lindsey Nelson, Kiner ended up being the longest tenured of the trio. Although Bell's Palsy slurred his speech later in life, he still made guest appearances in the Mets broadcasting booth right up through the season before he died.

Home run hitter and malapropist broadcaster, Ralph Kiner.

Groundbreaker, Frank Robinson.

Bobby Doerr was the oldest Hall of Famer I met on my travels.

Kiner's passing, in February of 2014, marked the first time that a Hall of Famer I had photographed while he was alive had later died. It was a difficult day for me. Although I had long ago stopped thinking of the members solely as statistics and plaques, I was surprised by how overwhelmed with emotion I was when I learned of his death. Not only did baseball lose a marvelous ambassador that day, but I lost a piece of my childhood. His death was also the moment when The Hall Ball became irreplaceable. The same combination of living players could never be duplicated. Kiner and Bobby Doerr were photographed back-to-back, both of them staged in the front lobby of a CVS drug store on Main St. On the day the photos were taken, Kiner was 88 and Doerr was 93.

The photo of Fergie Jenkins was taken in 2017. He was originally photographed at the same time as Gaylord Perry in 2011, during that first Induction Weekend. The lighting in the store was poor, and the photo was not the clearest. The day I took the photo seen here, he was doing a signing in front of that same CVS. He was in between autograph seekers and was just admiring the crowds. Seeing the opportunity, I quickly jumped in and asked him for the pic. He obliged and within seconds I had a new, cleaner photo. The experience highlighted the unpredictable nature of the project. Photographing some of the players has required hours, if not years, of patience. The photo of Jenkins was an unexpected lark and took less than a minute to execute.

Unfortunately, many of the indoor photos don't have the best composition, especially the early ones. Lighting is not always ideal in the gymnasiums and conference rooms where these events take place. I am also not a professional photographer and had decided from the beginning that I was going to consistently use my iPhone for the project. It was fast, and it did not necessitate setting up extra equipment. Over time you will see that the indoor photos improve, as

I switched from a 3s to a 4s to a 5s. I also learned the intricacies of taking pictures with an iPhone. Purists should know that, as with Jenkins's photo, whenever possible I have reshot a bad picture of a living member at a later date and replaced the earlier photos.

Wade Boggs, Roberto Alomar, and Andre Dawson were my first interaction with JP's Sports and Rock Solid Promotions. This also marked the time when I started telling the members the whole story. During the earlier Cooperstown interactions, I was concerned that the portion of the project involving cemeteries might make them think me a bit odd, a fear that later turned out to be not unfounded. But I decided it was only fair to the players to let them know the whole story. Besides, maybe the idea would click with one of them, and he might be willing to encourage his fellow Hall of Famers to participate when I came calling. Boggs did give it an enthusiastic, "Hey, that's cool man!" but that was as far as I got that day.

Fergie Jenkins is one of only two players photographed for the project in uniform.

Right-handed Wade Boggs held the ball in his left.

Roberto Alomar had been inducted only nine months prior to the taking of this picture.

Five and a half years after I shot the picture of Andre Dawson, I was fortunate enough to schedule a meeting with Jeff Idelson, president of the Baseball Hall of Fame. I ap-

proached him while he waited in line for his morning cup at the Stagecoach Coffee shop, and he agreed to meet with me. Idelson offered me his blessing to use his name as I continued to reach out to living players and even volunteered to try and put me in touch with Andre Dawson about this book. Dawson, it turns out, had gone into the funeral business in 2008. He thought The Hawk might be a fun choice to write a foreword. In the end, Dawson wasn't interested, but it was a kindness on Idelson's part that I wouldn't soon forget.

Soon enough I developed a "rap," a quick, four-sentence version of the project I told the players to give them maximum information in minimal time. Specifically, "My name is Ralph Carhart and I have been taking this baseball to all of the members of the Baseball Hall of Fame, living and deceased. If they are alive, I take a picture of them holding the ball, and if not, I take a photo of the ball at their grave. Once I have photographed all of them, it is my intention to donate the ball to the Hall of Fame. As of today I have photographed X members, I am hoping you will be number Y." When I gave the rap to Tommy Lasorda, he looked at me incredulously and asked me to repeat myself. I did, and he let me take the photo, but the look of bewilderment you see on Lasorda's face is genuine. He was the first who made it clear that he thought the project strange.

Two Phillies greats were clearly unimpressed with my idea. Steve Carlton was willing enough to pose and gave me a wide, toothy grin, but I heard him say to one of his compatriots as I walked away, "Boy, they will say anything, won't they?" Jim Bunning was the first who was rude. After he heard the rap, he refused to look at me, instead turning to Brian and coldly stating, "Take me to my plane." Thinking he was done with me, I thanked him for his time and started to leave. Before I could exit, he thrust out the right hand he used to strike out 2,855 major league batters, took the ball, and grimly stood for the photo. After I took a hurried picture, he thrust it back at me and I beat it out of the room.

The collaborator that got away, Andre Dawson.

The cheery, but skeptical, Steve Carlton.

The nonplussed Tommy Lasorda.

Jim Bunning, affable Senator from Kentucky.

The first Panamanian-born Hall of Famer, Rod Carew.

The result of my extended photograph session with Lou Brock.

Bruce Sutter's famous beard has been trimmed to a more modest goatee.

The interactions with Rod Carew and Bruce Sutter both fell into the category of unremarkable, but easy enough. Both were perfectly happy to hold the ball, and Carew, in particular, gave a winning, friendly smile. Lou Brock may have been my favorite moment with a living member over the life of the entire project. For most of them, the whole interaction was complete in under a minute, if they asked no questions. It was less than three minutes if they did. I spent 15 minutes with Brock. He was interested in the project, yes, but really it was because he was the first one who genuinely cared about what he looked like in the photo. He was having a bad hair day, and the slightly odd angle of his head in the picture is to hide a small tuft that was refusing to behave. He also wanted to be sure he was sufficiently lit because he knew his dark skin was a challenge for my amateur equipment. He treated it like a scheduled photo session and set a standard that I always longed for, but was never able to reproduce with any of the subsequent living players.

Groundbreakers

◆ OHIO ◆

The first game of major league baseball took place on May 4, 1871, on a chilly, 56-degree day in Ft. Wayne, Indiana. The Cleveland Forest Citys faced the Fort Wayne Kekiongas, members of the newly formed National Association of Professional Baseball Players. Fort Wayne had chosen to bat last that day (the home team had the option back then), making Cleveland catcher Deacon White the first batter in the game. He laced a double off of Bobby Mathews, the very first hit in major league baseball history. White was erased on a double play off the bat of the following hitter, Gene Kimball, and Fort Wayne went on to win, 2–0, in one of the lowest-scoring games in the history of the sport to that point.

Cleveland's long history with baseball goes back even further than their role in this seminal game. Historian Peter Morris points out that baseball had been played in the area since 1857, though it was not until after the war that the first organized team announced their formation. Since then, four additional major league teams have called Cleveland home, including the Blues, the Infants, and the Spiders. The city's most famous and enduring team is the Indians, who were also known as the Blues, the Bronchos, and the Naps before settling on their current name in 1915.

Elmer Flick

Crown Hill Cemetery, Twinsburg

A long day of driving meant an early start if we were going to reach all of the Hall of Famers who were buried in the area. Anna and I arrived at Crown Hill Cemetery, located in the Cleveland suburb of Twinsburg, so early that the sun was creating sharp, dark shadows on the stone of Elmer Flick.

They were near-impossible to photograph around. I had to stand above the marker and shoot it upside-down. That's why it appears to be at such an odd angle. When Flick died in 1971, just two days shy of his 95th birthday, he held the record for longest-lived Hall of Famer. He had surpassed the previous record holder, Connie Mack, by almost two years. Since then, four more Hall of Famers have passed Flick, including current king Bobby Doerr, who died at the age of 99 years, seven months and six days in November 2017.

A speedster, Flick often led the league in triples and stolen bases while playing outfield for the Indians.

Ruffing was one of many who were laid to rest above head height.

Red Ruffing

Hillcrest Memorial Park, Bedford Heights

When Charles "Red" Ruffing made his major league debut in 1924, the 19-year-old was the youngest player in the majors. When he retired in 1947, he was the second-oldest, trailing only his White Sox teammate Earl Caldwell, who was 24 days his elder. Ruffing's long career began miserably in Boston, where he led the league in losses with 25 in 1928 and again in 1929 with 22. It took being traded to the Yankees in 1930 for him even to finish above .500. In 15 years with the Yanks he won 231 games, including four straight 20-win seasons in 1936–1939. Today he is buried in the suburb of Bedford Heights at Hillcrest Memorial Park, in a mausoleum that offered no convenient way for me to stage the ball. Fortunately, this was one of the trips when Anna was with me. Ruffing's picture is just one of many that feature her hand holding the ball in a way that allowed me to photograph it from a distance, in order to capture it properly.

Ed Delahanty

Calvary Cemetery, Cleveland

The untimely death of Ed Delahanty is one of the more famous stories of a player's demise, because it was so unusual and dramatic.

There are enough Delahanty brothers buried in Calvary Cemetery to man every position of an infield.

Delahanty was an offensive powerhouse, leading the league in hits in 1899, in doubles for five seasons, in home runs twice, in RBIs three times, and in stolen bases in 1898. He batted better than .400 three times. He was also an alcoholic who was known for his fierce temper when drinking. On July 2, 1903, the 36-year-old Delahanty became rowdy on a train and was kicked off by the conductor on the Ontario side of the International Railway Bridge over Niagara Falls. Delahanty attempted to cross the bridge on foot. What happened next is uncertain. What is known is that there was a struggle with the night watchman followed by Delahanty falling off the bridge and plunging into the icy waters of the Falls. His body was found a few days later. A native of Cleveland, he was brought back home to be buried in the family plot, not far from three of his four brothers, all of whom had major league careers of their own.

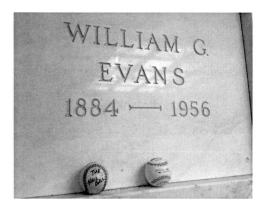

The photograph of Billy Evans belies the fact that his tomb is 12 feet off the ground.

The nondescript stone of "Rapid Robert" Feller and his second wife, Anne.

Billy Evans
Knollwood Cemetery, Mayfield Heights

Billy Evans, who was an umpire and later a team executive (1905–1951), was also buried inside a mausoleum. However, unlike Ruffing, Evans was stacked to a height of roughly 12 feet in the air, making it impossible for Anna to reach. She went to look for someone who worked for Knollwood Cemetery who might be able to assist us, and I started poking around for anything that might aid me. That was when I stumbled across a ladder tucked behind one of the velvet drapes. Hurrying to get the shot before Anna returned with an employee, who was certain to chastise me for doing something that I knew was against their insurance policy, I quickly scrambled up the ladder and snapped off a few hasty pictures. I've always wondered how the other ball got up there. Maybe that person found the ladder, too.

Bob Feller
Gates Mills North Cemetery, Gates Mills

It could be argued that the most famous Hall of Famer buried in Cleveland was also the Indians' greatest pitcher. "Rapid Robert," Bob Feller, was born in Van Meter, Iowa, but after his playing days were over, he made Cleveland his home.

A 17-year-old high schooler when he made his debut in 1936, he dominated the American League until he was 37 years old. Leading the league in wins six times, he won 20 or more games in each of those seasons. His lifetime win total of 266 was greatly reduced by nearly four prime seasons lost to World War II. His first season back in 1946 was one for the ages, as he led the league in wins (26), games (48), complete games (36), shutouts (10), innings pitched (371⅓), and strikeouts (348). Gates Mills North Cemetery, where Feller is buried, is one of the smallest visited in the entirety of The Hall Ball. Tucked into a small clearing surrounded by a grove of trees, Feller's unadorned grave features nothing but his name and dates. His legend lives on, however, as a decent-sized pile of balls has been left behind by fans to honor him.

*   *   *

Thanks in large part to the television show *M*A*S*H*, Toledo is the home of one of the most famous minor league teams in baseball history. The favorite squad of cross-dressing Corporal Max Klinger, portrayed by actor Jamie Farr, the Mud Hens got plenty of mention on the historic television show during its 12-year run. Farr himself was a Toledo native and Mud Hen fan and brought that element of the character with him. Because the show was filmed prior to the recent explosion in minor league baseball marketing, the program costumers often used a Texas Rangers cap as a stand-in, as they could not easily get their hands on the real thing.

Addie Joss
Woodlawn Cemetery, Toledo

The Mud Hens provided the first professional contract to Addie Joss, one of the premier pitchers of the first decade of the 20th century. Playing his whole major league career for the Cleveland Bronchos/Naps, his lifetime WHIP of 0.968 is the lowest all-time, and his career ERA of 1.89 is second only to Ed Walsh. Tragically, Joss, beloved by all he knew, died in 1911 at the age of 31 from tubercular meningitis. Joss's teammates defied league president Ban Johnson and refused to play a scheduled game so they could attend the funeral. Two months after his death, American League stars staged a contest against the Naps to raise money for his family. For decades, the Hall of Fame used its arbitrary "10-year rule" as reason not to induct Joss into its ranks. When he was elected into the Hall by the Veterans Committee in 1978, Joss became the first (and still only) player who appeared in fewer than 10 seasons to be inducted.

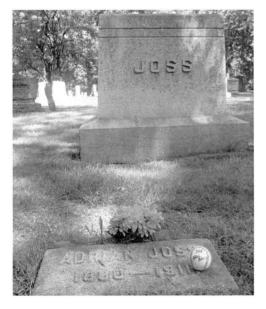

Joss, who died over a hundred years ago, still has fresh flowers placed at his grave.

Roger Bresnahan
Calvary Cemetery, Toledo

Buried six minutes away from Joss is his contemporary, Roger Bresnahan. A Toledo native, Bresnahan spent the bulk of his career in the National League, playing for the Giants, Cardinals, and Cubs. Versatile, Bresnahan manned all nine positions over the course of his career, although he made his greatest mark as a catcher. He is credited by multiple sources, including the Hall of Fame, as being the first backstop to wear shin guards, ignoring the scorn of spectators who questioned his manhood. In truth, Bresnahan did not don that final piece of the famous "tools of ignorance" (glove, mask, chest protector, and shin guards), until 1907. Bill James points out that a black catcher, Chappie Johnson, wore them almost five years earlier. Peter Morris found reference to them being used in the majors with regularity by 1904. The reason Bresnahan has been eternally linked to the innovation all these years is because he was, as Morris discovered, the first to wear them over his pants instead of hidden inside his uniform. As his playing days were winding down, Bresnahan used the money he had saved to purchase the Mud Hens in 1914 and owned the team until 1924.

* * *

The future of baseball changed irrevocably in 1869 when the Cincinnati Red Stockings, under the guidance of Harry Wright, had an unprecedented season. Professional baseball had existed for some time, with players collecting salaries for sham jobs that served as fronts for their true employment. The 1969 campaign marked the first time the NA included a professional division. Now able to offer a legitimate living, Wright was able to hire the finest talent. The Red Stockings had an undefeated season, sporting an impressive 57–0 record. They won the first 24 games of the 1870 campaign before finally falling to the Atlantics of Brooklyn, 8–7, on June 15.

Roger Bresnahan was a jack-of-all-trades, manning every position in his career.

Baseball's first superstar catcher, Buck Ewing.

The Red Stockings finished the year 66–7–1, still an impressive record by any measure, but local interest began to wane after the streak, and the team was disbanded the following season. Their dominant campaign has led to the claim that Cincinnati was the birthplace of professional baseball. From 1876, the first year of the National League, until 1989 the first game of each new season was played in The Queen City in recognition of the feat.

Buck Ewing

Mount Washington Cemetery, Mount Washington

The same year Roger Bresnahan made his major league debut, in 1897, the career of baseball's first superstar catcher was coming to a close. Buck Ewing first appeared with the weak Troy Trojans in 1880, but when he came to the New York Gothams in 1883, he seized the opportunity. He led the National League with 10 home runs that year, the first time anyone had ever hit double digits in the NL.

He also batted .303, .032 higher than his previous best. Ultimately, .303 was his lifetime average in a career that also saw him log time for the Players' League incarnation of the Giants, as well as the Cleveland Spiders, before finishing his playing days with his hometown Reds. Because Ewing had such a powerful throwing arm, he was unafraid of potential base stealers and became the first catcher to consistently crouch behind the plate. Elected to the Hall in 1939, Ewing was the first backstop tapped for the honor.

Waite Hoyt and Miller Huggins

Spring Grove Cemetery, Cincinnati

Buried at Spring Grove Cemetery, 650 miles from Yankee Stadium, are two of the most important pieces of that club's dynastic run of the 1920s. Waite Hoyt had a career record of 10–12 when he joined the Yankees in 1921. Over the next 10 years, he won 157 more for the Bombers, plus six World Series games. His finest post-season was 1928, when he held the St. Louis Cardinals to three earned runs over 18 innings, en route to his third and final championship ring. He played for eight more seasons after he left the Yankees in 1930, never with the same level of success, although he did post an impressive 15–6 mark with a 2.93 ERA for the fifth-place 1934 Pirates. Of all of the players photographed for The Hall Ball, Hoyt may be the one who would have most appreciated the quest. During the off-season, he supplemented his income by working as a mortician.

Hoyt's manager for virtually his entire run with the Yankees was the diminutive Miller Huggins. Clocking in at 5'6" and 140 lbs., "Mighty Mite" Huggins had a decent playing career from 1904 to 1916 in which he specialized in base on balls, leading the league in that category four times. When Huggins took over as manager of the Yankees in 1918, he had already logged five seasons as the skipper of the Cardinals, never finishing higher than third place. His first three years with the Yankees were more of the same, despite the addition of Babe Ruth at the start of his second season. It wasn't until 1921, after Hoyt joined the team, that Huggins won his first pennant. He won five more, and three championships, before he died just two weeks before the 1929 season came to a close. Three years after his death, the Yankees placed a monument to him in center field, which has evolved into one of the Stadium's defining features, Monument Park.

Miller Huggins had funerals at Yankee Stadium and the famous Church of the Transfiguration in New York, before being sent home to Cincinnati for burial.

Walter Alston
Darrtown Cemetery, Darrtown

As with Hoyt and Huggins, another native Ohioan made his name in New York, although this one left his mark in the borough of Brooklyn. Walter Alston had one at-bat in his major league career, striking out for the 1936 St. Louis Cardinals. He toiled for another 11 years in the minors before ending his playing days in 1947 and beginning a managing career that ultimately ended in Cooperstown. He took over the Dodgers in 1954 and the following season achieved the impossible. He brought Brooklyn the first championship in their history, defeating the hated Yankees. He accompanied the club on their exodus to Los Angeles and managed there for another 19 years until he finally handed the reins over to Tommy Lasorda at the tail end of the 1976 season. He won seven pennants, four World Series, and 2,040 games, still ninth all-time.

Sportswriter John Kieran tagged Waite Hoyt with the nickname "The Merry Mortician," because of Hoyt's off-season job.

A protégé of Branch Rickey, Alston was an unexpected choice by Walter O'Malley for the Dodgers' manager job.

The back of Brown's stone (not pictured) includes a highlight-filled biography.

Eppa Rixey

Greenlawn Cemetery, Milford

The final Cincinnati-area burial was born in Culpepper, Virginia, and is one of the lesser-known names from baseball's pantheon of greats. Eppa Rixey split his 21-year career between the Phillies and the Reds. A durable workhorse, Rixey pitched more than 200 innings 12 times, and more than 300 three times, including a league-leading 313⅓ in 1922, when he also led the league in wins with 25. Rixey holds the dubious distinction of being the pitcher in the Hall with the lowest winning percentage. His lifetime record of 266–251 equals a .515 mark, tied for 671st all-time as of the end of the 2018 season.

Ray Brown

Greencastle Cemetery, Dayton

The list of teams that Ray Brown played for over his 18-year career reads like a history of black baseball. He spent time with the Indianapolis ABCs, the Detroit Wolves, and the Philadelphia Stars, as well as Mexican League teams like the Mexico City Diablos Rojos and the Veracruz Azules. His longest tenure came with the Homestead Grays, whom he helped lead to nine League titles and two Negro League World Series championships. Perhaps his greatest moment came in the 1944 Series, when he used his tremendous curveball to pitch a one-hitter against the Birmingham Black Barons in Game Three.

Brown was married to the daughter of Negro Leagues entrepreneur and fellow Hall of Famer Cum Posey, owner of the Grays.

Jesse Haines

Bethel Cemetery, Phillipsburg

A one-game appearance for the Cincinnati Reds, five innings of relief work in 1918, was all that kept Jesse Haines from spending his entire major league tenure with the St. Louis Cardinals. In an 18-year career with the Cards, he won 210 games and had some fine seasons, including a 1927 campaign in which he led the league in shutouts and complete games. His election to the Hall, in 1970 by the Veterans Committee, remains a controversial one because although his career was notable, he ranks fairly low on all of the usual statistics used to measure Hall excellence.

The top of Haines's grave is a sundial that gives a nod to some of the Cardinals' championship seasons.

As of the end of the 2018 season, he ranked 98th in wins, 534th in strikeouts, and 542nd in ERA, the jewel stats in the pitching Triple Crown. A former teammate of Frankie Frisch, who served as Chair of the Veterans Committee in the early 1970s, his election is one that many think owes a greater debt to his old friend than to his actual accomplishments.

Billy Southworth
Green Lawn Cemetery, Columbus

Spending time with the Cleveland Indians, Pittsburgh Pirates, Boston Braves, New York Giants, and St. Louis Cardinals, outfielder Billy Southworth was well-traveled in a 13-year playing career. His final year as a player, in 1929, also gave him his first taste of managing when he took over the reins of the Cardinals. His tenure was brief, just the first 88 games of the season, but he crafted a respectable 43–45 record. For the next decade, he worked his way through the minor league ranks again, pursuing another managing position. He rejoined the major leagues in 1940, once again as manager of the Cardinals.

Southworth purchased his burial plot after the death of his close friend, former BBWAA President Robert Hooey, and shared the land with Hooey's family.

This time he won three pennants and two World Championships with the Cards before having his contract sold to the Boston Braves in 1946. He helped raise the Braves to respectability, winning his fourth pennant in 1948. His 13-year career as a manager is one of the shorter Hall resumes, but his level of success in those years speaks volumes. He retired with 1,044 victories and a .597 winning percentage.

Branch Rickey
Rushtown Cemetery, Rushtown

The final two baseball greats I visited in Ohio are spending eternity far away from the hustle and bustle of the state's more metropolitan areas. They are both giants in the sport, yet it is appropriate that they should repose in such rural areas. One's nickname came from the fact that he was so "country," while the other redefined the definition of the "farm."

When Branch Rickey first revolutionized baseball by organizing the previously informal farm system in the early 1920s, it is unlikely that the barely 40-year-old knew the lasting impact this change would have on the game. There is no question, however, that when he signed Jackie Robinson to a minor-league deal in 1946, the older, wiser Rickey knew exactly what he was doing.

There will always be debate as to whether Rickey signed Robinson for altruistic reasons or because he simply saw the financial benefit to his club being the first to finally destroy the abomination of the color line. With a man as brilliant and complicated as Rickey, the truth lies somewhere in the middle. He did, after all, raid the Negro Leagues for talent and saw little need to compensate the clubs from whence they came. What is indisputable is that without Rickey, there is no telling how many more years it would have taken for a black man to step onto a diamond wearing the uniform of a major league team.

The weathered stone of "the Mahatma" Branch Rickey.

His grave, at the remote Rushtown Cemetery, sports a substantial stone, although it is clear from the weathering that it does not receive the attention that it deserves.

Cy Young

Peoli Cemetery, Peoli

To the northeast of Rushtown lies the even smaller community of Peoli, home of Denton True "Cy" Young. The genesis of his nickname is somewhat in question. The most commonly cited reason today relates to an anecdote in which a minor league Young's fastball left a number of wooden fences in the ruined state of a cyclone. "Cy" was also a common appellation at the time for a country hayseed, which Young most certainly was. The true genesis may never be known.

There are not enough superlatives to describe the career of Young. Perhaps it is enough simply to recognize that the award that is handed out to the best pitchers in each league every year bears his name. It is interesting to note that while Young does hold the career records in wins and complete games, he also has the lifetime records for losses (316), hits allowed (7,092) and earned runs surrendered (2,147). Barring a sea-change in pitching, it is impossible for any of these records, good or ill, ever to be approached. Babe Ruth became a legend because in his time the records he set seemed unassailable. Today, Ruth retains the title in SLG and OPS, but most of his other marks have fallen. The same will never be said of Young.

Born in nearby Gilmore, Young moved to

Peoli in 1933 after the death of his wife. The home he lived in still stands today, serving as a small market and livestock pen for the Amish that currently represent the 10 homes still standing in the unincorporated community. We drove for miles through the heart of Amish territory to find Young's sturdy stone at the Peoli Cemetery. Along the way, every time we passed a farm or a horse-drawn carriage, the distinctive-looking members of this Mennonite sect smiled and waved.

Baseball, which prides itself on the fact that the game we watch today is relatively identical to the game that was played over a hundred years ago, would seem like a perfect pastime for a community that eschews electricity, as well as most other modern conveniences. Prior to 1995, this was the case. Then Amish church elders noticed that grown men were spending too much time playing a game instead of tending the fields. The sport became restricted to all but the unbaptized youth. This includes the adventurous souls on their *rumspringa*, the period of adolescence when the Amish are allowed to leave the farm and experience life on the outside before deciding whether or not they wish to become permanent members of the church. It is unknown if anyone has ever decided to forsake the farm because they instead found Annie Savoy's "Church of Baseball," but it is a fair guess that the children of Peoli know about an "English" hurler named Cy.

Cy Young's stone, adorned with a baseball bearing angel wings, mentions career highlights and is engraved with symbols of the Freemasons.

Hoosier Hopes
◆ INDIANA ◆

As mentioned in the chapter on Ohio, Indiana holds the distinction of being the other state involved in the very first major league baseball game. The Hoosier State was represented by the Fort Wayne Kekiongas during that initial 1871 season, the only year the club existed. After that, Indianapolis became the best hope for the state to field a major league team. Attempts in 1878 (the Blues of the National League), 1884 (the Hoosiers of the American Association), 1887 (the Hoosiers again, this time of the NL), and 1914 (one last Hoosiers team, this of the Federal League) were all short-lived. The state has never supported another major league squad since, although there are currently three affiliated minor league clubs in operation: the Fort Wayne TinCaps (Class A Padres), the Indianapolis Indians (Triple A Pirates), and the Class A South Bend Cubs. It was also an important piece of the famous minor Three-I League (Illinois, Indiana and Iowa) which ran intermittently from 1901 to 1961.

Oscar Charleston
Floral Park Cemetery, Indianapolis

Other than Stan Coveleski, who is buried along the northern border of Indiana in South Bend, the other five Hall of Famers spending eternity in the state are relatively clustered in the central and southwest regions. The two who are buried in the capital city were both native sons of Indianapolis. Oscar Charleston was born in 1896, 80 years after the state abolished slavery but only 10 years after the "Gentlemen's Agreement" barred blacks from playing organized ball. Charleston had one of the most important careers in the history of the Negro Leagues.

Enlisting in the U.S. Army at the age of 15, Charleston spent nearly five years in the Philippines. It was there that he learned to play baseball, and he became the only black man in the Manila League Baseball Association, playing for the Army squad. When he returned to the United States in 1915, he broke into black ball with his hometown Indianapolis ABCs. With the exception of an interruption in 1918 when he re-enlisted to fight in World War I, Charleston played for the ABCs consistently until 1923, with stops in St. Louis and Cuba along the way. He eventually played for many of the great teams, including the Harrisburg Giants, the Homestead Grays, and the Pittsburgh Crawfords. He took over as skipper of the Crawfords in 1933 and led them to their only undisputed title in 1935, defeating the New York Cubans for the Negro National League pennant. In the 2001 edition of the *Bill James Historical Baseball Abstract*, Charleston is labeled as the fourth-best baseball player of all time. He was the sixth Negro Leaguer chosen for the Hall when he was tapped in 1976.

After Charleston left baseball in 1944, he worked as a baggage handler for the railroad. He had one final dance with the game, managing the Indianapolis Clowns in 1954. He died of a heart attack within days of the end of that season.

The government-issued stone of Oscar Charleston.

His stone is military issue and highlights his service in World War I. Known as a fighter on the field throughout his playing career, it is fitting that his marker denotes his time on the front lines.

In that span, he never batted below .337, and in 1932 he won the National League MVP Award. He secured the Triple Crown in 1933 with a .368/28/120 line before the financially broke Phillies traded him to the Chicago Cubs prior to the 1934 season. His time in Chicago was brief, only two and a half seasons, before he returned to the Phillies, but his days of leading the league were over.

A comet who flashed across the sky briefly before fading into injury-plagued mediocrity, Klein wasn't elected into the Hall until 1980, 22 years after his death. Klein's modest stone is located in the same cemetery as those of Louis Chevrolet, the famed automobile designer, as well as his race car-driving brother Gaston Chevrolet, who won the Indianapolis 500 in 1920 before dying in a racetrack crash in California six months later.

Chuck Klein
Holy Cross/St. Joseph Cemeteries, Indianapolis

Few players made as much noise upon their arrival in the majors as Chuck Klein. He batted .360 over 64 games during his freshman year with the Phillies in 1928, but that was just a hint of what was to come. Over the next five seasons, Klein led the league in runs three times, hits and doubles twice, and home runs and total bases four times.

Klein was elected to the Hall after a letter-writing campaign led by his sister-in-law and a Philadelphia schoolteacher.

Ban Johnson
Riverside Cemetery, Spencer

An hour southwest of the capital lies the small town of Spencer, burial site of Ban Johnson. Born in Norwalk, Ohio, Johnson became one of the most powerful figures in baseball when he founded the American League in 1901. Rescuing the defunct minor Western League from the ashes in 1893, by 1899 he had renamed his newly revitalized league to its more familiar moniker. By offering higher-paying contracts than the National League, he was able to lure enough quality talent to the AL that by the first year of the new century, the teams were clearly of major league caliber. It took two more years for the National League to recognize Johnson's creation, but their resulting acquiescence led to the first World Series in 1903.

Despite his czar-like power (and an arrogance to match it), it all came crashing down on Johnson not long after the owners brought in Kenesaw Mountain Landis to revive public faith in the sport after the scandal of the Black Sox. Johnson was in part to blame for the fix.

Ban Johnson died just three hours after his AL President successor, Ernest Barnard.

A virulent enemy of Charles Comiskey, when the Old Roman approached him about whispers of potential gambler involvement in the 1919 Series, Johnson ignored him. After the election of Landis, Johnson's power quickly disappeared. In the middle of the 1927 season, he resigned and he and his wife retired to Spencer. Although Johnson died from complications due to diabetes in a hospital in St. Louis, his body was returned to his recently adopted home for burial. The substantial above-ground graves of Johnson and his wife bespeak of his considerable wealth and power in life, just as the devastating crack that runs through the center of the grave, splitting his name in two, perfectly symbolizes the fall of this great, but flawed man.

Mordecai Brown

Roselawn Memorial Park, Terre Haute

When Mordecai Peter Centennial Brown lost most of his right index finger to a childhood farm-equipment accident, it is doubtful many gave him much of a chance to be a successful major league baseball player. When a later accident broke his middle finger and paralyzed his pinky, it seemed unlikely that he'd even be able to work in the mines like so many of his kin and neighbors. He did, in fact, spend some time working in the mines.

Despite (or perhaps because of) how freely his nickname was used in the press, Mordecai Brown was not a fan of the sobriquet.

It was while playing for one of the company baseball clubs that were manned by those early diggers that he learned that his handicap gave him the ability to throw a curveball that was unparalleled. "Three Finger" Brown would have one of the most dominant careers of the early 20th century.

Debuting for the Cardinals in 1903, he was traded to the Cubs the following season, and it was in Chicago where he had his greatest years. Brown was an integral part of the championship seasons of 1907 and 1908, winning 49 games over those two years and excelling in the World Series. He appeared in three games over those two Fall Classics, winning all three and pitching to a 0.00 ERA over 20 innings. He won 239 games overall and sported a lifetime WHIP of 1.066 over 14 seasons, a mark that is still tenth all-time. His plain, flush-fitted grave marker makes no mention of his career or his distinctive nickname.

Edd Roush

Montgomery Cemetery, Oakland City

The final Indiana-native Hall of Famer left his greatest legacy in neighboring Ohio as a member of the Cincinnati Reds. Born in Oakland City, Edd Roush debuted in the majors in 1913, playing nine games for the Chicago White Sox.

Roush was voted the Reds' greatest player in 1969.

He jumped to the rebel Federal League the following season, returning home to play for the final major league incarnation of the Indianapolis Hoosiers and remaining with the squad when they moved to New Jersey and became the Newark Pepper in 1915. When the Federal League folded, he signed on with the New York Giants before being traded midseason, along with fellow future Hall of Famers Christy Mathewson and Bill McKechnie, to the Cincinnati Reds. It was in Cincy that a decent career blossomed into a Hall of Fame one.

He batted .341 in 1917, the first of 10 straight seasons in which he hit no lower than .321. He led the league in slugging in 1918, despite hitting only five home runs, and became a champion the following year when the Reds defeated the White Sox in the tainted World Series that ultimately cost Ban Johnson his power. After playing for the Giants again from 1927 to 1929, then sitting out 1930 due to a contract dispute, he played his final game for the Reds in 1931. He retired with a lifetime batting average of .323. Although he had one of the most successful careers in Cincinnati history, Roush remained in Oakland City after he left the game, becoming a civic leader. He lived to the age of 94, dying just before a Spring Training game in Bradenton, Florida, in 1988. He is buried next to his wife

Essie and his twin brother Fred, who died exactly one month and seven days before his famous sibling.

Stan Coveleski
St. Joseph Polish Roman Catholic Cemetery, South Bend

While he appeared briefly for the Philadelphia Athletics in 1912, the right-handed Stan Coveleski played his first full season in the majors with the 1916 Cleveland Indians. He spent nine years with the Indians, winning 172 games in that time, including more than 20 victories four seasons in a row, from 1918 to 1921. He was the hero of the 1920 season, winning 24 games during the regular year and three more in the World Series, including a masterful five-hit shutout in Game 7 that secured the championship for Cleveland over the Brooklyn Robins. Using his still legal spitball, Coveleski ultimately amassed 215 wins with an ERA of 2.89 in a career that also included time with the Washington Senators and the New York Yankees.

There were so many flowers on Stan Coveleski's grave the day I visited that his family name was almost hidden.

Coveleski was the opposing pitcher in the infamous Ray Chapman game. On August 16, 1920, Yankees hurler Carl Mays struck Cleveland's Chapman in the head with a pitch, leading to baseball's only on-field fatality. With everyone unaware of the mortal severity of the injury at the time, the game was played to completion, and Coveleski won, 4–3, notching his 19th victory of the season. It was an important victory for the Indians, putting them a game and a half ahead of the Yankees in the pennant race. One can't help but think that Coveleski and the rest of the Tribe would have gladly sacrificed the win to have saved their teammate. The tragedy spurred a new era in on-field safety, including, to the delight of the Spalding sporting goods company, the more frequent in-game replacement of used baseballs.

Unlikely Allies

◆ KENTUCKY ◆

For a long time, it really did look as though Louisville was destined to be a major league city. A founding member of the National League, the Louisville Grays had a respectable initial season in 1876 and an even better one the following year, finishing second out of six teams. But, undone by baseball's first gambling scandal involving Grays pitcher Jim Devlin, they quickly went out of business. Devlin had pitched every inning of the 1877 campaign, and his ouster spelled doom for the club.

The city returned to the majors as members of the American Association in 1882. Originally known as the Eclipse, by 1885 the club was called the Colonels. They were successful in the AA, even winning the pennant in 1890 and playing the Brooklyn Bridegrooms to a 3–3–1 stalemate in the 19th-century incarnation of the World Series. When the AA folded after the 1891 season, the Colonels were talented and profitable enough that they were absorbed into the National League.

Once in the National League, things fell apart. They never made it higher than ninth in the standings. When the NL decided to contract at the start of the 1900 season, the Colonels were cut. A partial owner of the team, Barney Dreyfuss, also had a controlling stake in the Pittsburgh Pirates. He was able to turn the loss of the Colonels into a boon for the Bucs, bringing over 10 of the best players, including future Hall of Famers Fred Clarke, Rube Waddell, and Honus Wagner. Kentucky, meanwhile, has never seriously competed for a franchise since. Today, modern economics and the huge fan base of the Cincinnati Reds, only an hour and a half away from Louisville, make it unlikely they ever will.

However, the city can boast of being the home of the most famous model of bat ever produced, the eponymous Slugger. While there are numerous bat manufacturers whose products are being used in the big leagues today, for a time the Hillerich & Bradsby Co. had a near monopoly on not only the majors, but on the dreams of children around the country. Everyone wanted their name emblazoned on the end of a Slugger. Today, there is a museum in Louisville dedicated to the famous lumber. Its collection of bats used by the game's immortals rivals the one in Cooperstown.

Pee-Wee Reese
Resthaven Memorial Park, Louisville

Twelve miles away from the museum is Resthaven Cemetery, burial site of a Hall of Famer who made his name far away from home, in the borough of Brooklyn. Harold Henry "Pee Wee" Reese will forever be linked to the kindness he showed Jackie Robinson, especially because his Southern background helped defy the expected narrative. To limit his career to that one facet does a disservice to one of the greatest field generals to set foot on a diamond.

Reese's grave features an image of him and his wife, Dorothy, affectionately known as "Dottie."

His statistics were never flashy. His lifetime batting average was a mortal .269. He led the league in bases on balls in 1947, in runs in 1949, and in stolen bases in 1952, and he was a 10-time All-Star. He batted .296 in the 1955 World Series, the year Brooklyn finally defeated the Yankees and Reese secured his lone championship.

What is most telling about Reese, however, is the award he never got. In the 16 years of his career, he finished in the top 25 in MVP voting 12 times. He was the captain of a team that came to symbolize guts and determination, earning him the nickname "The Little Colonel," and the voters could not ignore his driving influence. While Reese never got closer than fifth place in the voting, his annual appearance on the list is a testament to the power of intangibles.

Reese's gravestone is large, nearing six feet tall, and details some of the greater accomplishments in his career, including his time in the Navy and as a broadcaster. It is also extremely polished and, unfortunately on the day I was there, the sun was located directly

behind it. It was nearly impossible to shoot the photo so that all of the detail on the stone, including the etching of Reese and his wife, were visible simultaneously. However, I appreciate the streaks of light that were created, some of them so thick they almost look corporeal.

Happy Chandler
Pisgah Presbyterian Church, Versailles

Another important character in the drama of Jackie Robinson's entry into the major leagues is buried an hour east of Reese. Albert "Happy" Chandler played some baseball in college and managed to sign with the Class D Lexington Reds after graduation, but he knew his fate lay elsewhere. He went on to practice law before entering politics. He became the Governor of Kentucky in 1935 and a United States Senator four years later. So it was that, upon the death of Kenesaw Mountain Landis in 1944, the owners approached this affable, learned man about succeeding the old judge to the most powerful position in baseball.

Chandler ruled from 1945 until 1951, when he resigned due to a contract dispute with the owners. He addressed a number of issues during his tenure, including overseeing the establishment of the first pension fund for the players. His most significant act, though, was allowing Branch Rickey to sign Robinson to a minor league contract in 1946.

Happy Chandler was a man of many accomplishments.

No sentimentalist, Rickey knew that integration was impossible while Landis was in charge, and as soon as he possibly could (it took the owners nearly a year to install Chandler), he seized the opportunity. To his eternal credit, Chandler refused to stand in the way of progress.

He was later re-elected as Governor, serving a second term from 1955 to 1959. He lived until 1991 and was the oldest living member of the Hall at the time of his death. Today he is buried in a small churchyard, surrounded by horse farms in the remote countryside of Versailles. His tiered grave lists his notable political and baseball titles and features a brass seal of the Commonwealth of Kentucky.

Earle Combs
Richmond Cemetery, Richmond

During that brief time in which Chandler was a member of the Lexington Reds, he was a teammate of another native Kentuckian who would one day be elected to the Hall of Fame, Earle Combs. Like Reese, it was in New York City where this son of the South earned his ticket to Cooperstown. Combs joined the Yankees in 1924, with the club fresh off its first franchise World Series victory the year before. Combs appeared in four World Series for the Bombers over the next 12 years, the length of his career, and he won three championships.

Playing for the Yankees during the era of Ruth and Gehrig, it was Combs who set the table. With a lifetime on-base percentage of .397, and two of the greatest RBI machines to ever walk the earth batting behind him, between 1925 and 1933 Combs never scored fewer than 122 runs. He led the league in triples three times, including the "Murderers' Row" 1927 campaign in which he also led the league in hits, outpacing Gehrig by 13 knocks.

Earle Combs clearly embraced the duality of being a Yankee from Kentucky.

Combs was an alumnus of Eastern Kentucky University and, like Christy Mathewson, clearly felt an affinity for his alma mater as he chose to be buried in the school's backyard. Smart with money, he was a generous benefactor to the college, helping to fund the education of numerous students. In 1963, a dormitory was built and named in his honor, although the building was demolished in October 2014.

After his playing days were over, Combs spent some time as a member of Chandler's administration during his second term as Governor of Kentucky, serving as the state banking commissioner. The two old teammates, whose lives diverged and then reconnected in the most unlikely of ways, had become good friends over the years.

One of the five original members of the Hall, Christy Mathewson.

Roger Connor's grave, shared with his wife and grandchild, went unmarked for almost 70 years.

C2

The Harridge family niche, photographed the second time around.

Left: The first living Hall of Famer photographed, Yogi Berra. *Right:* The impressive mustache of Rollie Fingers.

The extended interaction with Ernie Banks is one of my favorite memories of the whole project.

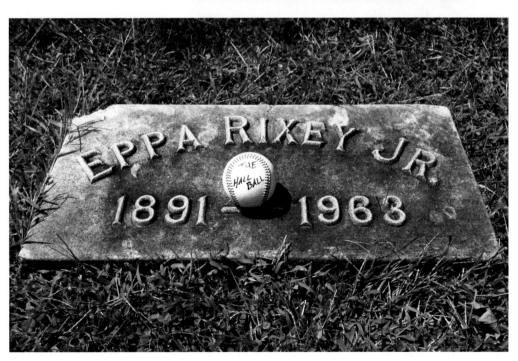

Although his winning percentage is unimpressive, Rixey held the NL record for wins by a left-hander until Warren Spahn.

Paul Krichell, the scout who signed Gehrig, once courted Greenberg for the Yankees.

I was never able to determine the secret meaning of the playing card affixed to Hank Greenberg's grave.

Of all my travels for The Hall Ball, Eagleville is the location I long to revisit the most.

The nimble-fingered Reggie Jackson.

Mel Ott and Carl Hubbell both died on November 21, 30 years apart, from injuries resulting from an automobile accident.

Top: The hand-painted grave of Joe McGinnity. *Bottom:* The Cleveland Indians were far more accommodating for the photo of Early Wynn, whose ashes had been spread on the mound, than the Cubs had been for Santo.

C8

Top: Three years after I visited, a plaque was placed on Piñones Beach, commemorating Clemente's life. *Bottom:* I find the image of Sparky Anderson's brilliant yellow seat to be one of the most striking in the project.

Hack
◆ WEST VIRGINIA ◆

Originally a part of Virginia, West Virginia seceded from its mother state in 1861 over ideological differences regarding the Civil War. In June of 1863, the state was formally accepted into the Union, much to the chagrin of the Confederacy. Born in the crucible of war, West Virginia unsurprisingly did not have its first verified baseball club until the end of 1865, when the Star and Anchor Clubs, both of Wheeling, established their charters. By 1867, there were over 20 clubs in the Wheeling area alone.

Hack Wilson
Rosedale Cemetery, Martinsburg

As of the end of the 2018 season, 120 native West Virginians have played major league baseball. Three of them have made it all the way to the Hall of Fame: Jesse Burkett, Bill Mazeroski, and George Brett. The one Hall of Famer buried there was actually not a native son. Lewis "Hack" Wilson was born in Elwood City, Pennsylvania, but moved to Martinsburg, West Virginia, as a 21-year-old when he made his professional debut with the Martinsburg Mountaineers of the Blue Ridge League.

He lived in the area for the next 20 years, although poverty forced him to move to Baltimore in 1941 to find work. When he died in 1948 from complications due to his alcoholism, he was virtually penniless. The city of Baltimore planned to bury him, but his ailing wife Hazel, an alcoholic herself and commit-

ted to an asylum by her family at the time of his death, arranged for his body to be buried in his adopted hometown. Ten months after his death, the marker you see was unveiled in a ceremony that was organized, in part, by his former manager Joe McCarthy.

Wilson's career was short by Hall of Fame standards, just 12 years. Only during five of those 12, all with the Chicago Cubs, was Wilson a consistent league leader. But what a run. He led the circuit in home runs four times, including an incredible 56 in 1930.

A giant stone for a giant man, Hack Wilson.

That mark remained the National League standard until Mark McGwire shattered it in 1998 en route to the PED-fueled destruction of Roger Maris's overall record. Wilson also led the league in slugging and walks in 1930, while batting .356, giving him a ridiculous OPS of 1.177. His crowning achievement of that remarkable season, however, was his mark of 191 RBIs. A record that stands to this day, it has been seriously challenged only twice, by Lou Gehrig in 1931 and again by Hank Greenberg in 1937. No one else has come within 15 RBIs of that legendary number. Since the expansion era, the closest has been Manny Ramirez, who clubbed a "mere" 165 in 1999.

The rapid rise and even faster decline of Wilson became a cautionary tale in the world of baseball. Well-liked, despite his self-destructive tendencies, Wilson's death began a reinvigorated push within baseball to address its alcohol problem. He was also a prime example of the necessity of baseball adopting a pension system, something that Commissioner Happy Chandler had instated just a year before Wilson's death, in 1947. Sadly, professional baseball's recognition of its responsibility to its veterans came a little too late for the man who, for a brief time, rivaled Babe Ruth when it came to the spectacle of his swing.

The Briefest Glory
◆ DELAWARE ◆

For one brief, shining month, Delaware was a major league state. The Wilmington Quicksteps were a part of the loosely organized Union Association for 18 games. Joining the league in August of 1884, four months after the eventual league champion St. Louis Maroons kicked off their season, they finished a dismal 2–16 and faded into obscurity almost immediately. Only a couple of names from their roster stand out. The first, Fred Tenney, is notable only because he shares a name with another player who had a healthy 17-year career, batting .294 and making frequent appearances in the recollections of the old-timers in Lawrence S. Ritter's groundbreaking book, *The Glory of Their Times*. The Quickstep Fred appeared in only 37 games with three UA teams in 1884 before disappearing into the mists of history, alongside his team.

The other noteworthy name is remarkable simply because it is so unusual. His birth moniker was Edward Sylvester Nolan, but he appears in Baseball-Reference (as well as the first edition of *The Baseball Encyclopedia*, published in 1969) as The Only Nolan. Nolan's major league career was slightly longer than Tenney's, with the pitcher appearing in parts of five seasons. He once led the league in walks, issuing 56 free passes as a member of the National League Indianapolis Blues in 1878.

There are various theories as to the genesis of his nickname. One guess states that it was a nod to the then-famous performer, The Only Leon, who was the age's preeminent practitioner of drag queen minstrelsy. A recent theory, posited by John Thorn and supported by the research of Peter Morris, attributes the name to his feats before Indianapolis became a major league club in 1878. The year before, when the team was a part of the newly formed League Alliance, which was itself an attempt to prevent the raiding of rosters after the rise of the successful International Association, Nolan reportedly had a season for the ages. He was rumored to have won an unprecedented 64 games, a number that is unmatched in the record books at any level of play. After his dominating year, Indianapolis ownership affixed the new nickname to Nolan when they advertised their popular pitcher. Despite his never rising to those heights of success again, the name stuck.

Vic Willis
St. John's Cemetery, Newark

Today, three Hall of Famers are buried in "The First State." Vic Willis had a devastating curveball and used it to win 249 games in a 13-year career. Making his debut in 1898 with the Boston Beaneaters, he won 25 games his freshman year. He won 20 or more seven more times and often sported an ERA below 3.00. Willis played for the Beaneaters until 1906, when he was traded to the Pittsburgh Pirates after his numbers started to decline. He responded to the move by winning 23 games, his most in four years, and finished with a minuscule ERA of 1.73.

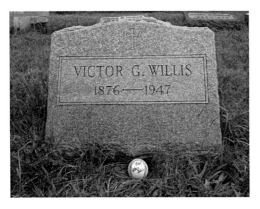

I enjoy the symmetrical simplicity of the photograph of Vic Willis's stone.

Willis appeared in one World Series, as a member of the victorious 1909 Pirates, and holds the distinction of being the starting pitcher in the first game ever played at Forbes Field, on June 30 of that championship season. He was selected for the Hall by the Veterans Committee in 1995, 48 years after his death.

Judy Johnson
Silverbrook Cemetery, Wilmington

The other two Hall of Famers in Delaware are buried near the old Quickstep stomping grounds in Wilmington. The first, William "Judy" Johnson, was born in Snow Hill, Maryland, but his family moved to Delaware when he was a boy.

Breaking into black baseball as a teenager on war-depleted semi-pro teams, he joined the Hilldale Club of Philadelphia in 1921, where he established a career as a solid third baseman. He played for the Hilldales for many years but, as with all black ballplayers of the age, he had to travel far and wide to make a living. He spent a season in Cuba and logged innings with two of the most successful teams in Negro Leagues history, the Homestead Grays and the Pittsburgh Crawfords.

In later years he had an impressive career as a scout for Major League Baseball, signing, among others, Dick Allen for the Phillies in 1960. He once claimed that he could have signed Henry Aaron for the Kansas City Athletics if only he could have gotten owner Arnold Johnson (obviously no relation) out of bed in a timelier manner, though his claim is likely apocryphal. When Judy Johnson was elected to the Hall in 1975, he was only the sixth Negro Leaguer so honored. Today, the Wilmington-area men's senior baseball league is known as the Judy Johnson League.

Judy Johnson may be my favorite baseball name.

The photograph of McGowan was bittersweet; it was the last picture from a long road trip.

Bill McGowan

Cathedral Cemetery, Wilmington

Buried a half mile away from Johnson is umpire Bill McGowan. One of the more colorful and demonstrative umpires in baseball history, McGowan came up through the ranks of semi-pro and minor league ball, logging 13 seasons before finally making his first American League appearance on April 14, 1925. He officiated eight World Series and four All-Star Games, and was something of an umpire Iron Horse, working 2,541 consecutive games. His call in 1931 contributed to the actual Iron Horse losing the home run title when McGowan determined that Lou Gehrig was out after he passed another runner on the basepaths following an April blast. He founded the Bill McGowan School for Umpires in 1938, which still exists today, although it currently operates under the name The Harry Wendelstedt Umpire School, having been taken over by Wendelstedt in the 1970s. McGowan is the umpire who famously told Ted Williams on the final day of the 1941 season, "To hit .400, a batter has got to be loose. He has got to be loose." Williams was.

Minor League Mecca
◆ NORTH CAROLINA ◆

Historians disagree about the effect the Civil War had on the spread of baseball. For years the narrative was that Union soldiers in Confederate prison camps introduced the sport to their captors, and play in the South expanded from there. Recent research, however, has revealed clubs in New Orleans as early as 1857. The first documented games in the state of North Carolina took place at Salisbury military prison in 1862, as contemporary diaries detail contests between soldiers as well as Union prisoners. It may be a romantic notion to imagine that baseball helped heal the divide after the war was over, but love of the sport was a rare point of agreement. As one captive noted in his journal, the games brought "as much enjoyment to the Rebs as the Yanks."

There has never been a major league ball club that has called North Carolina home. However, the state has figured prominently in minor league history. An "outlaw" Carolina League was formed in 1936, founded on the fertile talent pool of the local textile leagues, but that was crushed by organized baseball after three seasons. The current incarnation of the Carolina League, which is labeled class-A advanced, was founded in 1945. It originally featured five teams from the state, including the Burlington Bees, the Leaksville-Spray-Draper Triplets (three towns claimed ownership of the franchise, which in turn stayed in business for only three seasons), the Raleigh Capitals, the Winston-Salem Cardinals and, of course, the Durham Bulls. Made famous by the 1988 film,

Bull Durham, the club went out of business in 1967 before reforming in 1980 and serving as the home team for arguably the greatest baseball movie ever made.

Seven Hall of Famers were born in North Carolina. Two of them, Luke Appling and Hoyt Wilhelm, moved to Georgia and Florida, respectively, and were buried there upon their deaths. Another, Gaylord Perry, is ubiquitous on the autograph circuit. The other four chose to be interred back home, far away from the bright glare of the metropolitan worlds they encountered as major league baseball players. Another, Willie Stargell, was born in Oklahoma and lived throughout the United States before calling Wilmington home later in life.

Enos Slaughter
Allensville United Methodist Church Cemetery, Allensville

For Anna and me, the trip through North Carolina held special significance. We had met in the tiny town of Brevard, in the southwest region of the state, when we were both working for an opera festival 13 years earlier. We were going to visit old friends as well as discover some new places in this rural expanse that we both held so fondly in our hearts. Our first stop was the small Allensville United Methodist Church Cemetery in Roxboro. With a warning about bees from the woman in the church yard, we walked through the piles of recently mown grass to the man whose very nickname was "Country."

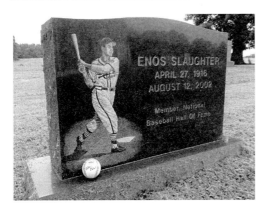

"Watch out for bees!" The grave of Enos Slaughter.

Enos Slaughter's most famous moment came in Game 7 of the 1946 World Series, when he made his unlikely "mad dash" from first base on a single to score the Series' winning run. While never a stolen base threat (his highest season total was nine, which he managed in 1946 as well as 1942), he twice led the league in triples, so Slaughter wasn't exactly dead weight on the bases. By blowing through the stop sign of third base coach Mike González, Slaughter not only secured the Cardinals' sixth title, but his place in history. After he left St. Louis in 1954, he played for the Yankees, the Kansas City Athletics, and the Milwaukee Braves. He retired after the 1959 season with the perfectly round batting average of .300.

Rick Ferrell
New Garden Friends Cemetery, Greensboro

When Rick Ferrell was elected by the Veterans Committee in 1984, his plaque highlighted his accomplishments as one of baseball's most durable catchers, spending 1,806 games behind the dish by the time he retired in 1947. It was an American League record that wasn't surpassed until 1988, when Carlton Fisk set the new mark. Ferrell also mastered the handling of the pesky knuckleball later in his playing career when he served as the backstop for the 1944 Washington Senators,

a team featuring four knuckleball pitchers, earning him his seventh All-Star appearance.

Ferrell's greater contribution, however, may have come as an executive with the Detroit Tigers. Spending 37 years in their front office, he oversaw two championships as general manager and, later, executive consultant. Famous for his astounding, computer-like memory, he spent 20 years as a member of the Major League Baseball rules committee. There he shaped the course of the game by being a part of changes to the pitching mound and the installation of the mandatory use of batting helmets. Ferrell, a Quaker, is buried in New Garden Friends Cemetery, not far from his brother Wes, whose career is perhaps even more Hall of Fame-worthy.

Rick Ferrell's brother, Wes, is buried very nearby.

Willie Stargell
Oleander Memorial Gardens, Wilmington

Born in Oklahoma, schooled in California, Willie Stargell became a legend in Pittsburgh. Playing all 2,360 games of his 21-year career for the Pirates, the man who was known as "Pops" was not only a leader in the clubhouse, but a monster at the plate. He led the league in home runs twice, in 1971 and 1973, and hit 20 or more dingers 15 times in his career. He played in the post-season six times, winning two championships. During the 1979 World Series, he hit .400, clubbing 12 hits, including four doubles and three home runs.

The horribly distant photograph of Willie Stargell's grave.

His greatest season may have been 1973, when he led the league in doubles, home runs, RBIs, slugging, and OPS, but he finished second in MVP voting to Pete Rose. He won the award only once, during the championship year of 1979.

Stargell's grave represented the first time I was faced with a problem I had been fearing for some time, ever since I had to find the ladder to shoot Billy Evans in Cleveland. Namely, he was just too high up to photograph. The selfie-stick had not yet been invented, and unlike previous instances of someone being up so high, there was no means of conveyance lying around to get me closer. There was a pole that was designed to grab the vases that decorate the graves, and I was able to use that to place the ball. The shot as you see it is a digital zoom, and a professional photographer would cringe to see what I've done. It was around this point that I simply accepted that not all of these pictures would be masterpieces. With over 300 photos in the project, some of them were destined to be clunkers. The Stargell photo is one of them. Ironically, I took this shot immediately after the photo of Tom Yawkey (see the chapter on The Symbolic Ones) which ranks as one of my favorites.

Catfish Hunter
Cedarwood Cemetery, Hertford

Jim "Catfish" Hunter established himself as one of the most reliable starters in the game after six seasons with the Kansas

City/Oakland Athletics, appearing in three All-Star Games by 1970. When he exploded to 21 wins in 1971, as well as lowering his ERA by nearly a whole run from the previous season, Hunter began a stretch that was not only dominant, but well-timed. He won more than 20 games for the A's four seasons in a row and led them to three straight World Series Championships from 1972 to 1974. He went 4–0 with a minuscule 2.19 ERA in seven Series appearances in that span. After winning the Cy Young Award in 1974, he got out of his contract when the team failed to make an annuity payment, as was stipulated. He then signed an unprecedented $3.2 million, five-year deal with the New York Yankees.

I had previously visited the graves of two Hall of Famers who felt such a deep connection to their colleges that they were buried in their backyards, Christy Mathewson and Earle Combs. Hunter, who never went to college, marked the first time I photographed one who lies in repose within sight of the baseball diamond at his old high school in Hertford, where Hunter was born and died.

His grave acknowledges his time with both the A's and the Yankees. He was diagnosed with amyotrophic lateral sclerosis (ALS), but died prematurely after a fall, at the age of 53. Hunter was the second Hall of Famer to suffer at the hands of this neurological disease. The first was, of course, the player whose name is eternally linked to the illness, Lou Gehrig.

Catfish Hunter spent 10 years in Oakland and five years in New York, but he gave them equal space on his gravestone.

The Negro Leagues' greatest first baseman, Buck Leonard.

Buck Leonard

Gardens of Gethsemane, Rocky Mount

Coincidentally, the final Hall of Famer buried in the state was known as "the black Lou Gehrig." While this may have more to do with Walter "Buck" Leonard being a first baseman than any actual similarity in the playing style between the two men, there's no doubting that Leonard was a legend. He appeared in 12 Negro League East-West All-Star Games, and Bill James named him the greatest first baseman in the history of organized black baseball. In 1972, Leonard and Josh Gibson became just the second and third Negro Leaguers elected to the Hall of Fame, following the induction of Satchel Paige the previous year. It was only appropriate that he and Gibson, who played alongside each other for 10 years, were inducted at the same time. After all, another likely reason for Leonard's comparison to Gehrig is that teammate Gibson was known as "the black Babe Ruth."

Lessons Learned

◆ GEORGIA ◆

The earliest documented organized game in the state of Georgia took place in Macon. Although today Atlanta is much larger, in 1860 the two were nearly identical in population, with both of them serving as home to approximately 9,000 souls. When the Macon-based Olympic Club played an intrasquad game on February 11 of that year, they became the first to do so under Association Rules. Less than a year later, in January 1861, Georgia became the fifth state to secede from the Union. As a result, it wasn't until May 12, 1866, that the first organized game took place in the capital city. The Atlanta Base Ball Club lost that inaugural game to the Gate City squad by a score of 127–29.

It took another 100 years for Georgia to get its first major league team. After 76 seasons in Boston, and another 13 in Milwaukee, the Braves moved to Atlanta in 1966. For the first 25 years, success was difficult for the twice-transplanted team to come by, as they appeared in just two post-seasons between 1966 and 1990, twice losing the NLCS without winning a single game. Thanks in no small part to Hall of Fame manager Bobby Cox and general manager John Schuerholz, the franchise's fortunes turned in 1991, when they won the first of 14 straight division titles. Although there was only one World Series victory during that unprecedented run of excellence, for the last 10 seasons of the 20th century and the first five of the 21st, the Braves were a part of October baseball.

Johnny Mize
Yonah View Memorial Gardens, Demorest

Roughly 80 miles northwest of Atlanta is the birthplace of Johnny Mize, "The Big Cat." For the first seven years of his career, Mize was simply dominant. While the Rookie of the Year Award was not issued until 1947, it is difficult to doubt that Mize's freshman campaign of 1936 would have been a sure-thing had the honor existed. Batting .329 with 19 home runs and 93 RBIs, his entry into the league with the St. Louis Cardinals was a harbinger. Over the following six years he hit 165 more home runs, leading the league twice in that category in 1939 and 1940, and in slugging four times. He was pressed into military service after the 1942 season, but when he returned in 1946, playing for the New York Giants, he picked up right where he left off, batting .337 and hitting 22 home runs in 101 games.

He led the league in home runs twice more, in 1947 (51) and '48 (40), but his skills quickly began to diminish during the 1949 season. He was traded to the Yankees that year and played a limited role in their run of five straight championships. Interestingly, 1949 was his first opportunity to play in the post-season, despite spending the rest of his career with the often successful Cardinals and Giants. In a cruel twist, the Cardinals, who could do no better than second place with Mize on the team, won the Series in 1942, his first year with the Giants.

Johnny Mize's stone highlights his career statistics and mentions the years he spent in the military.

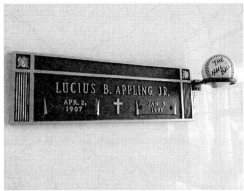

Luke Appling played an awful lot of games for a man nicknamed "Ol' Aches and Pains."

Meanwhile, the Giants, who appeared in three World Series between 1933–1937, had to wait until 1951 to make their next Fall Classic. By then, Mize was a part of the Yankees squad that defeated them.

Mize's grave is a rare one that not only notes his baseball career, but is centered around it. It mentions his election to the Hall and lists his lifetime statistics for games, at-bats, runs, hits, doubles, triples, home runs, RBIs, and batting average. It is perhaps a good thing that Mize lived and played in the time before the statistic-mad days of Sabermetrics that we are now experiencing, or he might have needed a bigger marker.

Despite his steady stream of physical complaints, Appling rarely played fewer than 140 games and usually hit better than .300, topping that mark 16 times in a 20-year career, all spent with the Chicago White Sox. He twice led the American League in batting, posting a sizzling .388 mark in 1936 as well as hitting .328 in 1943. His lifetime batting average of .310 is the eighth-highest in the history of the White Sox, and he is the club's all-time leader in WAR, with a 74.5, 6.3 points higher than runner-up Frank Thomas. Like his North Side counterpart, Ernie Banks, Appling has the dubious distinction of playing over 2,400 games without ever appearing in a World Series.

Luke Appling
Sawnee View Gardens, Cumming

As mentioned, Luke Appling was born in North Carolina, but by high school his family had moved to the Atlanta area. Famously nicknamed "Ol' Aches and Pains," Appling was labeled a hypochondriac by teammates, management, and the press. While impossible to prove at this point, there is the potential that the constant stream of backaches, headaches, and eye problems that plagued his career were actually due to an undiagnosed disease akin to fibrositis, now known as fibromyalgia. Since there is no medical record to support this theory, it's also possible that he just had a particularly low tolerance for pain.

Ty Cobb
Rosehill Cemetery, Royston

The final Georgian buried in the state is undoubtedly one of the most famous of them all, and possibly the greatest offensive force ever to play the game. Even though many of the names from the dawn of the 20th century have faded into history, Ty Cobb will be a point of comparison for as long as the game is played. Nicknamed "the Georgia Peach," Cobb's history is a complicated one. His effect on the field was undeniable. When he retired in 1928, after a 24-year career, he held the records for runs, hits, total bases, and even WAR, a modern metric. He still has the highest batting average of anyone to play the game, .366, a mark that will likely stand for all time.

His personal life has become more controversial. For decades, Cobb has been portrayed as a violent racist who was despised by teammates and opponents alike. Much of this opinion has been shaped by Cobb's autobiography, entitled *My Life in Baseball: A True Record*, written with the "help" of sportswriter Al Stump and published after Cobb's death in 1961. Stump later published two more biographies of Cobb, each painting the touchy legend in a worse light than the previous one. It was later discovered that Stump stole from Cobb and sold Cobb memorabilia that turned out to be forged, and that many of his claims in the books were fabricated.

A glance at newspapers of the time shows that many stories about Cobb had conflicting versions. A recent biography by Charles Leerhsen, entitled *Ty Cobb: A Terrible Beauty*, attempts to prove through contemporary accounts that not only is there little evidence of Cobb's racism, but his father was actually an abolitionist. Cobb did, in fact, throw out the ceremonial first pitch at the inaugural game of Hamtramck Stadium, home of the Negro League Detroit Stars, in May of 1930. Not long before his death, Cobb also spoke in favor of integration, stating that it helped improve the game. His obituary in the *Los Angeles Sentinel*, a black-owned newspaper, touted his support for African Americans.

He is a beloved prodigal son in his hometown of Royston, Georgia. Cobb was brilliant with money and a shrewd investor.

The recently visited family crypt of the extraordinary Ty Cobb.

He became one of the richest ballplayers of his age, and he spread the wealth. It was due to Cobb that the local hospital network was born. The Ty Cobb Museum and Franklin County Sports Hall of Fame is located in the lobby of the Joe A. Adams Professional Building of the Cobb Healthcare System. Hundreds of Georgian kids have attended college because of endowments established by Cobb.

The one aspect of his personality that even Cobb advocates like Leerhsen cannot deny was his burning desire to win. Perhaps it is a coincidence, but his impressive family mausoleum, which also houses the remains of Cobb's sister, Florence, and his parents Amanda and William Herschel, happens to stand on what appears to the naked eye to be the highest point in Rosehill Cemetery. When it's regarding a man as driven as Cobb, it's tough to think this was anything less than by design.

Sol White and the Negro Leagues Baseball Grave Marker Project

When the project began in August of 2010, I discovered that Sol White, the Hall of Famer located closest to my home, was buried in an unmarked grave. I quickly learned that this was a fate shared not only by two other Hall of Famers, but by dozens if not hundreds of former members of the Negro Leagues. Between 1920 and 1960, there were eight separate organized Negro Leagues. This number does not take into account the less organized barnstorming teams that began playing as soon as the infamous color line was drawn in 1887, and in some cases even before that. The original Cuban Giants, which featured no actual Cubans but was instead made up of members of the black waitstaff of the Argyle Hotel in Babylon, New York, began playing ball to entertain hotel guests in 1885.

The fact that the organized leagues resulted in some of the most successful black-owned businesses in the country rarely translated to even the modest wealth that white ballplayers were able to negotiate. Thus, when a black baseball player, who was forced to eschew all other trades and opportunities in order to concentrate and excel at his craft, found that his playing days were done, there were very few opportunities available to him. It was especially difficult for a former Negro Leaguer to escape the inexorable pull of poverty.

When many of them reached the ends of their lives, the players' families were forced to bury them without the luxury of a stone, if they even had any family at all. As is true for any professional athlete, the burden of travel can destroy relationships. For the Negro Leaguers who, even after the organization of the leagues, needed the barnstorming season just to make ends meet, the travel never ended. As a result, an inordinate number of former black players were afforded no stone to mark their presence when they died.

Enter Jeremy Krock and the Negro Leagues Baseball Grave Marker Project. As a child, Krock was told tales of the great Jimmie Crutchfield, who starred for the Pittsburgh Crawfords. Crutchfield had been born in the same small town where Krock's grandparents lived, Ardmore, Missouri. When Krock discovered in 2003 that this childhood idol was buried in Chicago at Burr Oak Cemetery, just two and a half hours from his home, he decided to pay his respects.

That was when he discovered that Crutchfield and his wife had no gravestone. Shocked by the indignity, Krock reached out to the Society for American Baseball Research's Negro Leagues Committee and put a fundraising effort in place. Enough money came in that Krock was able to mark not only the grave of Crutchfield, but also Candy Jim Taylor (brother of Hall of Famer Ben Taylor) and John Donaldson, who were also buried at Burr Oak. From there, a life's work was born.

When I returned home from my initial visit to Sol, it did not take me long to find Jeremy, and I quickly reached out to him. He was aware of Sol, of course, and grateful to have a representative so close who could serve as a point person with the cemetery.

It is not always easy for the NLBGMP to get permission to lay a stone, and such was the case with White. When White died in a state hospital on Long Island in 1955, his body was sent to Frederick Douglass Memorial Park in Staten Island, where he was buried in a grave that ultimately held eight more wards of the state. In such cases, it is rare that a cemetery will allow for a stone to be placed. After all, if all nine families of this particular plot came forward and each wanted an individual stone, where would the cemetery find room to place them?

I returned to Frederick Douglass and had an extended conversation with Virginia Footman, the lone administrative employee of this clearly financially-strapped institution. As Krock suspected, they were not initially willing to allow us to place a stone. I learned from Virginia that due to "mismanagement" (what my later research would clarify to be embezzlement by the previous director), they were in danger of the entire operation being shut down. I was able to convince her that the publicity of having a member of the Baseball Hall of Fame buried at her cemetery might be just what they needed to bring attention to their plight. Ultimately, Virginia acquiesced.

Krock was easily able to get the funding for the stone and, as a nod to my efforts, offered me the honor of writing the epitaph. It marks the first time that anything I've written has been chiseled in stone, and I cannot help but look upon the finished product with pride. In truth, the NLBGMP is such a well-oiled machine that I actually had little to do with the completion and placement of the stone. I didn't even know that it had been installed until months after the deed was done in 2012.

I did participate in the dedication ceremony. Working with Patricia Willis, the newly tapped CEO of Frederick Douglass, and Peter Mancuso, the head of SABR's 19th Century Committee, we were able to stage a ceremony for Sol White on May 10, 2014. Over 75 Negro Leagues fans, Little Leaguers, and government officials attended the hour-long ceremony which featured mu-

sical performances, a brief bio of Sol recited by yours truly, and a speech about Sol's impact on the game by the official historian of Major League Baseball, John Thorn. One of the most rewarding parts of the effort to honor White was the opportunity it offered me to get to know John. There is likely no other person on this earth whose depth and breadth of baseball knowledge can compare to his, and it is wrapped up in such a humble package that one can't help but be drawn to this national treasure.

Back in 2010, I had also driven across the Hudson River to Clifton, New Jersey, where Frank Grant was buried. The situation was nearly identical: a communal grave and cemetery rules which forbade the placement of a single marker. I had an initial meeting with them, but can claim even less credit for the ultimate success.

My words in stone, a personal first.

Grant is commonly thought of as the most talented black ballplayer of the 19th century.

Again, it was Krock who did the legwork. Around the same time that the stone was placed for White, another was quietly set for Grant.

Krock has, perhaps, no greater success story than his work with Pete Hill. At the start of The Hall Ball project, the official record stated that Hill represented the lone Hall of Famer of whose burial site we had no knowledge. (I ultimately learned that another Hall of Famer from the Negro Leagues may not be buried where we believed, but that tale comes later.) Records indicated that Hill had died in Buffalo, and legend had it that his body had been buried at Burr Oak in Chicago, the same cemetery where Crutchfield lay in an unmarked grave for 10 years. Burr Oak was unable to confirm this. Perversely, in the ensuing years since Krock first worked with them, it was discovered that four employees of Burr Oak had been digging up bodies and placing them in mass graves in order to resell the plots. At this point, so much misinformation was flying around that it seemed impossible that Hill would ever be found.

Finally, in November 2010, just three months after The Hall Ball was conceived and I first contacted Krock, he discovered that Hill's son Kenneth had lived in Chicago and had married a Roman Catholic. At some point, Kenneth purchased three plots at the nearby Holy Sepulchre in Alsip, though he himself was later buried in Gary, Indiana. However, in grave 3, lot 20, block 10, section 35 lies the body of his father, the incredible Pete Hill. Nearly 60 years after Hill's death, the equally impressive doctor/sleuth from Peoria had found what was believed to be the Hall of Fame's final missing piece. The NLBGMP placed a stone in 2013.

My experiences working with Jeremy have been so inspiring that I have recently become a founding committee member of the 19th Century Baseball Grave Marker Project.

The search for Pete Hill took nearly sixty years.

Along with John Thorn, Peter Mancuso, and baseball grave hunter extraordinaire Bob Bailey (who has visited thousands of ballplayer graves), we are working towards identifying and marking the lost graves of the pioneers of the game. The history of baseball runs deep, to an age when the tools and funds for permanent markers were not as common. There is no shortage of former ballplayers who lie unknown beneath the earth.

Our first stone, placed in May 2016, was for former stock broker and New York Knickerbocker stalwart, James Whyte Davis, who even did us the courtesy of writing his own epitaph. He is buried in the same cemetery, Green-Wood in Brooklyn, as Henry Chadwick. Davis's stone, in the shape of a modern home plate (a purposeful anachronism, since the home plate of Davis's day was round), certainly doesn't match the grandeur of Father Chadwick's grave, but it is fitting. Davis, who died in 1899, waited for over a hundred years to get his, despite a plea by the man himself to New York Giants owner Edward B. Talcott to make sure a gravestone was provided after he passed. Talcott never followed through on this request, and it would take the donations of the members of SABR, as well as a generous gift from MLB Commissioner Rob Manfred, to make it happen.

The Living Members
◆ II ◆

The Saturday of Induction Weekend, 2012, was the most successful eight hours in the entirety of The Hall Ball. Fourteen Hall of Famers, all of them living, were photographed in a single day. This was my first interaction with MAB Celebrity Services, who had taken over the first floor of the Tunnicliff Inn on Pioneer St. Originally built in 1802 as a general store, the Tunnicliff was converted into a hotel in 1848 and has borne the current name since 1916. When Prohibition was repealed, the Tunnicliff became the first establishment in Cooperstown to be issued a liquor license.

On this particular day, it was overflowing with Hall of Famers, all gathered by MAB owner Mollie Ann Braciglia. I did not meet Mollie that day, but I did meet Reggie Halloway, who was the man guarding the door. Pioneer St. was packed with people, and the lobby of the Tunnicliff is not large by any means. It was Reggie's task to regulate the flow of traffic. Despite having what is likely the most stressful job on the team at that moment, Reggie kindly listened to my rap and let me in. What followed was one photograph after another.

I pinballed between the likes of Paul Molitor, Dennis Eckersley, Ryne Sandberg, Eddie Murray, and Ozzie Smith. These were the men who starred in the tales of the game from my youth. It was an honor to meet the giants of the 1950s and 1960s, before I was born, and the project connected me with many of them. But there was something even more thrilling in telling my story to the men whose baseball cards I collected as an eager young fan. Eck-

ersley, Sandberg and Smith were particularly warm with the fans that day.

I had a quiet moment with Billy Williams. He had been signing for a while and the crowd had largely moved on to others at that point. I started making a habit of watching the players on the rare occasions they had down time. This never happened at an individual signing, for obvious reasons, but when there were group signings, the fans came in waves. I always wondered if the members were relieved for the break or if they were rather wondering why they weren't commanding longer lines. I imagine the answer varied based upon the player.

Sometimes the backdrops of the photographs are less than ideal, like Paul Molitor...

...or the bright window behind Dennis Eckersley.

Eddie Murray nearly broke into a smile for his picture.

Just months after this photograph, Ryne Sandberg got his first Major League managing job, with the Phillies.

Ozzie Smith is the Education Ambassador for the Hall and makes frequent appearances in Cooperstown.

Despite being 74 in this photograph, there is a youthful energy to Billy Williams's smile.

The only living Cuban in the Hall of Fame, Tony Perez.

Many of the players are wearing their Hall of Fame rings in their photographs. Joe Morgan's is displayed prominently.

Tony Gwynn became a vocal advocate for getting chewing tobacco out of the game.

The Hall Ball was dwarfed in Dave Winfield's giant hands.

I was able to capture two Cincinnati Reds icons, Joe Morgan and Tony Perez. By that point I had started developing a growing fascination with Cuban baseball, fed by my preparation for the trip I would need to take to complete the project. I began by researching the stories of those players who had left their homeland to play in the major leagues, many of them never to return, and I was particularly excited to meet Perez. I nervously tried to give him the rap in my broken Spanish, fully confident only of the heartfelt "gracias," I said as I walked away.

I was fortunate to get Tony Gwynn that day. He was the next Hall of Famer to pass after I photographed him, just four months after Ralph Kiner. When this photo was taken, he was a year removed from his first surgery for salivary gland cancer. He still had little control over the right side of his face, and the result is startling. If you mask the left side of the image (Gwynn's right), you can see the youthful smile still shining on the face of the man who was the youngest ballplayer in

the room at that moment. If you cover the opposite side, you see the haunted mask that is cancer. The happenstance of lighting intensified the moment, with his damaged side darkened by shadow.

I caught Dave Winfield after his signing session was technically over. He was settling in a removed corner, having just escaped from the throng. When I approached him, he said, "I'm not signing anything," before I could speak. When I explained that I only wanted the photo, he happily agreed. Even sitting down, he appeared to be a giant of a man, and the ball looked very tiny in his great hands.

Two Whiteys were photographed that afternoon, Ford and Herzog, and their reactions to the project were similar. Ford, who was 83 at the time, did not seem to understand what my intentions were with the ball. He didn't see the point if there wasn't a signature on it. When he finally understood that all I wanted was the picture, he posed with the ball, giving me a sardonic smile that I'm certain was a Chairman trademark. Herzog understood what I was doing, but seemed unimpressed. He was also in a poorly lit area, so I needed a couple of extra tries to get the picture. Apparently I took one too many because in the middle of the final shot he barked, "Oh, bullshit!" dropped the ball and let it roll across the table back to me.

The only other notable conversation that day was with Jim Rice. Everyone else was polite but quick, even Rickey Henderson. I was counting on the "Man of Steal" for a good quote, but he was remarkably taciturn. Rice willingly allowed me to take his photograph. It was not until after I was done that he got a good look at the ball, however. He asked me where I had gotten such a beat-up, old thing. I told him about Anna fishing the ball out of the creek (something I usually leave out of the streamlined rap), and he nodded grimly before declaring, "I thought it smelled a little fishy."

The two Whiteys, Ford...

I used to model my batting stance on Rickey Henderson's because I was short, and I wanted to make my strike zone impossibly small.

...and Herzog.

Jim Rice clearly thought I should have used a major league level baseball for the project.

Ernie Banks was one of the longer, five-minute interactions. He was beyond charming. We laughed throughout our chat, and he kept me around for a few moments after the picture had been taken to talk about baseball. The most beloved Cub in the history of Chicago's oldest franchise, Banks was an institution. His was a name from the annals of yesterday that has had enough time to reach mythic status. It would have been easy for me to be intimidated by him, but that was not his way. Instead, I felt like I was chatting with an old friend.

Jim Palmer, Luis Aparicio, and Phil Niekro were all originally photographed at JP shows. The Palmer photo you see is actually a make-up picture from a later show because the first one was so bad. Brooks Robinson, Carlton Fisk, and Don Sutton were at an MAB show at the Marriott in Hasbrouck Heights, New Jersey, my first visit to this location.

I was able to shoot Brooks Robinson outside of the room, in the well-lit lobby, and it is one of my favorites. I love the way his ruddy cheeks match the reds of the painting behind him. Fisk was a little gruff, but he posed for me. I was there that day with my friend Mel Schmittroth. She is an ardent Red Sox fan and was sporting her colors, a Boston t-shirt wrapped around a protruding, five-month-pregnant belly.

Perhaps not surprisingly, when she asked Fisk for a picture, the gruffness melted away and he swallowed her in a giant bear hug.

Sutton overheard me telling one of the representatives from MAB about the project and informed the promoter that there was no way he was going to pose for the picture until he had a chance to ask me a few questions. By then he was no longer backstage and was out on the floor, but he made the line wait. The four-time All-Star and 324-game winner proceeded to give me a brief competency hearing. He was disturbed about the part of the project involving the cemeteries, asserting that it was weird. I explained to him that I was attempting to honor these men, and there was no ghoulish intent. I must have been convincing because he let me take the picture, but not before he told me, "I still think you're a squirrel." Presumably, that's because I'm nuts.

I traveled to White Plains specifically for Orlando Cepeda. There was no one else appearing at the JP signing that I needed. This was one of the days in which I didn't get the photo until after the player was done on the floor, as opposed to beforehand, which I was sometimes lucky enough to do.

Jim Palmer redux, the first time I re-shot a living player.

The Aparicio photograph happened quickly, during a lull in his autograph line.

Phil Niekro was photographed in the same dimly lit auditorium as Aparicio.

You can tell, from the angle of the photograph, how much shorter I am than Carlton Fisk.

Squirrel-hunter, Don Sutton.

I waited hours before Cepeda finished his contracted time. Typically, Brian would introduce me to the player, but I saw Cepeda go off the floor and take a seat in the back room.

Orlando Cepeda began practicing Buddhism in the 1980s.

Brian was nowhere to be found, so I approached the "Baby Bull" on my own, the one outsider in a room full of JP employees, and made my pitch. He looked wary, giving the impression he was scanning the room for assistance. Ultimately, without speaking a word, he conceded and let me take the picture.

Greg Maddux was the quickest turnaround on any photo. Barely three weeks after his election was announced, he was appearing at a Long Island mall with Steiner Sports. Maddux was doubly cooperative. I suffered from a technology fail (okay, maybe it was user error) and needed to go back a second time to ask him to pose again. This particular signing also afforded me my first opportunity to speak with Brendan Herlihy, who has turned out to be one of The Hall Ball's most enthusiastic supporters. Brendan became such a fan that at one point he asked to be photographed with the ball.

Herlihy even arranged for me to have a private meeting with Joe Torre. Steiner is the exclusive licensor of many of the Yankees greats.

The first time I tried to photograph Greg Maddux, I accidentally turned on one of my iPhone's many filters. I had to get back in line and ask him a second time.

In addition to the public signings, they schedule private signings in which the fans don't actually meet the players, but can send in items to be autographed. Torre was going to be in their offices, and Brendan invited me to meet him. There is a gravitas to Joe Torre, as well as a warmth, that made me feel like I was talking to a beloved, but stern, uncle. Perhaps this was a necessary trait for managing the egos that go with baseball's most expensive payroll. He was very receptive to the project and wished me luck with a smile.

Frank Thomas and Reggie Jackson were photographed the same day. My then-barely two-year-old daughter Violet was with me, and at one point she was standing at Thomas's feet while I was getting ready to take the picture. Thomas is listed as 6'5" and 240 pounds according to Baseball-Reference, but at this point he was also five years past his playing days. Needless to say, he is a giant of a man and towered over Violet, who barely came to his knee. The image, while not captured for posterity, will remain burned in my brain for all time.

Joe Torre was the only time I was ever invited to attend a private signing.

Pen at the ready, Frank Thomas nearly signed the ball before I stopped him.

After the picture with the ball, Cal Ripken insisted on taking another posing with me. It's the only picture of me with a Hall of Famer.

As manager of the Braves, Bobby Cox oversaw the torture of your Mets fan author on an annual basis.

One of the most versatile men to ever play the game, Robin Yount.

Jackson was willing to take the picture but he wanted to have a little fun with me. Right before the first shot was taken, Jackson blurted out, "You want something like this?" and he proceeded to raise his middle finger prominently on the hand holding the ball. I quickly explained that I would *love* for that to be his photo (it would have been uniquely Reggie), but he hurriedly said, "Never mind. We should probably erase that," which he did before I could even protest. His smile in the photo is genuine as everyone in the room got a good laugh.

The Cal Ripken, Jr., meeting was unique because it was attached to a Q & A publicizing his book, *Squeeze Play*, part of a series of novels designed around teaching kids the importance of fair play and sportsmanship. Ripken spent much of the time in his interview extolling these virtues. He also revealed something I had never heard. As most know, Ripken's father, Cal Sr., had an unsuccessful playing career before becoming a fixture of the Baltimore Orioles organization, working for them in various capacities for 36 years. He even managed the club for a season in 1987. Despite this pedigree, it was actually Cal Jr.'s mother who taught the future Iron Man how to play ball. His father was often away when Cal was a child, and it was Violet Ripken who schooled him on the fundamentals, as well as drove him to all of his Little League games. He spoke emotionally about the time she was kidnapped and listed her as one of his greatest heroes.

Both the Bobby Cox and Robin Yount photos were courtesy of Steiner Sports, and although neither interaction was particularly noteworthy, both Cox and Yount had memorable one-liners once I finished the rap. Cox gave me a beaming smile and, in the parlance of a man who had spent nearly 30 years in Atlanta, stated, "Well, then, let's get it done!" Yount, long blonde hair flowing and stubbly beard covering his cheeks, looked like an acolyte of Jeff Bridges's Dude Lebowski. His appropriate response: "Wow, far out, man."

Unexpected Connection
◆ TEXAS ◆

The earliest record of a club organizing in Texas comes from a March 1, 1859, mention in the *Galveston Civilian and Gazette Weekly.* Perhaps expectedly, the three club officers, Ira Freeman, Alexander Davidson, and Edwin Van York, were all born in New York, although Freeman had been living in Texas since 1841. While no game records exist, the announcement stated that they would be playing "under the same rules as govern the clubs of the North," a banal sentence at the time that disappeared from Texas newspapers in just two short years.

Like the rest of the country, post-war Texas saw a rapid growth in the popularity of the game. Since the advent of minor league baseball, over 110 Texas locales have served as the home of a professional baseball team, more than any other state by a wide margin. It took until the expansion era, beginning in 1962, for the state to get its first major league team, the Houston Colt .45s, which changed its name to the now-familiar Astros in 1965. In 1972, the third incarnation of the Washington Senators moved to Arlington and became the Texas Rangers. Both clubs have had some success, with the Rangers making six post-season appearances and the Astros an even more impressive 10. The state was able to celebrate its first World Series championship when the Astros defeated the Los Angeles Dodgers in 2017.

While visiting the graves in the Lone Star State, I stayed with an old friend from college, whom I knew as Rebecca Ash, but at the time of my visit was named Rebecca Sassoon. She had married the nephew of the fashion icon, Vidal, but their marriage was ending and it wouldn't be much longer before she was an Ash again. She kindly let me stay with her and her menagerie of pets, including a mini-juliana mix pig named Pyewacket. My bizarre little project offered her a couple days of distraction.

Willie Wells
Texas State Cemetery, Austin

The first stop of day one was Willie Wells, buried at the Texas State Cemetery in Austin. Established in 1851, the cemetery was designed to be the final resting place of individuals who had made a significant contribution to the state of Texas, primarily politicians and military personnel. A whole section is dedicated to Confederate soldiers. One could also be buried there if he or she contributed to the reputation of the state in literature, the arts, or sports. Wells had originally been buried in nearby Evergreen Cemetery but his 1997 election to the Hall qualified him and led to his re-interment.

As a Negro Leaguer who spent considerable time playing in Mexico, the fierce competitor earned the nickname *El Diablo*, which was displayed proudly on the large monument that was erected next to the original, more modest stone that joined Wells on his journey from Evergreen.

123

A plaque at the base of Willie Wells's grave recognizes the influence of baseball ambassador Buck O'Neil.

Wells had speed and strength and was a power-hitting shortstop in the 1920s, more than half a century before the combination became a regular part of major league baseball. Upon his retirement, he ranked with the Negro Leagues leaders in extra-base hits as well as stolen bases. Though various designs had appeared frequently over the years, Wells was one of the first players to regularly use a batting helmet, after a beaning left him with a concussion in 1937. He fashioned it himself from a construction helmet.

One final note of curiosity regarding Wells: after a disagreement with Newark Eagles owner Effa Manley, Wells returned to Mexico in 1943. By 1944, he was playing for the Veracruz Azules in Mexico City under the leadership of a player-manager, the legendary Rogers Hornsby. They did not play together for long. In one version of the story, Hornsby resigned after nine games because team owner Jorge Pasquel chastised him for hitting a pinch-hit grand slam to win a game, thus lowering the potential box-office take

for what would have been a deciding third game in the series the following day.

Other sources allege that Hornsby was fired when he tried to get rid of Wells and three other transplanted Negro League players because he didn't want to play alongside blacks. Whatever the true reason, fate had decided that the two former teammates were going to spend eternity near one other. The next scheduled stop of the day was a mere 20 minutes away in Hornsby Bend, Texas.

Rogers Hornsby
Hornsby Bend Cemetery, Hornsby Bend

"The Rajah," Rogers Hornsby, is perhaps the greatest right-handed batter of all time. Seven batting titles, a three-time .400 hitter, two MVPs, and two Triple Crowns are just the tip of the iceberg when one tries to evaluate the career of a man who dominated the National League for almost 20 years. No discussion of the greatest hitters in the history of the game is complete without mentioning Hornsby, which makes the discreet circumstances of his grave that much more intriguing.

Thorough research and having a partner in the car proved to be invaluable in finding the small cemetery where Hornsby was buried. A dirt trail off of Farm Road 969, blocked by an aluminum fence plastered with "No Trespassing" signs, served as the entryway to this hidden plot of land. A single house, its lawn littered with automobile parts, used furniture and other detritus, all of which were guarded by a lean, loud German shepherd, stood at the head of the mile-long lane that led to the cemetery.

Once we made our way through the dense woods that surrounded the trail, Rebecca and I came upon not one, but two cemeteries, connected to each other. The entrance to Hornsby Bend Cemetery was framed by a clean, shiny, modern-looking sign and gate. The grounds themselves were well-groomed and relatively free of leavings by visitors.

Some of the balls at the grave of Rogers Hornsby had clearly been there for a while.

The gates to the Cemeterio Mexicano, on land donated by the Hornsby family.

One of the few exceptions was Hornsby's simple stone marker, which featured a number of baseballs left behind by well-wishers (one of which was inscribed with a plain black cross and the word "God"), as well as a toy plastic horse. The headstone featured his name, dates, and a picture of a pair of crossed bats and a ball. There was no mention of his achievements or his membership in the Hall of Fame, despite being inducted over 20 years before he died.

More interesting to me, however, was the adjoining cemetery, the Cementerio Mexicano, which featured a similar arched gate to its neighbor. Instead of clean, black box steel, this entrance appeared to be built from industrial pipe that had suffered under multiple layers of thickly applied silver paint. Rows of smaller headstones placed in more elaborately lined plots, with plenty of stone and brick landscaping, vibrantly colored plastic flowers, and even the occasional plastic molded chair one would normally find on a front porch, gave this cemetery a more visited feel.

With the help of Jenny McWilliams of the Texas Historical Commission, I learned that the land for the Mexican cemetery had been donated by the Hornsby family to be used as a burial ground for the large influx of Mexican and Mexican-American sharecroppers who lived in the area at the dawn of the 20th century.

This was illuminating because, as with the Willie Wells tale, there has always been a hint of racism tied to the anecdotal stories of Hornsby, including, according to his biographer, a semi-active membership in the Ku Klux Klan. To learn that Hornsby's family donated such an important and personal part of their land to immigrants back when Rogers was just a boy, served as another example that the myths surrounding baseball and race are more complex than most fans realize.

We left Hornsby Bend and headed back to Austin. I brought Rebecca home before heading to San Antonio, where Ross Youngs and Rube Waddell both lay in the Mission Park Cemetery South, just minutes from one of the most significant landmarks in American history. Nearly 70 years before the cemetery was founded in 1907, the Battle of the Alamo turned a small mission originally built by the Spanish in the early 1700s into a place as sacred as any burial ground.

Ross Youngs and Rube Waddell
Mission Park Cemetery South, San Antonio

After a brief visit to the near-silent Alamo grounds, I drove the rest of the way to Mission Park South. With a chapel, three funeral homes, two mortuaries, and three cemeteries, Mission Park has death in San Antonio covered. Youngs is buried in section three and Waddell in section five, just a few hundred yards from one other. Waddell played his final game seven years before Youngs made his debut in 1917, and the men had few similarities in personal history or habit. Youngs was from Shiner, Texas, and is the sole native San Antonian in the Hall. He was generous, serious about his sport (which also included golf), and respectful, making him a favorite of his manager, John McGraw. He hit better than .300 nine of the 10 years he played, seven of them consecutively. He was a model of consistency.

Waddell was born in Pennsylvania and has become better known for his flights of fancy than for his play. He was odd, often disappearing for days at a time mid-season to go fishing. He drank often, married frequently, and was known to climb into the stands during a game, sometimes to beat up a spectator and sometimes to find the exit so he could chase a passing fire truck. He was also the most lights-out pitcher of his generation, leading the American League in strikeouts six years in a row. His fastball was lightning, and he had an incredible curve to match.

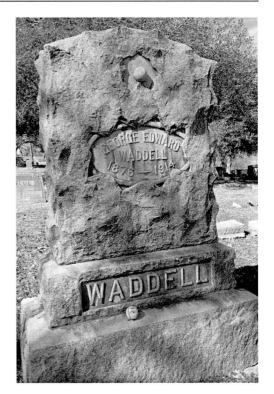

The stone of Rube Waddell, as unique as the man himself.

The image of crossed bats on Ross Youngs's marker was a recurring theme on many stones.

Despite the differences, there is a poignancy to the two of them ending up buried in the same cemetery as there is a similarity to their ultimate fates. Youngs contracted kidney disease, what was then called Bright's disease, and died before his 30th birthday, making him the shortest-lived member of the Hall of Fame. Waddell contracted pneumonia while stacking sandbags against a flooding river in Hickman, Kentucky. His already abused immune system failed him, ultimately leading to tuberculosis. Connie Mack and fellow A's owner Ben Shibe paid for Waddell's medical expenses and placed him in a sanitarium in San Antonio, where his family had settled. He died at 37.

Both perished too young and, as a result, their final statistical totals do not measure up to some other Hall of Famers. It took 36 years after Waddell's final major league game, and 45 years for Youngs, for their respective Veterans Committees to elect them to the Hall.

I visited Willard Brown just after Christmas, and the field of stones featured a sea of identical wreaths, one placed on each grave.

Willard Brown
Houston National Cemetery, Houston

The final stop of my first day in Texas was the Houston National Cemetery. Unlike the Texas State Cemetery, which highlighted veteran burials in its mission but allowed exceptions, this was a traditional National Cemetery. Willard Brown was a Tech Corporal in the U.S. Army during World War II and the first black man to hit a home run in the American League.

Brown joined the Kansas City Monarchs in 1935 and had a career that lasted 22 years, winding through the Negro Leagues, Mexico, Puerto Rico, and Canada. An extremely talented player, he was also a bit of a showboat and was rumored to fail to play his best on days in which there wasn't much of a crowd. He interrupted his career in 1944 to serve in Europe, hauling ammunition and guarding prisoners in Normandy, as well as playing on an integrated ball team in France.

He got his chance in the majors in July of 1947, when he was signed by the St. Louis Browns. Unfortunately, neither St. Louis nor Brown was ready. He was chagrined by having to play on such a bad team, and the racism he suffered from his own club's fans as well as his fellow players was more than he could bear. His tenure was brief; he played his last major league game in August, finishing with a .179 batting average.

His historic home run, coming off Detroit's Hal Newhouser, was an inside-the-parker, a fitting homage to the small-ball style of Negro Leagues baseball.

* * *

The following day my first stop was in a town that, because of my age, will forever live in my mind in infamy. While I remember it as the location of the botched government raid of the Branch Davidian cult, the official website of the city of Waco mentions it as the birthplace of Dr. Pepper, as well as the home of the Texas Sports Hall of Fame and the Texas Ranger Hall of Fame (the lawmen, not the ball club). The city also has quite a history with baseball. Waco first got an organized team in 1889 as part of the Texas League and eventually housed a minor league franchise for the Pittsburgh Pirates. Babe Ruth and Lou Gehrig played an exhibition there in 1929. The Baylor Bears finished first in the NCAA Big 12 conference in 2012 and have had 134 players drafted by MLB teams.

Andy Cooper
Greenwood Cemetery, Waco

Waco was also the home of Andy Cooper. Playing the bulk of his career with the Detroit Stars and the Kansas City Monarchs, Cooper was a dominating pitcher who was part of the final class of Negro Leagues inductees in 2006. Not known for his tremendous speed, Cooper pitched with his brain along with his command of four different breaking pitches. In an age when many Negro Leaguers never finished high school, Cooper graduated from Paul Quinn College in 1918, where he starred on their baseball team, the Tigers.

The subtlety of Cooper's gravestone made it a difficult one to locate.

The grave of Tris Speaker and the wife that belies a legacy of hate.

Tris Speaker
Fairview Cemetery, Hubbard

The next stop of the day was scheduled for Hubbard, about a half-hour drive along Texas Rte. 31. Hubbard is a city of just under 1,500 individuals and has five municipal lakes, numerous Victorian era homes and is the location of the only public pool in Hill County. It was also the lifelong home of Tris Speaker, the "Grey Eagle." Eternally linked with longtime friendly rival (and eventual teammate) Ty Cobb, he shared not only a rough and tumble style of play, but success at bat. Speaker still holds the career record for doubles with 792, greater than 200 more than the nearest active player, and ranks sixth all-time in batting average. In addition to his plate acumen, Speaker excelled in the field in ways that Cobb never did. He remains the all-time leader in center field assists with 322, 106 more than the man in second place, Max Carey.

Speaker could be volatile, contentious, and complicated. As with Hornsby, there is some evidence that he was on the rolls of the KKK, though in later years Speaker was a booster of Larry Doby. He had a long-standing feud with Hugh Duffy, along with other Catholics in the league, which led to rumors of a virulent anti–Catholic streak. Seemingly at odds to that popular legend, Speaker was married to a Catholic woman named Mary Frances Cuddihy. Their wedding ceremony took place in a Catholic church and was performed by two Irish-Catholic monsignors. There was a damning implication made by Dutch Leonard in 1926 that Cobb and Speaker had conspired to fix a game during the 1919 season. Commissioner Landis exonerated both men, but it signaled the end of Speaker's long career in Cleveland. He played only two more seasons, one in Washington in 1927 and another in Philadelphia in 1928, where he and Cobb finally played together as teammates.

Speaker's grave lies at the base of the cemetery flagpole, which itself is graced at the top by a sculpture of an eagle. In addition to his understated stone, which mentions his Hall induction, there is a plaque at the base of the flag, stating that the pole itself was placed in honor of the U.S. and Confederate veterans who were buried within the sacred grounds of Fairview. It also points out that the grey eagle sculpture perched atop the pole was in honor of Hubbard's favorite son.

From there it was off to the final stop of my brief tour of Texas, which also involved meeting up with a former student. The previous summer, Casey Drane, a promising alum, had directed a production of Stephen Sondheim's *Assassins* for the college's summer festival. *Assassins* tells the based-on-truth stories of nine attempted (with four of them being successful) United States presidential assassins, all of them simultaneously existing in a very unreal Limbo. The final scene in the play is chilling; the Presidential killers, past and future, converge on the Texas School Book Depository to convince a frightened, suicidal Lee Harvey Oswald to murder John F. Kennedy and make his mark on history.

Casey and I were meeting in Dallas.

I knew that once I had photographed the last grave of the day, we were going to Dealey Plaza. Before that, however, I needed to visit a Hall of Famer whose name is writ in the American mythos in letters possibly as large as Kennedy's. Within the pink granite walls of the mausoleum at Hillcrest Memorial Park, in the North Saint Mathew section, lies Mickey Mantle.

Buried below Mantle are his sons, Mickey Jr. and Billy, both of whom died before they were 50.

Mickey Mantle
Hillcrest Memorial Park, Dallas

There's little I can say about Mantle that hasn't already been written. He's special to me because of my father. Like every other little boy born in New York right after World War II, my father idolized the Mick while he was growing up. One Christmas, I gave Dad Jane Leavy's *The Last Boy*, an unflinching look at the good and the bad within this American icon. I was nervous giving him the book because I knew it didn't sugar-coat the Mick's rougher side. Mantle was a god to my father, and I feared tearing him down. As with many of the curveballs I've thrown my old man, he took it in stride, his idoliza-tion unshaken. Someone had left a copy of the book leaning against the base of Mantle's tomb.

After the photos were taken, Casey (whose hand you can see in the photo) and I decided that we would meet in downtown Dallas and park near Dealey Plaza. I have a box of JFK memorabilia on my front porch, collected by my mother, Julia, in 1963 and early 1964, when she was 12 years old. Newspaper clippings, magazine articles, even a '64 half-dollar are all pasted inside two scrapbooks. There are three more fat folders of unsorted clippings, a few copies of *Look* magazine, and a number of books. I was raised revering John F. Kennedy. There was even a synchrony within the calendar. I was born on November 21, just one day before the ninth anniversary of his murder.

That was when I began to realize just how unusual this final leg of my Texas tour was. Not only do two of the most influential names in American history, Mantle and Kennedy, share a connection just a few short miles from each other, but there was a completely unexpected personal intersection I had failed to consider before my trip. Dallas, a city that no one in my immediate family had ever visited, was the location where my mother's hero died and my father's was laid to rest. On the drive back to Austin, I spent the next three hours thinking about legends and the holes they leave behind.

Meeting Friends and Family
◆ MICHIGAN ◆

Baseball scholar Peter Morris believes that the first club to exist west of New Jersey was the Franklin Club of Detroit. Made up primarily of printers from the *Detroit Free Press*, they formed in August of 1857. Twenty-four years later, the city became a major league town for the first time when the Detroit Wolverines joined the National League in 1881. In the eight years the team existed, four future members of the Hall of Fame played for the Wolverines, including Dan Brouthers, Ned Hanlon, Deacon White, and Sam Thompson, who remained in Detroit after his death. They won the 19th-Century incarnation of the World Series, taking the crown in 1887 after defeating Charlie Comiskey's St. Louis Browns 10 games to five.

After the Wolverines went out of business following the 1888 season, Detroit needed to wait until the arrival of the American League charter franchise Tigers in 1901 to satiate its major league thirst. Despite their longevity, the story of the Tigers is not one filled with much success. They didn't win their first championship until 1935 and have won only three more since. Recent teams have done well, appearing in four straight post-seasons between 2011 and 2014, but they were swept in four games in the 2012 World Series by the San Francisco Giants.

My journey to Detroit was inspired by the Negro Leagues. For the first time, I attended a Jerry Malloy Negro League Conference, sponsored by SABR, and the host this year was the Motor City. Each year the conference highlights an individual and dedicates a larger amount of research to the subject. This particular year it was Turkey Stearnes, who also happened to be my first stop in the state.

Turkey Stearnes
Lincoln Memorial Park Cemetery, Clinton Township

I woke early on the morning of the first day of the conference and visited Stearnes, who is buried in Clinton Township, about an hour west of Detroit. Turkey was an all-around offensive threat. A speedster who could slug tape-measure home runs, he consistently hit better than .300 for the entirety of his nine-year career playing for the Detroit Stars between 1923–1931. After he left Detroit, his presence on the roster contributed to championships for the Chicago American Giants in 1932 and 1933 and the Kansas City Monarchs in 1940 and 1941. When his playing days were done, Stearnes returned to Detroit, worked in the copper rolling mills and, with his wife Nettie, raised two daughters and was a doting grandfather.

It was a thrill to learn that Nettie, who was 17 years Turkey's junior, and their two daughters, Rosilyn and Joyce, were special guests at the conference. Nettie was 96 when I met her, and her Alabama roots were still clear in her loud voice, which sang the gospel of Jesus and Turkey Stearnes loud and clear, to the delight of the conference attendees.

The plaque marking Turkey Stearnes's grave was installed after his election into the Hall.

One of the most touching moments was when one of Stearnes's grandsons, so moved by discussing his trips to the ballpark with his legendary grandpa, broke into tears and had to leave the room. I was able to share the story of The Hall Ball, as well as Stearnes's photo from the project, with his granddaughter Vanessa Thompson, who herself was a Division 1 basketball player. It marked the first time I received vocal support for the project from a member of a Hall of Famer's family.

Charlie Gehringer and Harry Heilmann

Holy Sepulchre Cemetery, Southfield

When I wasn't at the conference filling my notebook with various tales from the black game, I managed to find time to visit the other graves I needed for the project. Charlie Gehringer and Harry Heilmann were buried in the same cemetery, Holy Sepulchre. Heilmann made his debut in 1914 and, with the exception of two final seasons in Cincinnati, spent the entirety of his 17-year career with the Tigers. Gehringer came up with Detroit in 1924 and played 2,206 games manning the second sack for the team, never calling another city home.

Heilmann was a lifetime .342 hitter who led the league four times in batting average. In each of those four seasons he hit above .390, including .403 during the 1923 campaign. Gehringer had a career .320 mark and only led the league in average once, in 1937, but it was enough to secure him his lone MVP award that year. The two of them, sandwiched in between Ty Cobb and Hank Greenberg, were part of a legacy of hitters who should have led the Tigers to greater post-season glory than they ever achieved. Heilmann never even played in the post-season. Gehringer played in three World Series, helping to secure the lone championship of his career in 1935 when he hit .375 in a six-game victory over the Chicago Cubs.

Gehringer's widow did not die until July 2018, twenty-five years after her husband. She was 100 years old.

Harry Heilmann was the first former player to be hired by a team as a radio announcer.

Holy Sepulchre is the resting place of multiple ballplayers, including Al Cicotte, Steve Gromek, Dick Radatz, and Vic Wertz, who hit the long fly ball Willie Mays famously turned into an out with "The Catch," during the 1954 World Series. It is also where one can visit the graves of both Frank Navin and Walter Briggs, who between them owned the Tigers for 44 years, serving as the bosses for the entirety of the combined careers of Heilmann and Gehringer.

Hal Newhouser
Oakland Hills Memorial Gardens, Novi

Twenty minutes west in the town of Novi is the grave of Hal Newhouser. After debuting with the Tigers in 1939, Newhouser spent his first four full seasons as an occasional starter who could also perform out of the bullpen. His work was impressive enough to have already earned him two trips to the All-Star Game when, in 1944, he became a regular in the rotation. He responded by winning 29 games and collecting the first of two back-to-back MVP Awards. He won the second in 1945, posting 25 victories and crafting a skinny 1.81 ERA. He won two games in the World Series that year, securing the only championship of his career.

His period of greatness was short. After 1950 he never won more than nine games and, despite one last gasp in 1954 with Cleveland, was effectively done before he was 30 years old.

A favorite nickname for a Shakespeare-nut such as myself, "Prince Hal" Newhouser.

He won 207 games in that brief time, and it took the Veterans Committee until 1992 to recognize Newhouser because of his short resume. He stayed in baseball as a scout, last working for the Astros in 1992, when they ignored his advice to draft a kid from the University of Michigan named Derek Jeter.

Sam Thompson
Elmwood Cemetery, Detroit

The last Hall of Famer buried in the city is the previously mentioned Sam Thompson. After his time with the Wolverines ended, he played for the Philadelphia Quakers/Phillies until 1898. With Philadelphia, he twice led the league in home runs, smacking 20 in 1889 and 18 in 1895 during an era when the home run was a rarity. His 1889 total marked only the fifth time that a player had surpassed the 20+ plateau, the previous four all occurring in the homer-mad season of 1884.

In addition to the claim of two .400 seasons, Thompson's stone disagrees with Baseball-Reference on virtually all of his lifetime totals.

His 166 RBIs in 1887 (historian Herm Krabbenhoft argues that the total should be 167) was the standard for 34 seasons before Babe Ruth passed him in 1921, when he knocked in 168. Thompson nearly matched his own feat in 1895 when he batted in 165. He returned to Detroit in 1906, eight years after he played his previous major league game, and batted .226 for the Tigers, while knocking in three more runs in 31 at-bats, at the age of 46.

Thompson died in 1922, and originally his grave featured a plain, small stone bearing only his name and dates. In 2000, a larger stone was set by his family, which details his career statistics, his election into both the Baseball and the Indiana Halls of Fame (Thompson was born in Danville), and has a fierce-looking wolverine etched into the center. It incorrectly states that Thompson hit better than .400 twice, when in fact he only accomplished the feat once, batting .415 in 1894. Despite his torrid average that season, he actually came in *third* in the batting race, behind Tuck Turner, who hit .418, and Hugh Duffy, who achieved a nearly unbelievable average of .440.

Larry MacPhail

Elkland Township Cemetery, Cass City

Larry MacPhail had a hand in the building of three separate major league franchises, leaving a lasting impact on each one and the sport in general.

Larry MacPhail was a veteran of two wars, making him and Ted Williams the only two Hall of Famers to have made that sacrifice.

While serving as the architect of the Cincinnati Reds, he partnered with team honcho Powel Crosley, Jr., a radio manufacturer and station owner, to make the broadcast of Reds games a regular occurrence. His vision disproved the conventional wisdom of the time, that radio would hamper attendance at the stadiums. Instead, attendance for the Reds increased, a fact that was aided when MacPhail also ushered in the era of night baseball in 1935. He left the Reds in 1937 and joined the Dodgers the following season. Four years later, the Dodgers celebrated their first pennant in 21 years. In 1945 he put together a syndicate that bought the New York Yankees, where his success continued, including a World Championship in 1947 over a Dodgers team that still bore numerous reminders of his tenure.

Unfortunately, his tempestuous nature, fueled by his alcoholism, brought about his ruin. He had a meltdown the night the Yankees won the Series, yelling at players and attacking a reporter after he was insulted by his former ally, Branch Rickey. His career with the Yankees, and in Major League Baseball, was over. His son, Lee MacPhail, was also elected to the Hall in 1998, making them the only father/son pair to share the honor.

Kiki Cuyler

St. Anne Cemetery, Harrisville

Hazen Shirley "Kiki" Cuyler was one of the names that was completely unfamiliar to me when I began the project. Splitting his career between the Pittsburgh Pirates, the Chicago Cubs, the Cincinnati Reds, and one final season with the Brooklyn Dodgers, Cuyler was perhaps a man who excelled at the wrong thing at the wrong time in history.

He played in exactly one game with the Pirates in each of the 1921 and 1922 seasons, and it took until 1924 for him to become a regular. Once he made it, however, Cuyler became a run scoring and base stealing machine. Unfortunately for him, this was early in the home run era ushered in by Ruth.

Kiki Cuyler's grave is a literal stone's throw from his eponymous grill.

The public's attention was more focused on the long ball than on the subtleties of the stolen base. He hit .321 over his career and was a prominent part of the Pirates' 1925 championship season, when he finished second in MVP voting.

Cuyler's distinctive nickname, pronounced "kai-kai" as opposed to "key-key," was a play on his last name. I learned this when I stopped at Ki Cuyler's Dugout, a restaurant located just across the street from Cuyler's grave at St. Anne Cemetery in Harrisville, four hours north of Detroit and situated roughly around the tip of the pointer finger that is the mitten of Michigan. Cuyler not only lent his famous name to the bar and grill built by his son, Harold, but entertained customers with tales of his playing days and even lived in the apartment upstairs. It was owned by the family until 1994, when they sold it to Bob Pelton, who despite having sold the bar himself in 2006, happened to be having a drink the day I wandered in. He cheerily shared a little bit about the history of the place. We raised a glass to Kiki, surrounded by the faded newspaper clippings of his deeds, framed on the knotty pine walls, doing their best to help the world remember one of the Hall's less famous members.

So Many Brewers
◆ WISCONSIN ◆

Baseball came to Wisconsin as early as 1858, and possibly even sooner. An ad in *The Chilton Times* of April 29 of that year announced that the local ball club would be holding their "regular" meeting that Saturday. The earliest game results we have are from a November 1859 contest played at the State Fair Grounds. With only seven players to a side and four innings of play, it is clear that this game did not follow the rules adopted in 1857 by the National Association, even if they were playing the New York Game.

Milwaukee made a very early stab at becoming a major league city when the Milwaukee Grays joined the National League in 1878. They lasted only a season, finishing in last place. Their roster was never graced with a Hall of Famer, although it did have the lyrically named Abner Dalrymple. Largely forgotten to history, Dalrymple was a local hero when he joined the Grays, having been born in Gratiot, just 130 miles west of Milwaukee. While playing for Chicago, he hit a fence-busting 22 home runs in 1884, an aberrant season when the White Stockings' advantageous ground rules led to inflated totals. Dalrymple played until 1891, finishing his career with the American Association Milwaukee Brewers.

Those Brewers were the second major league club to bear the name. An earlier squad made a late entry into the 1884 Union Association season, winning eight of the 12 games they played. It became impossible to know if they would have been able to repli-

cate the small sample of their early success when the UA folded after just a single year. Dalrymple's Brewers fared little better, playing only 36 games in their sole season in the AA.

It took another decade for the major leagues to return to Milwaukee, this time as a part of the newly formed American League. One could argue that the league was officially born in Milwaukee, when Ban Johnson, Connie Mack and Charles Comiskey incorporated their teams during a meeting in room 185 of The Republican House hotel in March of 1900. One of the founding franchises of the eight-team league was the third major league team to be named the Milwaukee Brewers. They were managed by 34-year-old Hugh Duffy, who also played 79 games in the outfield that first season for the Brewers en route to the Hall. The team finished in last place, and the following year they moved to St. Louis and became the Browns.

After the Brewers vacated in 1902, it took another 51 years for major league baseball to return to the city, this time in the form of the recently emigrated Boston Braves. The Braves had immediate success at their new address, vaulting from seventh place during their final year in Boston in 1952, all the way to second place after the move in 1953. It took them until 1957 to bring a championship to the beleaguered city, but along the way the citizens of Brew Town got to watch the dawn of the career of Henry Aaron, along with fellow future Hall of Famers Eddie Mathews and Warren Spahn. Milwaukee was heart-broken when, after the 1965 season, they were abandoned again, this time by the Braves for the southern climes of Atlanta.

The team currently playing as the Milwaukee Brewers came into existence in 1970. Born the year before as the Seattle Pilots, this time it was Milwaukee that purloined another city's club. Initially the Brewers were members of the Western Division of the American League, before shifting to the Eastern Division in 1972. Then, with the introduction of the wild card and realignment in 1994, they moved to the Central Division before finally making the rare migration to the National League in 1998 to accommodate inter-league play. Milwaukee has been one of the most changeable major league cities in the history of the game and, perhaps not coincidentally, the Braves' championship in 1957 remains the sole one of which it can boast.

Dave Bancroft
Greenwood Cemetery, Superior

Because I was entering Wisconsin via the Upper Peninsula of Michigan, my first stop was in Superior, six hours north of Milwaukee on the coast of the eponymous Great Lake. Born in Sioux City, Iowa, Dave Bancroft made his professional debut playing for the Superior Blues of the Minnesota-Wisconsin League of 1909.

He spent three seasons there, marrying local woman Edna Harriet Gisin, and made Superior his home for the rest of his life. His career as a ball player took him to Philadelphia, New York, and Boston. Later he managed an all-girls team, which afforded him the chance to travel to South America and Cuba. But it was isolated, rural Superior that Bancroft called home.

Despite some solid seasons, including five years batting over .300, Bancroft's numbers are weak when compared to other Hall of Famers. A lifetime average of .279 with only 32 home runs and 145 stolen bases (plus being caught stealing 75 times), ranks him far below the median statistics. One of seven veterans elected to the Hall in 1971, Bancroft also had a number of former teammates on the selection committee. As a result of this election, the Hall changed the rules, allowing the Veterans Committee to select only two players and one non-player annually. Those rules have since been updated repeatedly.

Burleigh Grimes
Clear Lake Cemetery, Clear Lake

Two hours south of Superior is Clear Lake, the burial site of another controversial Hall of Famer. It's more difficult to argue with Burleigh Grimes's statistics than Bancroft's.

After his playing days were done, Dave Bancroft worked for a local pipe company.

Inez was Grimes's third wife, out of five. His fifth wife was 38 years his junior.

Grimes won 20 or more games five times, twice leading the league, and was an absolute workhorse, topping the circuit in innings pitched three times. He threw more than 300 innings five times in his 19-year career. Ultimately, he won 270 games to the tune of a 3.53 ERA and an inflated 1.365 WHIP. The debate in regard to Grimes is less about the numbers but instead how he came by them.

The spitball was banned in 1920, forbidden to all but a select few whose usage of the pitch was grandfathered in with the implementation of the rule. Grimes, for whom the spitter was his money pitch, was a mere lad of 26 at the time. He was able to use the illegal pitch for another 14 years, capitalizing on the loophole to confound batters in a way that was off-limits for most pitchers. Grimes was the last of the 17 legal spitballers to retire, outlasting fellow Hall of Famers Stan Coveleski and Red Faber. To say it gave him an advantage is an understatement. If one were to look at the numbers of Jack Quinn, the next-to-last spitballer to retire, his 247 wins, 3.29 ERA, and 1.300 WHIP are close enough to Grimes's stats to call into question either Burleigh's election or Quinn's lack thereof.

Al Simmons

St. Adalbert's Cemetery, Milwaukee

The final Hall of Famer in the state, Al Simmons, is buried in Milwaukee. Simmons was an outfielder who saw playing time with seven teams in a 20-year career, the greater portion with the Philadelphia Athletics. He never hit below .300 in Philadelphia and twice led the league in batting, including a punishing .390 in 1931. He helped the A's to three consecutive pennants from 1929 to 1931, but Simmons became another casualty of Connie Mack's post-championship fire sales. After leaving the A's in 1933, Simmons reached the post-season only once more, with the 1939 Reds, a series they lost to the Yankees. Simmons retired with a lifetime average of .334 and was just 73 hits shy of 3,000 for his career.

Al Simmons's stone contains his less wellknown birth name, Aloysius Szymanski.

Before I visited Simmons, I made an unlikely pitstop in Oshkosh. Earlier that summer, it had been my pleasure to direct a play entitled *The Signal Season of Dummy Hoy,* written by Allen Meyer and Michael Nowak. Hoy played in the major leagues for 14 seasons. His own statistics, which include 596 stolen bases and a lifetime WAR of 32.5, are borderline Hall-worthy. When one takes into account that he was able to accomplish these statistical feats all while completely deaf, his numbers become even more impressive.

The play tells the fictionalized tale of Hoy's first season in the minors, playing for the Northwestern League club in Oshkosh under the management of future Hall of Famer Frank Selee. I stopped in town for dinner and visited East Hall Park which, when Hoy made his debut in 1886, served as the grounds on which the Oshkosh club played. Today, the land hosts four diamonds, situated in a circle with their backstops meeting at the center of the park. Surveying the grounds under the magical spell of twilight, I thought of Dummy and his unlikely journey.

One of Hoy's Northwestern League opponents that season was yet *another* Milwaukee Brewers team. If one throws in the Northwestern League, Western Association, Western League, and minor-league American Association (which is different from the 1891 league of the same name) incarnations of the Brewers, that brings the total number of teams to share that name up to eight. Either the people of Milwaukee aren't very original at coming up with nicknames, or they really are as fond of their beer as we think they are.

A Forbidden Land

◆ CUBA ◆

While records of informal play date to 1864, professional baseball in Cuba is nearly as old as its American counterpart. Established in 1878, just two years after the National League, the *Liga de Base Ball*, Cuba's first professional league, had a decidedly short season that inaugural year. The champion club from Havana had a record of 4–0–1. The Red Lions, as they were originally known, also set a precedent for dominance that would make the New York Yankees green with envy. The capital city won 30 of the 73 championships that took place in the Cuban professional leagues before their dissolution after the 1960/61 season.

The manager and catcher of that original Havana squad was Esteban Bellán. A Cuban student at St. John's College (later a part of Fordham), Bellán learned the sport in the Bronx before spending three seasons with the Troy Haymakers and New York Mutuals from 1871 to 1873, becoming the first Cuban, as well as the first Latino, to play in the major leagues. After his American career ended, he returned to Cuba and the turbulence of the Ten Years' War, Cuba's first attempt at declaring independence from Spain. It was the conclusion of that war, in 1878, that allowed for the frivolity of something like an organized league to come into being, and the baseball-mad populace embraced the chance.

Despite serving as a symbol of civic pride throughout the nation's volatile history, the league eventually became a casualty of Fidel Castro's revolution. In 1961, all professional sport was abolished in the country, including the game most beloved by the enigmatic leader. It was replaced by an amateur system that still exists today and has produced some of the most successful squads in the history of international competition. In the five times that baseball was played at the Summer Olympics (1992–2008), Cuba took home three gold medals and two silvers. They took second place in the inaugural World Baseball Classic in 2006 and dominated the Pan American games from 1971 to 2007, winning all 10 tournaments from that era. They rejoined the Caribbean Series in 2014 after a 54-year hiatus and, although they stumbled in their initial try, finishing last that first year, they bounced back to become champions in 2015.

It is because of this rich and varied heritage of baseball history that Kit Krieger created Cubaball in 2001. Recognizing a desire from his fellow Canadians (and perhaps even more so from Americans whose legal options for visiting the island are limited) to experience the non-commercial joy of Cuban baseball, Krieger founded an annual pilgrimage to the Pearl of the Antilles. When it came time for The Hall Ball to visit the graves of Negro Leagues legends José Méndez, Cristóbal Torriente, and Martín Dihigo, who records stated were all buried in their homeland, I knew that Cubaball would be my best bet. Not only could they guide me through the legal morass that results when an American citizen tries to visit the restricted island, but I was looking forward to experiencing this exotic locale with a group of like-minded baseball nuts.

One of the initial stops during our first full day in-country was, conveniently enough, the *Cementerio de Cristóbal Colón*. Within this most famous of all Cuban cemeteries are two Monuments to Baseballists. Constructed in 1942 and 1951, these monuments were funded by the *Asociacion Cristiana de Players, Umpires y Managers de Base-Ball Professional* and hold the remains of some of the most revered *peloteros* (ballplayers) in Cuban history.

First, however, a note on the specific nature of burial rituals in Cuba. The Europeanization of Cuba goes back to Columbus, who landed on the island in 1492. Havana itself was founded in 1519, 257 years before the United States declared its independence. Couple this antiquity with the fact that Cuba is a small island, just under 69,000 square miles (only slightly larger than its neighbor, Florida), and it quickly becomes apparent that space is an issue. To compensate for this, Cubans have adopted the practice of the ossuary. A few years after the deceased has been placed in an above-ground grave, the bones are removed and placed inside a smaller vessel, freeing up the initial space for another burial.

It is because of the nature of these ossuaries that something like the Monuments to Baseballists could even come into existence. A single burial site housing the remains of the most revered men to ever play the sport would be a logistical impossibility in the United States. But in Cuba, because the dead eventually become portable, it is fittingly appropriate that they have chosen to keep their most respected under the confines of a single monument. Or, in this particular case, two monuments.

The monument from 1942 is the more elaborate of the two, featuring a sculpture of a player atop a tiered pedestal that stands over the four grave spaces below. As with much of the country's architecture, the salt-laden air and communist infrastructure have not been kind to the marble. Over the years, the stone

pelotero has lost not only his legs, but the bill of his cap. Also like the rest of the country, there is a fragile beauty to this crumbling relic. Krieger has reached out to the cemetery, and the government, about restoring this truly special piece of baseball history, even offering to fund it. To date, he has had no luck.

José Méndez and Cristóbal Torriente

Cementerio de Cristóbal Colón, Havana

It is the monument from 1951, however, that was integral to my quest. The plaque adorning the front is inscribed with 54 names of Cuban-born players who had an impact on the sport, at home and abroad. Many of the names are difficult to read, but the three faces carved above the list are clearly labeled. Of those three, only 19th-century batting champion Antonio García is not in the American Hall of Fame (although he is in the Cuban incarnation). The other two are José Méndez and Cristóbal Torriente.

It was the mark they left in American Negro Leagues history that led to their enshrinement in the Hall, but it was on the playing fields of Cuba where these two greats learned the game. Méndez made his first appearance in the Cuban League during the 1907-08 season for Almendares.

The 1951 Monument to Baseballists, final resting place of dozens of Cuban players, including Méndez and Torriente.

Of all of the clubs in Cuban professional history, only Almendares rivaled Havana for dominance. Méndez burst upon the scene with an incredible run of pitching heroics, including 25 innings of scoreless baseball in a series of exhibition games against a visiting Cincinnati Reds squad. Over the next 20 years, he split his time between Cuba and the Negro Leagues, playing for the Cuban Stars of Havana, the Chicago American Giants and the Kansas City Monarchs. He died in 1928, just two years after he retired as a player, and it was believed that his ossuary was placed in the monument in 1951.

The story of Torriente's eternal rest is more complicated. The conventional wisdom, for decades, had been that after Torriente's death in New York City in 1938, his body was returned to Cuba. When I reached out to Krieger about participating in the trip, I mentioned the impetus for my desire to join him. It was then that he pointed out that he believed that Torriente was not actually in the monument. In fact, as far as Kit knew, no one in Cuba knew where he was buried.

Krieger put me in touch with Sigfredo Barros, baseball beat writer for *Granma*, the official newspaper of the Cuban Communist Party. "Siggy" confirmed that a check of the cemetery records showed no information about "The Cuban Babe Ruth." I had a new mystery on my hands, and my short stay in Cuba (as well as my weak Spanish) meant I wasn't going to solve it while I was there. I only hoped he wasn't buried somewhere else in Cuba, necessitating a return trip. It seemed unlikely that I would be returning to Cuba any time soon.

Unlike the trip to the *Colón* Cemetery, the *Cementerio Municipal Cruces* was not a scheduled part of the Cubaball itinerary. Each journey differs for a Cubabalista (our nickname amongst ourselves), as the tour is always scheduled around which baseball teams are still playing. The National Series, Cuba's highest baseball league, has a system and schedule that is unmatched in world baseball. There are 15 provinces (and one "special

municipality") in Cuba, and each has its own team, with the players coming almost entirely from their home region. The season begins sometime in the fall/late summer and has a varying number of games, depending on the year. The first half of the season ends around the beginning of the new year, and the various all-stars usually break away from their teams to play for the Cuban national squad in international competition. When league games resume later in the winter, only the top eight teams from the first half continue to play. At the completion of the regular season schedule (roughly 90 games total), the top four teams proceed to the post-season.

In the 2014-15 campaign, the team from Cienfuegos, the province containing the town of Cruces, did not make it to the second season. As a result, we were not scheduled to stop at this remote village that served as the home for the most revered player in the history of Cuban baseball, Martín Dihigo. This assessment is not merely a personal opinion. At one point, the tour had been introduced to a group of roughly 10 veterans of Cuban baseball, and when asked whom they felt was the greatest Cuban *pelotero*, each man stated Dihigo, without hesitation.

I broke away from the majority of the group, accompanied only by fellow travelers Larry Phillips and Bob "Pepito" Krieger. Pepito is Kit's brother and had been on many a Cubaball trip in the past. He was joining me because over the years, he had formed a very special friendship with a current resident of Cruces, and he was looking forward to seeing him again. That man was Martín Dihigo, Jr.

In a twist of fate that I couldn't have predicted when I was planning the trip (and most certainly not when I began the project), I was going to have the unprecedented opportunity of taking The Hall Ball to the grave of a member while being accompanied by his child. Dihigo Jr., who himself was a former minor leaguer in the Reds organization and played alongside Pete Rose and fellow countryman Tony Perez, had baseball stories of his own. I was looking forward not only to taking the photograph under such special circumstances, but also to having a chance to speak with this remarkable connection to the past.

The town of Cruces does not have much, but it does have a museum and a bar. We visited both. The museum, which opened their doors that day solely for us, was ostensibly dedicated to the town of Cruces. There were multiple rooms of relics from the 1895 War of Independence as well as the aboriginal tribes that predated the Spanish. It was the room dedicated to their hometown hero, though, that grabbed the imagination of our little band. Documents, photos, game-used equipment, and a blanket woven by Mexican fans which bore his image were the highlights of a veritable trove of treasures connected to *El Immortal*. When it comes to *artefactos de Dihigo*, Cooperstown's got nothing on *El Museo Municipal de Cruces*.

From there we went to the bar where I was able to conduct an interview. Martín Jr., is a large, warm, funny man whose English far exceeds my Spanish. We talked about his career, including his difficulties with racism when he came to America in the early 1950s. We spoke about his father and why he was such a dominant force on the mound. And we discussed his father as a man. Because of the nature of the game, and the necessity of leaving one's family behind, there are few baseball biographies that espouse what a great parent their subject was. It was a nice change to hear from Martín Jr., that his father was an important, guiding influence in his life.

Martín Dihigo
Cementerio Municipal Cruces, Cruces

We ended our visit with the trip to the cemetery. Dihigo's grave is traditionally Cuban, placed above ground. This one, however, is also covered in white ceramic tiles, an elaborate flair. A stone book atop the grave is inscribed "*Recuerdo al Immortal Martin Dihigo Llano *1906 *1971.*" That is all. Nothing more elaborate or instructive than this for the man

universally accepted around the nation as the most talented Cuban to ever pick up a ball. But the mere semi-permanence of the grave, without the typically accessible lid, speaks to a level of reverence that is unusual, if not unique. I would later learn that Dihigo's remains were once housed in his wife's family's tomb until a previous Cubabalista arranged for the icon to have a grave of his own. That intrepid do-gooder? Stew Thornley.

It was after taking the photo that the single-most poignant moment not only in the project, but possibly in my baseball experience took place. I had created a ritual whenever I visited one of the graves. I would toss the ball in the air a couple of times and say thanks to the player for their service to the game. I liked to think of it as "playing catch." This time, I asked Martín Jr., if he'd be willing to play with me. After he returned to Cuba, discouraged by his time in the minors, the younger Dihigo gave up baseball and turned his attention to basketball. He didn't often toss *la pelota* around these days. His deep affection for Pepito and the other Cubabalistas who had come to visit his father in the past made him acquiesce. We threw the ball back and forth three times. The timer on the video shot by our driver, Manuel, shows that the whole exchange took less than a minute. But each second of that minute will forever be retained in the most sacred space I have for memory.

The decorated grave of *El Immortal*.

The ball signed by all the Cubabalistas, a gift to Martín Dihigo.

We had one final thing to do before we got back in the cab to join the rest of the group. We were, after all, anxious to get on the road to Victoria de Girón Stadium to catch the end of a contest between that year's most dominant club, the Matanzas Cocodrilos, and the perennial powerhouse, the Havana Industriales. However, there was one more photo I had to take.

Earlier in the trip, each of the Cubabalistas had signed a ball. I had been given instructions by Kit to leave it behind. Pepito presented it to Martín Jr., and we placed it on his father's grave, where I took one more picture. This time, it was I who was leaving the memento. It was something that I had not done on the quest, instead choosing to leave the graves as I had found them. This time, however, was different. I had traveled almost 1,400 miles from my home to visit a forbidden land. The moment called for something significant, and Kit's request was a perfect way for me to celebrate just how special this part of the journey had been.

When we arrived in Matanzas, we learned that Orestes "Minnie" Miñoso, the Cuban Comet, had died that day. Miñoso's major league career spanned from the time of the U.S.-backed government of dictator Fulgencio Batista to the dissolution of normalized relations between his native land and his adopted home. He was a beloved ambassador of the game, especially in Chicago, where he spent 12 years playing for the White Sox. Despite appearing on multiple Veterans Committee ballots, including the most recent one before his death, Miñoso never got the call to the Hall. He even got a do-over with the Baseball Writers' Association of America after he appeared in two games for the White Sox in 1980, 16 years after he had initially retired. Originally jettisoned from consideration in 1969 when he only got 1.8 percent of the vote, his stunt appearance at the age of 54 allowed him to reappear on the BBWAA ballot, where he got enough consideration the second time around to last until 1999. He was one of the last surviving links to professional baseball on the island that had come to mean so much to me in my brief visit, and Miñoso's death was a powerful coda on an already memorable day.

Fire and Ice
◆ ARIZONA ◆

Arizona was the last of the contiguous states to gain statehood, joining the nation on February 14, 1912, but its history with baseball began decades before. Originally played during the 1870s at the military camps that dotted the frontier, baseball's true growth in the region boomed a decade later. Phoenix was incorporated in 1881 and, after it was connected to the Southern Pacific Sunset Route with the construction of the Maricopa and Phoenix Railroad in 1887, became an important hub on the burgeoning railroad lines. Those cross-continental steel engines brought with them the game that was captivating the nation.

The first squad in the area was funded by local entrepreneur Elmer Patton, who also built a ball field at what is now East Lake Park. The Phoenix Base Ball Club began play in 1895 and hosted matches against other prominent Arizona clubs, such as Tucson and Prescott. The city made its initial foray into minor league baseball in 1915, with the Phoenix Senators of the short-lived Rio Grande Association. Arizona accounted for three of the six clubs in that D-level league that lasted only a single year and also featured teams from New Mexico and Texas.

Today, Arizona is known as one of the two homes of Major League Baseball Spring Training, namely the Cactus League. The Detroit Tigers were the first major league club to use the state for pre-season practice, playing at Riverside Park in Phoenix in 1929. Today 15 of the 30 MLB clubs call Arizona

home for the month of March. It took 70 years after the Tigers first arrived for technology to create retractable dome roofs, finally allowing a big league club to withstand the blistering summer heat. The Diamondbacks became the first major league club in the state's history, playing their inaugural game on March 31, 1998, a 9–2 loss to the Colorado Rockies.

For me, Arizona was the first leg of a massive road trip that would span the entire West Coast and include California, Idaho, and Washington (with a day and a half of driving through Oregon as well). I put out feelers to friends who lived along the route and might be willing to house an itinerant traveler. The first to step up was another dear friend from college, Meredith Brennan (nee Haswell). Mere and her husband David had just bought a house in the Phoenix suburb of San Tan Valley a few months prior, and she opened her home to me.

When we had gone to college, Meredith was sharp-witted, quick-tongued, and could intimidate the hell out of a person. Little of that has changed about her, although she has been softened by becoming the mother of two children. She moved to Arizona because David's work had the flexibility, and the two of them had found a mammoth house, with 18-foot ceilings and a swimming pool, for the same price as they were paying for their modest home in upstate New York. It turned out to be convenient for me that they did, as it gave me a place to crash.

A little less than an hour to the northeast of San Tan Valley, with the beauty that is the Superstition Mountains in the passenger window throughout the drive, lies Scottsdale. Despite its small size, at least when compared to its neighbor Phoenix, Scottsdale happened to be the location of both of the Hall of Famers I needed to visit in the state.

Jocko Conlan
Green Acres Cemetery, Scottsdale

Jocko Conlan was a part-time outfielder for the 1934–35 Chicago White Sox when he was pressed into service one day to act as an emergency umpire, after original arbiter Red Ormsby passed out from the heat. Realizing he had a natural impartiality when he called the game (he got in trouble with manager Jimmy Dykes for calling a teammate out on a close play), Conlan decided his real future lay in the position behind the catcher. Over a 25-year career, he was on the field for some of the most dramatic moments in baseball history, including Bobby Thomson's "shot heard 'round the world." He retired to Scottsdale so he could play golf all year long, dying there in 1989.

Not far from Conlan rest the remains of one of the great colossuses from the history of the game, whose death became the fodder for tabloid headlines for months.

Ted Williams
Alcor Life Extension Foundation, Scottsdale

When John Henry Williams announced that he and his sister were going to cryogenically preserve their legendary father, Ted, with the hopes of someday reanimating him, a firestorm of controversy erupted. Ben Bradlee, Jr.'s book, *The Kid: The Immortal Life of Ted Williams*, goes into great detail about the legal maneuvering that took place, including the question of whether or not the documents approving the freezing bore the Splendid Splinter's signature or were forged. Bradlee's take seems to be one of sympathetic skepticism about their validity. One person who is thoroughly convinced that the documents are legitimate, however, is Diane Cremeens, membership department coordinator for the Alcor Life Extension Foundation, where Williams' body is being kept.

Ms. Cremeens gave me and another guest a tour of their facility and was very eager to explain who they are and what they do. The idea of cryonics was first presented (beyond the world of science fiction, anyway) with the publication of Robert C. W. Ettinger's *The Prospect of Immortality* in 1964. To Ettinger, and those at Alcor, Williams is not dead, as much as he is in a state of suspended animation.

The umpire's brush left at Conlan's grave came from Cooperstown Dreams Park, a youth baseball complex not far from the Hall of Fame.

Privacy concerns kept me from discovering which of the pictured dewars contained the "Splendid Splinter."

Their website clearly states that "cryonics … is not an interment method or mortuary practice. Alcor intervenes as soon as possible after legal death to preserve the brain … to prevent loss of information." In his book, Bradlee clarifies that despite the myth, Williams's was a full-body freeze and not solely his head, or what Alcor calls a "neuro."

To date, over 180 individuals are contained within the freezing containers, called dewars, at Alcor's warehouse. There are another 1,800 signed up for the service in the future. While the lobby of the Alcor offices is covered in photos of "members" who have willingly allowed their images to be displayed, they are very protective of their clients. Ms. Cremeens attempted to get me closer to the Kid's dewar, but her boss denied the request. Somewhere in the room you see pictured, along with roughly 179 other souls, are what's left of Ted Williams, as well as John Henry, who himself died of cancer less than two years after his father.

Despite having nearly concurrent careers (Williams played from 1939 to 1960, while Conlan umpired from 1941 to 1965), the two greats appeared on the same field only three times, in the 1947, 1950 and 1958 All-Star Games. They played in different leagues, and regular season interleague games were still decades away. Today, the two men are a study in fire and ice, with one spending eternity baking under the Arizona sun and the other waiting, at sub-zero temperatures, for science to catch up to the dreams of his son.

The Longest Road Trip
◆ CALIFORNIA ◆

The story of California and its oversized role in the development of baseball could fill a book in its own right, and has, many times over. Most fans know that major league baseball first came to the West Coast with the shocking moves of the Dodgers and Giants before the 1958 season. It is now the state with the most franchises, with five teams calling the massive region home, including the San Diego Padres, the Oakland Athletics, and the absurdly named Los Angeles Angels of Anaheim.

There is also a rich minor league tradition in California. Perhaps the most historic and famous of the minor leagues, the Pacific Coast League, centered around the state from its formation in 1903 until roughly the 1950s when the leagues' teams began to spread to the interior of the country. The current president of the PCL is Branch B. Rickey, the grandson of the legendary Hall of Famer.

There is a myth that Hall of Famer Alexander Cartwright brought baseball to California in 1849, when he moved west to seek his fortune panning for gold. It is unlikely that this story is true. At least, it is no truer than the stories of the multitude of fortune-seekers from the cities of the East who brought the nascent sport with them. The game was becoming popular just as they were loading their wagons and placing their fates in the hands of blind luck. The earliest verified mention of the game in California is a November 1858 note in the *New York Clipper* about the popularity of the sport in La Porte.

Its dynamic history with baseball made California the richest remaining source in my attempt to complete the project. There are a verified 20 Hall of Famers buried there, the most of any state. I also wanted to stage five of the symbolic photos (more on them, later) in California, meaning that with just under 90 more photos to take, I could cross off more than a quarter of them in one epic, week-and-a-half-long marathon.

Bid McPhee
Cypress View Mausoleum, San Diego

I entered the state from the south, having first gone to Arizona. My first trip to California in my life began with a stop in San Diego to visit the grave of one of the Hall's lesser-known members, Bid McPhee.

If you look closely you can barely make out McPhee's name through the reflection on the glass.

147

To look simply at the offensive stats of McPhee would be uninspiring. In his day, he was known for his tremendous defense. He joined the 1882 Red Stockings of the American Association and spent 18 years playing in Cincinnati, staying with the team when they jumped from the AA to the National League in 1890. He was elected by the Veterans Committee in 2000, and his election was significant. It marked the first time a second baseman whose career took place primarily in the 19th century was finally recognized.

Unfortunately, McPhee was one of those examples of circumstance making a decent photo impossible. The glass panel covering his niche reflected light in every direction, making it difficult to see the details on his urn. On his website, Stew Thornley mentioned getting a cemetery official to open the niche for him, but my attempts to do the same failed. I guess I'm not as convincing as Stew.

Duke Snider
Masonic Cemetery, Fallbrook

An hour to the north of San Diego is the unassuming town of Fallbrook, burial place of one of the most beloved figures in Dodgers history and one of the three best center fielders of the 1950s, according to Terry Cashman's infectious song, "Talkin' Baseball."

Duke Snider was the Boy of Summer with the matinee idol looks and the sweet left-handed swing that resulted in over 400 home runs. As a young player, he often struggled emotionally with the pressures of playing in Brooklyn, a fact that irritated some of his tougher teammates and often went unnoticed by a public that was enamored with his majestic power at the plate and athleticism in the field. His stone is a standard military issue and mentions his real, full name, Edwin Donald, and his service in World War II.

Biz Mackey
Evergreen Cemetery, Los Angeles

Los Angeles was one of the most fruitful locations in the whole project, as nine Hall of Famers were buried in the city and its surrounding environs. For the quantity of Hall of Famers buried in California, it was somewhat surprising to learn that Biz Mackey is the only Negro Leagues player (there is also one owner, mentioned shortly) spending his eternal rest on the West Coast. Mackey is considered one of the greatest catchers in baseball history, and his tutelage fostered the early careers of Roy Campanella, Larry Doby, and Monte Irvin, along with many others. Mackey spent 18 winters playing in the California Winter League, the first integrated league in the United States in the 20th century.

The "Duke of Flatbush" and Fireman 2nd Class of the U.S. Navy, Duke Snider.

The lone Negro Leagues player buried in California, Biz Mackey.

Off-season exhibition games against major and minor league talent gave black players a chance to shine, and Mackey was no exception. He batted .366 in California and apparently loved the state so much that he moved there after he retired from baseball.

Sam Crawford and Bobby Wallace
Inglewood Park Cemetery, Inglewood

Two contemporaries who often squared off on the diamond, but never played on the same team, are now buried near one another at Inglewood Park Cemetery. Bobby Wallace's major league career spanned from 1894 to 1918, while Sam Crawford's tenure lasted from 1899 to 1917. Both men started in the National League, Wallace with the Cleveland Spiders and Crawford with the Cincinnati Reds, and both quickly joined American League clubs within two years of the founding of the league in 1901. Wallace was a strong-fielding shortstop whose election in 1953 is often questioned, while Crawford still holds the lifetime record for triples, with 309. The man in second place on that list, Ty Cobb, was Crawford's teammate on the Tigers from 1905 to 1917, meaning that the people of Detroit at the turn of the century likely witnessed more three-baggers than any other fans in the history of the game.

Sam Crawford was one of the more memorable interviews in Lawrence Ritter's *The Glory of Their Times*.

After his playing days were done, Bobby Wallace stayed active in professional baseball for another three decades.

Hank Greenberg
Hillside Memorial Park & Mortuary, Los Angeles

One of the most important figures in regards to the social impact of the game is buried not far away at Hillside Memorial Park in Los Angeles. Hank Greenberg was a power threat who twice won the American League MVP Award, in 1935 and 1940. In 1938, he challenged the Babe's single-season record when he slugged 58 home runs on the year. Like his contemporary, Ted Williams, Greenberg's lifetime totals were greatly hampered by almost four full seasons lost to service in World War II. He was also, at a time when the world was watching Adolf Hitler cast a terrifying shadow over all of Europe, a hero for American Jews. After his playing days ended, he continued a successful career as a general manager and team owner. He is buried in one of the most famous Los Angeles-area cemeteries, Hillside Memorial Park, which serves as the final resting place for, among others, Jack Benny, Leonard Nimoy, Moe Howard (of the Three Stooges) and Dinah Shore. Shore is located just a few panels away from Greenberg, whose grave featured a five of hearts playing card on the day I visited, a loving nod to Greenberg's number.

Holy Cross Cemetery, in nearby Culver City, has an even greater share of famous residents, including Jimmy Durante, Bela Lugosi, Jack Haley *and* Ray Bolger (the Tin Man and the Scarecrow from MGM's *The Wizard of Oz*), and Bing Crosby, just to touch the tip of the iceberg. Crosby was a minority owner of the Pittsburgh Pirates and was influential in bringing Greenberg to the team in 1947 for one final season. Lesser-known names Peanuts Lowrey, Jerry Priddy, Erv Palica, Tim Layana, and Fred Haney represent the world of baseball at Holy Cross. Actor John Beradino is also buried there. Beradino was a member of the original cast of *General Hospital* and was featured on the soap opera until his death in 1996. Before he played Dr. Steve Hardy, however, he spent 11 seasons playing the infields of the St. Louis Browns, the Cleveland Indians, and Crosby's Pirates, playing under his original name, Johnny Berardino.

Walter O'Malley and Effa Manley

Holy Cross Cemetery, Culver City

The two most famous names connected to baseball at Holy Cross are also two of the most influential owners in the history of the game. Walter O'Malley was as reviled by the people of Brooklyn as he was beloved by the people of Los Angeles. By moving the Dodgers across the country, he shook the very foundation of baseball and inspired a period of expansion and franchise relocation that still has lasting effects on the game. The move had immediate effects on the Dodgers as well. The team had won one World Championship between 1884–1957 while in Brooklyn. They won three more in the first eight years after they moved to Los Angeles. Brilliant and unsentimental, O'Malley ushered in the first era of real success for one of baseball's most storied franchises.

A few sections away from O'Malley is the sole female member of the Hall of Fame, Effa Manley. Co-owner of the Newark Eagles with her husband, Abe, Effa was the

one with the business acumen and the skills to make Newark a continual force in the Negro National League, eventually winning the championship in 1946. Manley was sophisticated, bold and not intimidated by her male counterparts or the players. Her own racial history is murky, as her white mother was married to a black man, but claimed that Effa was the result of an affair with her white employer. She was raised with her six siblings and lived her life as a black woman, becoming one of the great voices in civil rights, staging anti-lynching days at the ballpark and organizing boycotts of stores in Harlem that wouldn't hire black clerks. Her unassuming grave reads, "She Loved Baseball."

Brooklyn villain Walter O'Malley died less than a month after his wife of 47 years, Katherine.

Effa Manley's husband, Abe, is buried all the way across the country at Fairmount Cemetery in Newark, New Jersey.

Even Leo Durocher's grave mentions his thirst for competition.

A larger plaque, detailing Stengel's numerous accomplishments, hangs not far from the stone pictured here.

Leo Durocher
Forest Lawn Hollywood Hills, Los Angeles

Born in West Springfield, Massachusetts, Leo Durocher's career took him to New York, Cincinnati, St. Louis, Brooklyn, back to New York, Chicago, and ultimately Houston. It seems only fitting that the man they called "The Lip" spends his eternal rest in Hollywood. Durocher originally moved to Tinseltown because it's where he lived when he was married to Hollywood starlet Laraine Day. Durocher was a larger than life character, a perfect fit for an outsized movie about the National Pastime. Brash, confident to the point of arrogance, and foul-mouthed, Durocher won three pennants and, in 1954, a World Series as the manager of the Giants. Durocher never said, "Nice guys finish last" (he actually said, "The nice guys [the 1946 New York Giants] are all over there, in seventh place,"), but the fact that the truncated sentiment has long been ascribed to him speaks volumes about the way he is remembered in the game. He even took ownership of the quip, and used it as the title of his memoir.

Casey Stengel
Forest Lawn Glendale, Los Angeles

Another perfect character for our imaginary movie is buried in nearby Glendale.

Casey Stengel became famous for his witticisms, for his steerage of the Yankees from 1949 to 1960 (winning seven championships and 10 pennants in that time), for his grandfatherly ushering-in of the fledgling New York Mets, and for his longevity. He played his first major league game as a raw rookie for the Brooklyn Dodgers in 1912, and he managed his last game for the New York Mets in 1965. He was a fixture in New York baseball for half a century, but he moved to Glendale when he married Edna Lawson in 1924. Stengel lived in the house built for him and Edna by her father for the rest of his life.

Frank Chance
Rosedale Cemetery, Los Angeles

The final stop on my whirlwind tour of Los Angeles was at the less grandiose Rosedale Cemetery. After the readily apparent wealth that was clear at the Forest Lawn cemeteries of Durocher and Stengel, the more reserved Rosedale, with its front office of flickering fluorescents and hospital colors, felt institutional. Frank Chance was an institution in Chicago for the first decade of the 20th century. The first baseman in the famous trio of Tinker to Evers to Chance, he was so linked to his fellow infielders that someone left a Joe Tinker bobblehead at the base of the granite cup that served as his marker.

Eternally linked to Chicago, Frank Chance was from Fresno, about three hours north of Los Angeles.

He was also the manager of the Cubs during the one dominant run in their history. Between 1906 and 1910, Chance's Cubbies won four pennants and two World Series, including their final one before 2016.

Eddie Mathews
Santa Barbara Cemetery, Santa Barbara

Eddie Mathews joined the Braves in 1952, the final year the team was located in Boston. He stayed with them during their entire tenure in Milwaukee (1953–1965) and even spent a year with the club after the move to Atlanta in 1966, making him the only person to have played for the team in all of their homes. In that time, he left a legacy that was unrivaled by Braves third basemen until the arrival of Chipper Jones. He twice led the league in home runs and finished his career with 512, good enough for sixth all-time when he retired, and still tied (with Ernie Banks) for 23rd today, even after the homer-happy days of the early 21st century.

Breaking the norm, Mathews's grave has a single bat instead of the frequently used crossed-pair.

After retiring in 1968, he returned to the Braves in 1972 as their manager, a mid-season replacement for Lum Harris. He himself was replaced halfway through the 1974 season and spent several years after as a coach and scout.

Harry Hooper
Aptos Cemetery, Aptos

Exemplary defense and top-of-the-lineup reliability made Harry Hooper an ideal and worthy exception to the normal statistical milestones required for Hall induction. Hooper was a key figure in the early–20th century Boston Red Sox dynasty, playing for four World Championship teams. A lifetime .281 hitter, he batted .293 over the four Fall Classics. His heroics in the decisive Game 5 of the 1915 World Series, two home runs including the game-winner in the top of the ninth off fellow future Hall of Famer Eppa Rixey, made him beloved by the Boston faithful. An educated man, he left behind a series of diaries and letters that serve as a wonderful insight into that period of time when the game transitioned from rowdyism to professionalism.

*   *   *

A six-hour drive up the I-5 brought me to the other piratic city, San Francisco.

Harry Frazee once claimed the one player he would never trade was Harry Hooper. Two years after that statement, Hooper was sent to the White Sox.

Despite arranging for roses to be placed on Marilyn Monroe's grave for nearly 20 years, DiMaggio chose to be buried six hours away from her.

For all the vitriol spilled over O'Malley, little is said about Horace Stoneham packing up the National League's *other* New York franchise and shipping it across the continent. Without the Giants, and the ease on the travel schedule their simultaneous move to California provided the Dodgers, expansion west may have never happened. Unlike the Dodgers, the Giants did not see immediate success after they moved. It took them until 2010 to raise their first World Series flag in the Pacific Time Zone.

Further cementing the connection between New York baseball and the journey west are the five Hall of Famers buried in the San Francisco/Oakland area. Each of them made his mark on baseball in the Big Apple long before 1958, and all of them came home to the Bay area when their careers were over. Only one did not live to see major league baseball come to his hometown.

Joe DiMaggio and George Kelly
Holy Cross Cemetery, Colma

Buried in Holy Cross Cemetery in Colma is one of the most famous Yankees of all time. He is so ingrained in the mythos that his nickname has the word "Yankee" in it. Joe DiMaggio was born a fisherman's son and became a legend so large that songs were written about him. He was the backbone of some of the most memorable Yankees squads in history, and he crafted the single greatest streak of excellence in all of sport when he successfully hit in 56 straight games. His grave, which is nearly as tall as a person, has the look of a Greek temple, apropos for a man who, for the final years of his life, insisted on being introduced as the "Greatest Living Ballplayer." When I visited his grave, it sported a few baseballs, a bright yellow softball, two bats, and two Yankees hats.

The elusive stone of George Kelly.

The separate stone at the front, which features his full name and dates, reads, "Grace, Dignity and Elegance Personified."

In the same cemetery is a man who made his career on the other side of the river from DiMaggio, playing for John McGraw's Giants during the first half of the 1920s. George "High Pockets" Kelly was an RBI machine from 1920 to 1925, nearly winning the MVP Award in that final year. After he was traded to the Reds in 1927, he saw his playing time dip considerably. He had one more full season in 1929 but after that he became a part-time player.

Due to his relatively short period of excellence, Kelly's election to the Hall is a controversial one. Kelly's grave is one of the more frustrating memories of the project as well. Sometimes, despite Stew's detailed descriptions and helpful reference photos, a grave is just not easy to find. Anna and I searched for over an hour on a hot, sunny day to locate Kelly hidden in a sea of similar-looking graves. The stone was low-lying and difficult to read from a distance. The moment we snapped that picture and left for Mountain View Cemetery, in the comfort of our rental car's air conditioning, could not have come soon enough.

Ernie Lombardi
Mountain View Cemetery, Oakland

Ernie Lombardi made his name with the Cincinnati Reds, but he began his career with the Brooklyn Dodgers and ended it with the New York Giants, bookending one of the finest careers of any catcher in the City That Never Sleeps. He has the fourth-highest career average for a catcher, behind Mickey Cochrane, Bill Dickey, and Mike Piazza. Lombardi was the backstop for the Reds when Johnny Vander Meer pitched his consecutive no-hitters, a fact that is often overlooked when that trivia nugget gets perpetually dusted off. Sadly, his later life was one of tragedy that included a suicide attempt. Today, he is buried in a high-enough tier of outdoor crypts that Anna had to hold one of the poles used to set vases in the holders so that we could get the ball near enough to him for the picture.

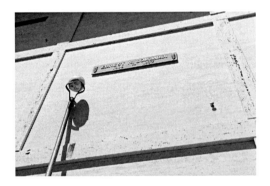

Ernie Lombardi was famously one of the slowest runners ever to play the game.

Tony Lazzeri
Sunset Mausoleum, El Cerrito

The New York/Bay area connection continues with Tony Lazzeri, the Italian-American infielder who was a force to be reckoned with in the vaunted Murderers' Row of 1927. On a team that featured Ruth, Gehrig, Earle Combs (who batted .356 that year), and Bob Meusel (.337), Lazzeri finished 11th in MVP voting in '27, a testament to the respect the then 23-year-old kid had already earned. He won five World Series with the Yankees and was a featured player in the story of Pete Alexander's shining moment of glory, in Game 7 of the 1926 World Series.

Arriving late in the day, we had to ask the groundskeeper to open the locked doors of the mausoleum of Tony Lazzeri.

In 2017, Lazzeri's great-nephew, Marty Peronto, and his wife Tisha reached out to me to express their enthusiasm for the project. I ended up roping Tisha in completely, and she wrote a number of the player bios for the website.

Lefty Gomez
Mount Tamalpais Cemetery, San Rafael

The final great Yankee who called the San Francisco area home was Lefty Gomez. Buried in San Rafael, about half an hour north of the Bay, Gomez was a seven-time All-Star who played for some of the greatest Bronx Bombers squads in history.

His terrific 1934 season, in which he won the pitching Triple Crown with 26 wins, a 2.33 ERA and 158 strikeouts, along with 25 complete games, was good enough for third place in MVP voting. He won the Triple Crown again in 1937, with an identical 2.33 ERA. Gomez was equally famous for his wit, much of which was based on a self-deprecating perspective of his career. His most famous line persists in modern parlance, even outside of the world of baseball. After being rescued by the stellar play of his outfield in one particular game, he sagely told reporters, "I'd rather be lucky than good."

Chick Hafey
Holy Cross Cemetery, St. Helena

While the career of Chick Hafey was on the shorter end of the Hall of Fame spectrum, much of it riddled with illness, there is little question about his skills. A lifetime .317 hitter, he was the model of consistency. His 1928 and 1929 seasons for the St. Louis Cardinals are so statistically similar they qualify as bizarre: at bats—520 vs. 517, runs—101 both seasons, hits—175 both seasons, doubles—46 vs. 47, average—.337 vs. .338. He followed that up by batting a nearly identical .336 in 1930. He appeared in four World Series with the Cards, winning the championship in 1926 and 1931.

The stone of Lefty Gomez is emblazoned with an image of himself and his wife, actress June O'Dea.

Chick Hafey had one of the shortest Hall of Fame induction speeches of all time, clocking in at 63 words.

Hafey had the distinction of being one of the first early stars to sport glasses. Remarkably, he did not start wearing them regularly until 1929, despite years of trouble with his vision. After a period of adjustment, they clearly helped, as his average jumped to .349 in 1931 (the only year he won the batting crown) followed by .344 in 1932. Hafey played in the first All-Star Game in 1933, knocking a single off of Lefty Gomez in the top of the second. But sickness and multiple sinus surgeries spelled a quick end for his career. He missed all but 15 games of the 1935 season as well as the entirety of 1936. He gave it one last try in 1937, but he was a part-time player, and the dissatisfied Hafey retired before the 1938 season. He was elected to the Hall in 1971 by the Frisch-led Veterans Committee.

Arky Vaughan

Eagleville Cemetery, Eagleville

Arky Vaughan's lifetime statistics aren't some of the flashiest in baseball history, though he crafted an impressive lifetime batting average of .318. He had a brilliant year at the plate in 1935, when he led the league in batting (.385), on-base percentage (.491), and slugging (.607). Unfortunately, he was an island that season as he labored on an unsuccessful Pirates club that finished in fourth place. Vaughan spent the first 10 years of his career with the Bucs and the last four with the Dodgers. After sitting out three seasons because of a salary dispute, Vaughan returned to the Dodgers in 1947, just in time to meet Jackie Robinson. A native of Arkansas, Vaughan was one of the Dodgers who refused to sign the famous petition calling for Robinson's ouster. Robinson later cited Vaughan's kindness to him during that first season as one of the things that gave him the strength to carry on in the face of such adversity.

At the end of his career, Vaughan chose to retire on the ranch that he had bought in far northeastern California, near the remote town of Eagleville. He bought the land because of the great fishing it provided, and it was fishing that killed him. Near the end of August in 1952, when Vaughan was just 40 years old, he and a friend went angling on Lost Lake, and their boat capsized. It was reported that Vaughan was attempting to help his friend, who could not swim, and both men drowned. His grave is the most remote of any Hall of Famer in the continental United States. Located six hours from San Francisco and six hours from Boise, Eagleville may be even smaller than Cruces, the tiny village in Cuba I visited to honor Martín Dihigo. According to the 2010 census, there were exactly 59 souls living in the "census-designated place," including a grand total of one between the ages of 18 and 24.

The immense quiet that permeated the air as I completed the California section of the quest was profound. The Warner Mountains, snow-capped and immense, appear in the background of Vaughan's picture. Their grandeur, impossible to capture in an iPhone photo, left me breathless. As I stood in this secluded place, the scent of wild sage everywhere, I thought about the seven previous days. I had never been to California before. In just a week, I had driven the entire length of it, immersing myself in its rich baseball history as I went. I saw so many nods to the game along the way. I ate dinner at Lefty O'Doul's restaurant in San Francisco (now out of business). I saw a statue of a 19th century player, posed in mid-throw, in Golden Gate Park. I saw Little League trophies on the counters at gas stations, and fat heads (those giant cardboard cutouts of real people) on the walls of bars. The history of baseball in California is old and vast, and in the quiet moments after I snapped Vaughan's photo, I let it wash over me.

Hometown Legend
◆ IDAHO ◆

In the March 28, 1868, issue of the *Idaho Statesman*, an announcement was placed stating that the Pioneer Base Ball Club had been formed on the Wednesday prior. It was an appropriate nickname for the club, and not only because they were the first team to organize in the far-flung territory. Franklin, the first town in the region to be settled by individuals of European decent, had only come into existence eight years prior. It was a largely uncharted land, home to only the hearty souls who were still making their way towards manifest destiny, as well as the original residents of the area, the Shoshone-Bannock Indian Tribe.

By the time Idaho was admitted into the Union on July 3, 1890, professional baseball was nearly 20 years old. It took another 67 years for the major leagues to expand any farther west than Kansas City. These obstacles, coupled with the fact that even today there are barely more than 1.5 million people who call the state home, means that there have only been 30 major leaguers who have hailed from The Gem State. For certain, the one Hall of Famer born and bred in this remote land is a jewel.

Sixty miles west of Boise lies the small town of Payette, just minutes from the Oregon border. The greater portion of my journey to Payette, which took place right after I visited Eagleville in northern California, was through the mountainous southeast region of Oregon. My time physically in Idaho was limited to visiting this small town that,

in June of 1936, gave witness to the birth of Harmon Clayton Killebrew.

Harmon Killebrew
Riverside Cemetery, Payette

Discovered by Washington Senators scout Ossie Bluege, the kind, quiet Mormon left home for the first time when he graduated from high school. As a bonus baby, Killebrew was contractually obligated to be on the major league roster despite being as green as an unripe potato. He made his first appearance in Chicago on June 23, 1954, six days shy of his 18th birthday. That day, which also marked the first time in his life he had set foot in a major league baseball stadium, he was inserted as a pinch-runner in the top of the second inning. He made it as far as second base before he was pulled from the game. He didn't set foot on the field again for almost three weeks.

Such was the story of the first five years of Killebrew's career, when he appeared in a total of only 113 games. It was clear the kid had power, but he couldn't hit a lick. It was with the dawn of the 1959 season that he finally put it all together. While he never hit for average, finishing with a lifetime mark of .256, he became a dominating power hitter feared by American League pitchers for 17 more seasons. He led the league in home runs six times and hit more than 40 homers eight times.

157

In the years immediately before I started The Hall Ball, Harmon Killebrew was a fixture at Induction Weekend.

Despite his low batting average, he developed a tremendous eye at the plate. He led the league in walks four times. He never struck out more than 96 times at any point after 1967, spanning the final eight years of his career. His incredible plate discipline turned a .276 batting average into a .427 on-base percentage in 1969 and won him his sole MVP Award. Killebrew's 573 lifetime home runs still rank as 12th all-time.

After the Senators moved to Minnesota and became the Twins in 1961, Killebrew became perhaps the most beloved figure in the Twin Cities' baseball history. But their idolatry is nothing compared to the people of Payette. For the last 20 years, they have celebrated Harmon Killebrew Payette Days, an annual festival in which the man himself used to be a primary piece. He gave instruction to the school baseball team, hosted a charity golf tournament, and signed autographs for the town. The festival has continued after his death, raising money for various causes.

Perhaps Killebrew's most poignant legacy can be seen at the newly built field behind the town middle school. Part of the Miracle League, the Harmon Killebrew Miracle Field is a specially-designed diamond for children with disabilities. The rubber surface makes it possible for all kids, even those in wheelchairs, to participate in a ball game. Killebrew and his wife, Nita, were responsible for the construction of numerous Miracle fields throughout the country, but the one in his home town stands as a monument to the giving, gentle spirit of a man ironically nicknamed "The Killer."

His stone is located near the entrance to the cemetery and is larger than average. A relief of a ballplayer in mid-swing stands at center. The bat, which was likely designed to appear as though it were in the forced-perspective of a completed swing, looks comically small. Or perhaps this was the artist's nod to the fact that in the giant hands of this mountain of a man, even the bat looked tiny.

The Farthest Corner

◆ WASHINGTON ◆

An item in the February 23, 1867, edition of the *Vancouver Register* notes the formation of the Occidental Base Ball Club, signaling the birth of organized ball in the state of Washington. They played a match against the Pioneer Club of Portland, Oregon, on May 29 of that year, and lost, 79–62. The game was a controversial one. There was some debate about player eligibility, and the umpire, after three botched calls, was removed in the middle of the second inning. He was replaced by a member of the Clackamas Club of Oregon City, who had joined the caravan to view the interstate contest.

The real heart of baseball in Washington has always been, predictably, Seattle. Both Spokane and Tacoma have had their fair share of teams, including a legacy that lives today in the form of the Tacoma Rainiers, the triple-A squad of the nearby major league Seattle Mariners. Seattle has supported a professional franchise almost consistently since 1901. The names of the teams have changed, including such memorable monikers as the Hustlers, Yannigans, Clamdiggers, Siwashes, Turks, Giants, Rainiers, Indians, Steelheads, and Angels. They have also shifted league affiliations, spending time in the Pacific Northwest League, New Pacific League, Pacific Coast League, Northwestern League, and the unaffiliated West Coast Baseball League.

Because of its consistent ability to field a minor league franchise, the city of Seattle was awarded its first major league team in 1969, in the form of the American League Seattle Pi-

lots. The team remained there for only a single season before they moved to Milwaukee. When the Pilots departed, the city was without professional baseball for two years, the first time this had occurred since the dawn of the century. In 1972, the Seattle Rainiers of the Northwest League moved into historic Sick's Stadium, but when Major League Baseball decided to give the city a second try in 1977, they were replaced with the Mariners.

Despite one of the least successful beginnings in baseball history, finishing in sixth or seventh place in the seven-team division for 11 of their first 16 seasons, they have survived. Things have even looked up a bit in the last 20 years. Ken Griffey, Jr., became the first Mariner inducted into the Hall in 2016. Both Ichiro Suzuki and Alex Rodriguez are likely Hall of Fame-bound, even if Rodriguez's scandal-tainted career delays his entry. Edgar Martinez, whose own candidacy was hampered by the fact that he was a long time designated hitter (a role he assumed after being injured in a collision on the field), was inducted in 2019, after *The Hall Ball* was completed.

All began their major league service with the Mariners, with Martinez spending his entire 18-year career with the club. Those four played central roles in Seattle making four post-season appearances between 1995–2001, making it as far as the American League Championship Series in 1995, 2000, and 2001. That 2001 squad shocked the baseball world when they won a major league-record 116 games, tying the mark set by the 1906 Chicago Cubs.

Anna and I were fortunate enough to be invited to stay with Elizabeth Rothman, the aunt of our dear friend Daniel, while we were in Seattle. A former (okay, maybe still) hippie who grew up in Brooklyn, Elizabeth now lives in a charming home within sight of Safeco Field, the current home of the Mariners. She was a supporter of The Hall Ball early on, even donating money to the cause. By also opening up her home to us, Elizabeth quickly elevated her status as a full-fledged contributor to the project.

Amos Rusie
Acacia Memorial Park, Seattle

Only one Hall of Famer is buried in Seattle. Born in Mooresville, Indiana, and nicknamed the Hoosier Thunderbolt, Amos Rusie did not move to the Seattle area until years after his retirement in 1901. The 19th-century hurler was so dominant that he, along with Bob Gibson seven decades later, ranks as one of the few people to almost single-handedly lead to a rule change. Rusie's pitches were so fast that hitters could barely swing the bat in time to make contact. It is no accident that he led the league in strikeouts *and* bases on balls five times in each category. There was little chance for a batsman to create any other result.

Amos Rusie is buried next to his wife, May, who died just two months before him.

Between 1890 and 1892, when the pitcher's mound was still just 50 feet from home plate, Rusie struck out 341, 337, and 304 batters, respectively. After the league moved the mound back in 1893, to its now-standard 60 feet, six inches, he saw that total drop to 208, still enough to lead the league. Rusie won 20 or more games eight times and more than 30 games four times. Often pitching more than 400 innings a season, an arm injury essentially ended his career in 1898 at the young age of 27. He managed to come back in 1901 to appear in three games for the Cincinnati Reds, giving him just enough service time to squeak in under the wire of the 10-year minimum requirement for induction into the Hall.

Rusie is buried in Acacia Memorial Park, also the final resting place of Emil Sick. A pioneer in Northwest baseball, Sick was the owner of the Seattle Rainiers and was responsible for the construction of Sick's Stadium, home of Seattle baseball from 1938 until the Mariners moved into the Kingdome in 1977. A philanthropist who served as the Chairman of the Washington March of Dimes, he made his money in the brewing industry. Sick died in 1964, so he was spared the painful irony of his hometown Pilots, who played in the stadium which bore his name, being whisked away to Milwaukee to become the Brewers.

Earl Averill
Grand Army of the Republic
Cemetery, Snohomish

The only other Hall of Famer buried in the state is resting 30 miles north in Snohomish. Born in that small suburb of Seattle, Earl Averill earned his fame in Cleveland. There, he was a constant threat at the plate, batting better than .300 eight times in his 13-year career. A six-time All-Star, Averill also frequently appeared in MVP voting, though he never got closer than third place. His 1936 season may have been his finest, as he led the league in hits and triples and batted a career-high .378.

The tiny section on the top right of Earl Averill's stone recreates the text from his Hall of Fame plaque.

He lost the batting crown that campaign to Luke Appling, who also had a career year, hitting .388.

Averill spent the last two years of his career with the Detroit Tigers and Boston Braves, and appeared in his lone World Series with those 1940 Tigers. Averill, by that point a 38-year-old part-time player, went 0-for-3 in three pinch hitting appearances en route to the Tigers' Series loss to the Reds. After his retirement, with a lifetime batting average of .318 and 238 career home runs, Averill became very vocal about his worthiness to be elected to the Hall of Fame. In 1975, 34 years after his last game, the Veterans Committee finally agreed with him. Coincidentally, just 10 days after I visited Averill's grave, his son, Earl Averill, Jr., who had spent seven years in the majors himself, died in Tacoma.

The visit to Averill's grave was the final one in a two-week odyssey that had begun with Ted Williams in Arizona, had encompassed the entire length of California as well as the brief sojourn in Idaho, and ended in the Evergreen State. Over 30 graves had been added to the project, bringing me closer than ever. But it also marked the last significant travel I could make for the project for some time. Thus it was, with a combination of satisfaction and sadness, that I boarded the plane to bring me home. Yes, I was closer than ever, with only 53 more photographs to take, but that closeness made the desire to finish that much more powerful.

The Living Members
◆ III ◆

I had missed the 2013 Induction Weekend, which was particularly frustrating. No living players had been elected that year, meaning that the crowds had been more subdued and I likely would have had better access to the players. In the middle of directing a production of *Romeo and Juliet*, there simply wasn't an opportunity to pause the rehearsal schedule that summer. I made sure to create a break for myself in 2014 because I wasn't going to miss another opportunity that rich. It just so happened that a year after zero living players were named, 2014 marked the election of a historic six living members. The town was once again wall-to-wall fans, most of them sporting Atlanta Braves gear supporting new inductees Bobby Cox, Tom Glavine, and Greg Maddux.

Pat Gillick offered one of the funniest summations of the project. It was one of the rare times when I was able to jump in ahead of the crowd, the room virtually empty except for me and three of my targets that day. I approached Gillick first, and when I got to the part of my rap that explained that "I either photograph the ball in the hands of the living player or at his grave if he is no longer with us," he quickly quipped, "Well, I'd rather you got me on this side than the other." He, I, and everyone within earshot, which included Bert Blyleven and Al Kaline, immediately burst out laughing. I love that I was able to capture that moment.

Johnny Bench had the most unexpected reaction. I finished my pitch, and he looked at me with watery eyes and said, "So, you're that kind of asshole." Dumbfounded, even more so than by Jim Bunning's terseness, I could only feebly reply, "Yes, sir, I'm that kind of asshole." He sighed and picked up the ball. He wouldn't stop slowly swaying, and so most of the shots I took of him are a little blurry. When I was done, I was glad I never needed to ask any more favors of Johnny Bench.

Pat Gillick's laugh was authentic.

Bert Blyleven is one of only 12 major leaguers who were born in Netherlands.

Mike Schmidt image courtesy of Sean Morgan.

Al Kaline partnered with fellow Hall of Famer George Kell to call Tigers games for a quarter-century.

Bob Gibson is actually looking at Anna and Violet in the photograph.

The blurry photograph of Johnny Bench.

Mike Schmidt and Bob Gibson were photographed at a Fanatics Authentic show in Philadelphia. During my first interaction with the organization, they were initially very resistant to giving me access to Schmidt. He is one of the more expensive signers, running around $150 a shot, and FA rep Sean Morgan was having trouble reconciling giving me something that expensive for free. Having dragged the entire family down to Philadelphia for the weekend, I was unwilling to give up too easily. It was only when I said that I would let Sean take the picture without me that he finally relented. Schmidt became the first Hall of Famer the ball had met, but I had not. There would be others.

Gibson had grown to be a bit of a nemesis. He was one of the aforementioned players who had told me "no," he wasn't interested in being a part of the project. In fact, he denied me twice. Philadelphia was my third opportunity, and I had decided that three was enough. For the first time since that initial induction weekend in 2011, I paid for a photograph. Gibson, who had seemed so fierce and brooding in my previous two attempts, was in high spirits that day. He joked with Anna and Violet while I took the shot. Maybe I should have had them with me the first two times.

By the time I photographed Barry Larkin, I had become comfortable navigating the card shows. I knew how to hunt down where the players were being stashed both before and after their signings. I had also learned that as long as it looked like I belonged, I could often find my way into places where I wasn't technically allowed. Such was the case with Larkin. I walked into the gym at Hofstra University, made a beeline for the area shielded by pipe and drape, stuck my head in, and immediately spotted Larkin. Seeing him alone, I walked over and gave my pitch. He took the ball and that was that. Less than 10 minutes after I parked the car, it was done. That easy efficiency was a rarity.

The taking of Barry Larkin's picture was over quickly. By that point I had started to resent how long I had to wait for some photographs.

A personal favorite of your humble author, Pedro Martinez.

Pedro Martinez was doing a signing for Steiner Sports. I was accompanied by my Red Sox-loving friend Mel (who was with me for the Fisk picture) and Violet. Pedro was receptive to the project, agreeing to the photo before I even finished my spiel. He told me that he thought it was "a really cool thing you are doing," even saying that he would visit the website. More importantly, though, he was charmed by Violet and took the time to let her know just how adorable he thought she was.

I have always been fond of Pedro Martinez. His playful, yet competitive, attitude, as well as his unprecedented run of dominance lasting from 1997 to 2005, were a pleasure to watch. His WHIP of 0.737 in 2000 is the lowest single-season mark in the history of the game and is probably the greatest extended pitching performance I've witnessed in my lifetime. Despite his mixed success and injuries, I especially enjoyed his four-year run pitching for my Mets near the end of his career. Now, after giving an adorable three-year-old her due, he had skyrocketed near the top of my list of all-time favorites. What can I say? I'm a dad. We're suckers that way.

To me Mike Piazza will always be Atlas; a Titan who, for a night, held the heavens aloft.

The Tony La Russa photograph marked a rare moment of decent lighting.

He immediately took the ball as I was finishing my explanation and asked, "Am I the last living guy?" I said, no, there were still quite a few to photograph. He replied, "Oh, never mind. I want to be last," and started to hand the ball back to me. I stared dumbfounded until he said, "Just kidding," and posed for the picture, a devilish smile on his face.

The Mike Piazza photo was perhaps the most emotional for me. There was not only the usual amplified energy that went with requesting a photo, but Piazza was a key figure in the single most important baseball moment in my life to date. I personally witnessed the Twin Towers fall, not on television like most of the country, but from the street outside the small theater I managed, 15 blocks away in downtown Manhattan. Like all New Yorkers, there was little joy for me in the ensuing days. The home run that Mike Piazza hit on September 21, 2001, the first game in New York after the attacks, didn't just defeat the Braves and briefly rekindle the playoff hopes of the Mets. It was also the first time in 10 days that I felt anything resembling hope, and the catharsis of that moment left me a sobbing wreck as I listened to the pandemonium at Shea Stadium on my transistor radio. In the end, the experience of taking the picture was greatly aided by just how nice Piazza was. He was soft-spoken and gentle, allowing me to settle my shaking hands for the photo and maintain my composure in front of a man who rescued me from one of my darkest hours.

Prankster Tom Glavine.

Tony La Russa and Tom Glavine were both photographed during Induction Weekend 2015. Again aided by MAB, I took the photos in the back rooms of the Tunnicliff. The exchange with Glavine was particularly memorable.

Craig Biggio and John Smoltz were both photographed at the Tunnicliff. The sole photos taken during the 2016 Induction, they were shot almost back-to-back. There was a little time after the first photo, while I waited for the crowd around Smoltz to thin, so I took a seat not far from Biggio. While I waited, the last of the Biggio autograph speakers had dispersed. On a whim, I decided to take the opportunity to tell him about the 19th Century Baseball Grave Marker Project. Having just listened to my story about The Hall Ball, and the connected graves portion of the quest, hearing this new bit of information about my dedication to the dead may have been more than enough evidence for Mr. Biggio that I was little daft. He remained polite, but I could tell that he was hoping that I would soon move on with my day and free him from this most peculiar fan.

The photos of Red Schoendienst and Bill Mazeroski were firsts in the history of The Hall Ball. Both Schoendienst and Mazeroski were making appearances (in St. Louis and Pittsburgh, respectively) in the fall of 2016, but work commitments prevented me from going. Luckily for me, by this point The Hall Ball had a "Super Fan." Tony Milito had been an advocate of the project almost as soon as I created the website.

He wrote dozens of bios for the site, tagged The Hall Ball in every relevant Facebook post, and donated substantial money to the project. He was the only person at that point, besides Anna, whom I trusted with the ball.

John Smoltz is in the same position in the room where, two years earlier, Johnny Bench was seated when I photographed him.

Craig Biggio was kind enough to listen to me talk about the 19th Century Grave Marker Project during some down time.

Red Schoendienst image courtesy of Tony Milito.

Bill Mazeroski image courtesy of Tony Milito.

I hijacked Carl Yastrzemski as he smoked a cigarette before his signing.

He also happened to be retired and recently widowed. He was eager for something to do and available. Using his own money, he flew to St. Louis and drove to Pittsburgh to take the two pics. They have a slightly different look than the other photos in the project because Tony doesn't have an iPhone, and every photographer frames their pictures differently. I have come to respect and cherish Tony's commitment to the project. Knowing I was likely never going to be able to complete this on my own, I had always envisioned The Hall Ball as a crowd-sourced enterprise. Tony was the first, best example of that ideal.

The Carl Yastrzemski photo was once again taken with Mel Schmittroth, although enough time had passed that the fetus that was embraced by Carlton Fisk was now a little boy. Xavier, and his older brother Orion, charged the hallways of the Marriott Hotel in Burlington, Massachusetts, where they and their intrepid mother waited for their chance to meet one of her childhood idols. While they were giddily racing through the lobby curtains, I saw Yaz snake through a cluster of people and head to the other end of the lobby.

I followed him and found him outdoors smoking a cigarette on the patio. I gave him the rap and he gruffly agreed. He even offered to pose in two separate locations so I could get a better angle from the sun.

The picture with Tim Raines was one that necessitated some waiting. Wearing a puffy jacket and a winter hat, Raines looked more like he was on a ski slope than sitting in the overly warm back room of the convention center. Long past waiting to be ushered in by Brian or Mollie, I approached him and took the picture. The first few photos featured the hat and then, seemingly realizing he was wearing it, he pulled it off, and I was able to shoot a couple that gave a clearer view of his face.

Randy Johnson was the second player, besides Bob Gibson, to refuse to cooperate. At first, I thought he was going to agree because he took the ball. He then explained that he would hold the ball but refused to allow his face to be in the picture. Remembering the earlier jocularity of Tom Glavine, I assumed he was joking.

Tim Raines was elected only two months prior to the taking of this photograph.

One of the few photographs in the project that does not spark joy in me, Randy Johnson.

When I said so, his response was to tersely tell me that actually, no, in fact, he didn't want his picture taken at all. I walked away empty-handed. My second opportunity came when he was making an appearance with a company I had never had any interactions with before, GT Sports Marketing. Unlike the other promoters, they would not give me any access to Johnson unless I bought the ticket, even refusing my offer for them to take the photo for me.

So as with Gibson, I ultimately paid for this photo. What was particularly painful is that Johnson charges what is possibly the highest autograph fee of those who make regular appearances, almost $200. I had never paid that much for a photograph and hoped never to do so again. For a project that was born from an idea to exempt it from commerce, it was a bitter picture to take.

Tickets, Both Meal and Traffic
◆ OKLAHOMA ◆

The first recorded game of baseball in Oklahoma took place in 1869. Soldiers of the 7th U.S. Calvary and the 19th Kansas volunteers squared off at the newly established Fort Sill. Named for Civil War casualty Brigadier General Joshua W. Sill, the original fort was constructed during one of the campaigns of the U.S. government to slow down Indian raids on the borders of Texas and Kansas. To this day, both the 7th Calvary and Fort Sill survive.

Oklahoma has never had a major league team but is currently home to two minor league teams. The Pacific Coast League (triple-A) Oklahoma City Dodgers and the Texas League (double-A) Tulsa Drillers, both Los Angeles Dodgers affiliates, carry on a baseball legacy that is young by many measures. The first professional team didn't come to Oklahoma City until 1904, when the OKC Mets joined the Southwestern League as part of a four-team circuit that included franchises in Guthrie, Enid, and Shawnee.

Six Hall of Famers were born in Oklahoma: Willie Stargell, Paul Waner, Lloyd Waner, Bullet Joe Rogan, Johnny Bench, and Mickey Mantle. Only one, Lloyd Waner, is buried in the state. Waner, born in Harrah, was a mainstay on the Pittsburgh Pirates teams of the late 1920s and 1930s. The younger brother of Hall of Famer Paul Waner, they are one of three brother duos to accomplish the feat, including Harry and George Wright, as well as Rube Foster and his half-brother, Bill.

Lloyd Waner
Rose Hill Burial Park, Oklahoma City

Lloyd came into the league like gangbusters. He registered more than 200 hits in four of his first five seasons, leading the league in 1931. Lloyd and Paul combined to help the Pirates reach the 1927 World Series, Lloyd's first year in the majors. The younger Waner batted an impressive .400 in the Series, but the Pirates were swept in four games by the mighty Yankees, and neither brother ever saw post-season play again in their careers. Lloyd's stone highlights his 53-year marriage to his wife Frances Mae and features the double-headed eagle signifying that he was a member of the Scottish Rite of Freemasonry. The small 31 at the center of the symbol indicates that Waner was an Inspector Inquisitor.

It took the Pirates 55 years after his Hall election to retire the uniform number of Lloyd Waner.

Carl Hubbell died from injuries suffered in a car accident on my 16th birthday, the day I got my driver's permit.

Carl Hubbell

Meeker New Hope, Meeker

A little less than an hour east of Oklahoma City is the town of Meeker. Although he was born in Missouri, Carl Hubbell's family moved to Meeker when he was 13, and the humble hurler called the town home for the rest of his life. Nicknamed "Meal Ticket" because of his consistency, Hubbell was a master of control. In six of the 16 years he pitched, Hubbell led the league in the modern metric of WHIP. He led the league in ERA three times and twice won the MVP award, in 1933 and 1936. He spent his entire career with the New York Giants and appeared in three World Series with them. The most memorable of those was the 1933 Series, when Hubbell pitched the first and fourth games, winning both. His second appearance was a game for the ages when he pitched all 11 innings of a 2–1 victory. Hubbell's final line on the '33 Series included two wins in 20 innings pitched with zero earned runs allowed. It was his lone championship. His legacy was cemented when, during the 1934 All-Star Game, Hubbell struck out Babe Ruth, Lou Gehrig, Jimmie Foxx, Al Simmons, and Joe Cronin consecutively.

Joe McGinnity

Oak Hill Cemetery, McAlester

When "Iron Man" Joe McGinnity made his major league debut in 1899, it was the end of one age and the dawn of another. The American League was still two years away, and home runs were still a rarity. Pitchers also finished what they began, and Iron Man McGinnity was no exception, completing 314 of the 381 games he started in the majors. In a brief major league career that saw him play for four franchises in 10 years, McGinnity led the league in wins four times, twice topping the 30-win mark, in 1903 and 1904. He won his sole World Series in 1905, pitching 17 innings, including a shutout, and surrendering no earned runs. After he played his final major league season, he pitched 14 more years in the minors.

The Hall of Fame keeps a file on each man ever to appear in a major league game. Interestingly, McGinnity's file is one of the thickest I observed, despite the fact that he is not one of the more well-known names in the Hall. This is in large part because McGinnity had an extensive number of kin, many of whom have provided thorough genealogical information on the family. Included in the file are photographs of the monument maker adding the finishing touches of paint to McGinnity's unique updated stone, installed by his family in 2006, 77 years after his death.

Warren Spahn

Elmwood Cemetery, Hartshorne

The final Hall of Famer buried in Oklahoma is easily the most famous of the four. Warren Spahn was born in Buffalo, New York, and made his major league debut in 1942 for the Boston Braves, the franchise he stayed with for 20 seasons. He appeared in only four games that first year before enlisting in the Army. He trained at Camp Gruber near Tulsa, where he met his future wife, LoRene Southard. LoRene convinced her husband to move to Oklahoma and, in return, her real estate acumen made the Spahns wealthy people.

For his part, Spahn was simply the greatest, most durable left-handed pitcher in baseball history.

Warren Spahn's grave denotes baseball, his military service, *and* his devotion to his family.

First in career wins for lefties, with 363, Spahn pitched for 21 seasons, despite losing three years to the war. In a remarkable numerical coincidence, 21 turned out to be a recurring theme for the venerable pitcher. In addition to it being the number of seasons he played in the majors, he was born in 1921, wore the number 21, and *eight times* in his lengthy career won 21 games in a season, a statistical consistency so unlikely it is almost impossible to believe. The last time he accomplished the feat, in 1961, he was 40 years old. He notched a 23-win season two years later at the remarkable age of 42.

The visit to Spahn's grave marked the third and final speeding ticket I got over the life of the project. I understand that three sounds excessive and paints me as someone with a heavy right foot. This would be a good time to point out that between the start of the project and its completion, I drove approximately 20,162 miles (and flew an additional 24,724). That is nearly two years worth of driving for the average American. When considered from that perspective, it doesn't seem that bad at all.

For the Love of It
◆ KANSAS ◆

On a mild Christmas Day in 1858, the citizens of Emporia, Kansas, celebrated the holiday as much of the rest of the country did, with one exception. The townsfolk took advantage of the weather by celebrating in the square with a game of ball. All of the males, young and old, gathered together to play a match that lasted from morning until dark. The day featured much debate over the relative merits of "base" versus other games like "bull pen" and "cat ball," and it was considered one of the more memorable Christmases on record. This is the first recorded instance of what was likely baseball in the Sunflower State.

Kansas has never been able to support a major league team. Even today, there are only two minor league squads in the sparsely populated state, the Salina Stockade and the Wichita Wingnuts, both of the independent American Association. Over 200 major leaguers have been born there, including Walter Johnson and Joe Tinker, and 91 of them have chosen to spend their eternal rest there. The lone Hall of Famer from that latter group is Fred Clarke.

Fred Clarke
St. Mary's Cemetery, Winfield

Originally from Winterset, Iowa, Clarke made his professional debut as a 20-year-old when he answered an ad in *The Sporting News* seeking players. He split the 1893 season between the Southern Association Montgomery Colts and Western Association Saint Joseph Saints. Clarke played his first major league game in 1894 for the Louisville Colonels, having a first game for the ages, going 5-for-5 with four singles and a triple. That year also served as the beginning of a relationship with team owner Barney Dreyfuss that had profound effects on the young player.

Clarke credited Dreyfuss as the guiding influence who helped him change from a callow youth to one of the most admired leaders in baseball. Clarke was known for his calm demeanor and was quoted by one paper as espousing the philosophy of "smile, smile, no matter how things break," though, ironically, he was once arrested for assaulting a fan while skipper of the Pirates. Clarke was an early adopter of the "scientific" methods of the game, and he had tremendous success both on and off the field. By the age of 24, he was pulling double duty manning the outfield as well as serving as the manager of the Colonels, a position he maintained when the Colonels folded and Dreyfuss purchased a controlling interest in the Pittsburgh Pirates.

As manager of the Bucs, he secured them four pennants, including the 1903 flag which afforded his club the honor of appearing in the first modern World Series. The Pirates lost that Series, five games to three, with Clarke himself hitting an ordinary .265 over the eight games. It was not until 1909 that he achieved the ultimate glory of a Series victory, when the Pirates defeated Ty Cobb and the Detroit Tigers, securing Clarke his lone World Championship. He himself hit two home runs in the Series.

A brilliant businessman, he was a millionaire by the end of his life, his fortune made when an oil speculator discovered crude on the ranch Clarke had bought with his baseball earnings. He also had vested interests in coal mines and wheat futures. His farm, called "Little Pirate Ranch," was, at one point, over 20,000 acres. He used his tremendous wealth to become a philanthropist of sandlot baseball in his adopted home of Winfield. In the days before the creation of Little League in 1939, and during the ensuing decades while the new organization gained a foothold, kids played baseball in impromptu games on the local diamond. This testament to a time when there was enough interest in the game that 18 children could be corralled on any given day resonated with Clarke, and he did what he could to support it.

Beyond his sandlot efforts, Clarke stayed active in baseball for years after he retired from the majors, serving in various capacities in local non-professional baseball.

Fred Clarke may have been the most successful player-manager of all time.

Aided by his wealth, his was a life spent in service to the sport, even without the lure of major league dollars. In August of 1959, he was honored during the opening night ceremonies for the 25th annual National Non-Pro Baseball Tournament, sponsored by the National Baseball Congress. He died less than a year later of pneumonia, at the age of 87.

The Truth About Pete
◆ NEBRASKA ◆

Baseball precluded statehood in Nebraska. In July of 1867, just four months after Nebraska joined the union, the Occidental Base Ball Club of Denver challenged the Omaha BBC to a championship match game. Strangely, the game was never played, but baseball continued to thrive in the state. By 1870, the Otoe Club of Nebraska City had become legitimate enough to join the National Association of Base Ball Players.

While there has never been a major league team in Nebraska, Omaha can boast of being the home of the Storm Chasers. Previously known as the Royals (1969–1998), the Golden Spikes (1999–2001), and the Royals again (2002–2010) before settling into their current name in 2011, the Storm Chasers have the distinction of being the sole triple-A affiliate of the Kansas City Royals since the parent club's inception in 1969. Given the often volatile shuffling of minor league affiliates that happens across baseball, that is a remarkable testimony to organizational harmony.

Despite Nebraska never having a major league team, over 150 future major leaguers were born there, including seven Hall of Famers, a substantial number. Richie Ashburn, Wade Boggs, Sam Crawford, Bob Gibson, Billy Southworth, and Dazzy Vance all hailed from the Cornhusker State. Perhaps Nebraska's favorite son, however, is the legendary Grover Cleveland "Pete" Alexander. Nowhere is this truer than in St. Paul, the removed city of fewer than 3,000 people where Alexander spent the latter years of his life.

At the heart of this county seat is one of the most unexpected shrines to baseball a person could imagine. At the Museum of Nebraska Major League Baseball, every person ever born in the state who has spent a day in the majors is given a plaque honoring the achievements that brought them to the pinnacle of the sport. Curated by Loren Studley, who also works at the Bryan Jensen Clothing store across the road, the museum has an impressive collection of artifacts, including a substantial amount of game-used equipment from various Nebraskans.

Grover Alexander
Elmwood Cemetery, St. Paul

Loren was kind enough to re-open the museum on the day of my visit and give me a tour, as I arrived just minutes after they closed. He also made sure, during my tour, to do his part to dispel one of the most enduring myths surrounding Alexander's career. After his decisive Game 6 win in the 1926 World Series, holding the Yankees to two runs while the Cardinals pounded out 10, everyone figured Alexander's season was complete. But manager Rogers Hornsby shocked the baseball world when he called in Ol' Pete to pitch the Cardinals out of a bases-loaded jam in the seventh inning of Game 7. Alexander responded by striking out Tony Lazzeri and then completing two more flawless frames, securing the Cardinals their first World Championship.

The legend that has always surrounded these facts is that Alexander was hung-over when he struck out Lazzeri. Pete, a veteran of World War I who spent time at the front, returned from the war deaf in his left ear, injured in his right arm, and shell-shocked. He dealt with his trauma by drinking and battled alcoholism for the rest of his life, a poorly kept secret. Of course, people assumed that, after the Game 6 victory, Alexander would have celebrated. However, Studley, and none other than Rogers Hornsby, tell a different tale.

Hornsby was partially responsible for the genesis of the myth. When questioned by reporters as to Alexander's sobriety for the big game, Hornsby jokingly quipped that he would rather have Alexander pitch for him while drunk than another man that was sober. Reporters took the answer as a tacit "yes," and a legend was born. Alexander maintained, for the rest of his life, that he was sober when he pitched the last 2⅓ innings of Game 7, and Hornsby later supported that. Hornsby regretted making the quip and later told interviewers that he had a feeling after Game 6 he might need Alexander and had specifically requested Pete not go carousing. He later went on record saying that the two men had a quiet dinner together that night.

No matter the truth, Alexander's 1926 World Series performance stands out as one of the greatest in post-season history. Alexander won 373 games in his career, trailing only Cy Young and Walter Johnson on the all-time list. He was, for the first 10 years of his career, as dominant as Johnson or Christy Mathewson. When he died, he was issued a military stone to which was later affixed a smaller plaque mentioning his election to the Hall in 1938. I was guided directly to the marker by Alexander's loudest modern advocate, Studley, who has made it his mission to rescue the reputation of this tarnished hero.

While he survived the war, the damage it did to Pete Alexander lasted long after the battle was over.

The Home of the Negro Leagues
◆ MISSOURI ◆

The state of Missouri has been a presence in the world of baseball for a long time. The first verified reference to the game in the state can be found with a notice in the September 3, 1859, edition of the *New York Clipper*. It reads, "CLUB ORGANIZED,—A base ball club was organized in St. Louis, Mo, on the 1st inst. It boasts of being the first organization of the kind in that city, but will not, surely, long stand alone." The article's prophecy was on point, as seven more squads were formed in St. Louis alone by the end of 1860.

Major league baseball arrived in the state in 1875, when both the St. Louis Brown Stockings and the St. Louis Red Stockings were members of the National Association. From the dawn of the modern era, in 1901, until 1954, when the Athletics moved from Philadelphia to Kansas City, St. Louis was the western-most city in the American or National Leagues. In addition to the two National Association clubs, four other major league teams have called St. Louis home, including the Maroons of the Union Association, the Terriers of the Federal League, the Browns of the American League (which still exist today as the Baltimore Orioles), and of course, the Cardinals, the most successful franchise in National League history.

Over on the western half of the state, six major league teams have also called Kansas City home. Three different franchises have gone by the name Kansas City Cowboys, appearing in the Union Association, the National League, and the American Association. The Kansas City Packers were members of the short-lived Federal League. The Athletics, who moved after the 1954 season, just two years after the Braves went to Milwaukee and one year after the Browns went to Baltimore, were a part of the migration that signaled the first great schism in the baseball map in nearly half a century. The A's tenure was brief, only staying in Kansas City until 1967, but they were quickly replaced by the Royals two years later.

Even with the rich major league history in Kansas City, the city's greatest contribution to baseball may be its role in the Negro Leagues. The famous Kansas City Monarchs were the longest surviving franchise to engage in continuous play in the Negro Leagues. The Monarchs were formed in 1920 and lasted all the way until 1965, three years after the final official league, the Negro American League, folded. Kansas City is home to the Negro Leagues Baseball Museum, the single greatest repository of blackball artifacts in the world, even outshining the collection at the Hall of Fame. Among their multiple treasures is a gigantic collection of baseballs signed by Negro Leaguers that was donated to the museum by Geddy Lee, Canadian-born lead singer of the band Rush. Not surprisingly, four of the six Hall of Famers buried in Kansas City made their impact in the Negro Leagues.

J. L. Wilkinson, Hilton Smith and Kid Nichols

Mount Moriah & Freeman Cemetery, Kansas City

Mount Moriah & Freeman Cemetery is a treasure trove of baseball legends. Early 20th century catcher Johnny Kling and 1980s pitching whiz Dan Quisenberry are buried there, along with three Hall of Famers: J. L. Wilkinson, Hilton Smith, and Kid Nichols. James Leslie Wilkinson was born in 1878 in Iowa, where he discovered the sport that changed his life on the local sandlots. Wilkinson was a founding owner in Rube Foster's Negro National League, when he formed the Monarchs in 1920. He had ventured into the world of ownership previously. He put together a women's team called the Boston Bloomer Girls in 1902 and a mixed-race barnstorming squad called the All-Nations in 1912.

He owned the Monarchs for 28 years, introducing the world to some of the most legendary names in black baseball, including Cool Papa Bell, Willard Brown, José Méndez, Cristóbal Torriente, Buck O'Neil, Bullet Rogan, Ernie Banks, and Jackie Robinson. A Caucasian, Wilkinson was famous for his fairness and integrity and was an important figure in the effort to bring some measure of equality to his players.

He was an early proponent of night games, purchasing a portable set of flood lights in 1929 so his barnstorming Monarchs could entertain the working populace after dark.

Although various attempts to play at night had been attempted since 1880, the first official major league game to be played under lights took place six years after Wilkinson made it standard practice for the Monarchs.

One of Wilkinson's most successful pitchers was Hilton Smith. An effective right-hander, Smith spent much of his career playing in the very long shadow of Satchel Paige. Smith was as quiet and serious as Paige was loud and flamboyant, so they made for an odd pair. Yet their dominance can easily be seen in the incredible success the Monarchs had.

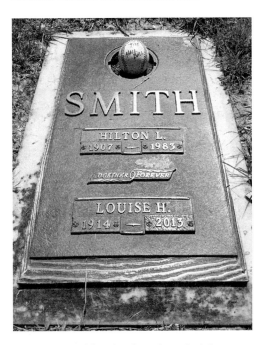

At the time of his death, Hilton Smith was an occasional scout for the Chicago Cubs.

Alone on this trip, I had to stretch to get Wilkinson's full name into the picture.

Kid Nichols pitched in an old-timers' game in 1939, at the age of 70.

The tandem led their squad to six titles between 1937 and 1946. Smith possessed a dizzying array of pitches with pinpoint precision, readily placing his lightning quick fastball, his swift curveball, and his baffling screwball. Smith himself once claimed that one of his greatest thrills was beating Dizzy Dean in an exhibition game at Wrigley Field in 1942.

The final Hall of Famer buried at Mt. Moriah wasn't a Negro Leaguer but instead was a man whose major league career began just three years after the cursed "gentlemen's agreement" barred blacks from baseball. Kid Nichols joined the Boston Beaneaters in 1890 and made an immediate splash, winning 27 games in his rookie year. He ultimately won 361 contests, including seven seasons in which he won 30 or more. Nichols once pitched three games, on three consecutive days, in three different cities, and won them all. After he retired, Nichols became a successful coach of college baseball.

Zack Wheat and Satchel Paige
Forest Hill & Calvary
Cemetery, Kansas City

Just five miles north of Mount Moriah is Forest Hill & Calvary Cemetery, where two Hall of Famers, and a third who should be in the Hall, all lie. The first immortal spent 18 years toiling on the Brooklyn Dodgers during the storied franchise's very lean years. Zack Wheat joined the club in 1909 (when they were known as the Superbas). It took until 1912 for him to play a full season in which he batted above .300. Twelve more above-.300 seasons followed. One of the most popular Dodgers of his time, it was surprising that it took 32 years for him to be inducted into the Hall after he retired. It could be attributed to a bias against Brooklyn during that time in the Hall's history. When he was elected, Wheat was only the second player who spent his career primarily as a Dodger, behind Dazzy Vance. It is perhaps not a coincidence that Wheat's recognition came almost immediately after Brooklyn won its first championship.

One hundred ten years after his first game, Zack Wheat still holds numerous Dodgers offensive records, including games played and hits.

Satchel Paige's stone includes his rules for "how to stay young."

Buried a short distance from Wheat's modest marker is perhaps the single most recognizable name in Negro Leagues baseball, Satchel Paige. His story is famous, and tales of his escapades and successes are oft told and do not need repeating here. Instead, I will mention his gravestone and his home. The stone you see here with the Ball was installed when Paige's wife, Lahoma, died in 1986. His original marker, which can be seen at the Negro

Leagues Baseball Museum, was much simpler and featured only his name and, in a posthumous bit of Paige inspired wit, his birth year displayed simply as a question mark. That stone spent years in storage at the cemetery until the museum opened in 1990.

After finishing at the cemetery, I visited Paige's home, which Lahoma bought and managed with Paige's earnings during his vagabond career. Paige died in the house on June 8, 1982, (the very day Anna was born) during a blackout in Kansas City. On the day I visited, the house was a dilapidated wreck. Still owned by the Paige family but in too much disrepair for them to afford the renovation, it is a sad symbol of the rapidly fading memory people have for the Negro Leagues. What should be a museum is instead an eyesore. The front porch had collapsed, and bricks from the staircase spilled across the front yard. In 2018, the house suffered further damage when it was the victim of a fire that was later deemed arson.

On the day I was there, for the first time in all my Hall Ball travels, I took something I discovered on my journey (other than a photograph). One of the bricks from the crumbling porch rests in my home, a reminder that it is my duty, and that of all historians, to keep these stories alive lest they crumble to dust.

The individual who is buried in Forest Hill who should be in the Hall but is not is none other than Buck O'Neil. I try not to engage in the debate of who does or does not belong in the Hall. I am not a member of the Baseball Writers' Association of America nor on any of the Veterans Committees. I do not have a say in who is chosen, and my opinion has no more weight or merit than any other knowledgeable fan's. However, the case for O'Neil, including his work as an ambassador of the game, his time as a coach in the Majors, and his days as a player in the Negro Leagues, makes him the most deserving of candidates. The Hall has tried to correct the oversight by creating the Buck O'Neil Award, given out every three years to an individual whose efforts have furthered the positive impact of baseball on the greater society.

The nearly life-sized grave marker of Buck O'Neil.

Bullet Rogan
Blue Ridge Lawn Memorial Gardens, Kansas City

The final Hall of Famer buried in the Kansas City area is, predictably, one more Negro Leaguer. Bullet Rogan's descriptive nickname came from his blazing fastball, one that Bob Feller was quoted as calling "the best.... I ever saw." Like many Negro Leaguers, Rogan also spent time in the field when he wasn't on the mound. Frequently comparing him to Paige, his supporters point out that while Paige was often removed late in the game for a pinch-hitter, Rogan was batting cleanup. His effective fastball was all the more impressive because Rogan never wound up. He just threw the ball with a speed that mystified hitters. After his retirement from baseball, he spent the majority of the remainder of his life working for the Post Office. His grave was not an easy one to find, a ground flush marker in a poorly mowed section of the lawn. It took me some time to locate him.

After the mammoth stones of Paige and O'Neil, it was a challenge to locate Bullet Rogan.

Jake Beckley
Riverside Cemetery, Hannibal

Jake Beckley had a long career that began in Pittsburgh in 1888, during the turbulent early days when the National League squad was known as the Alleghenys. After briefly jumping ship to the Players' League, Beckley returned to the Pirates until 1896. He split the next 12 years between the Giants, Reds, and Cardinals. He was a lifetime .308 hitter from Hannibal, Missouri, and his grave offered me a unique opportunity.

In all my life's travels, for The Hall Ball and beyond, I had no recollection of ever seeing the Mississippi River, though earlier trips had brought me close to it. It was still a mythical place in America to me, with the pictures in my head taken from the pages of Mark Twain's *Huck Finn*. Riverside Cemetery's name is understatedly appropriate. Located at the top of a steep hill, Beckley's grave afforded a breathtaking view of the iconic river, with Illinois on the other side. Because of topography, the river seemed to twist around two-thirds of the portion of the cemetery where Beckley lies. The view did not disappoint, with the late-day sun casting harsh streaks of light on the water, washing out details but somehow expanding the size of this already massive body of water.

It should not be lost that Beckley and Twain, Hannibal's most famous native son, were contemporaries for a time. Twain was 36 years older than Beckley, and at the very beginning of his fame when the future ball player was born in 1867. By the late 1880s, Beckley was a legitimate star of the game, and Twain was still writing masterpieces like *A Connecticut Yankee in King Arthur's Court*.

Perhaps Twain was giving a nod to his fellow Hannibalian when he had his "Yankee" protagonist school the monarchs of the land on how to play baseball. The attempt to teach them the game is marred by the fact that the assembled kings are unwilling to remove their armor, and thus never move out of the way of inside pitches because they fear no injury. Beckley, who was hit with 183 pitches in his career, still 11th all-time, could have used some of the armor that Arthur's Bessemers squad refused to eschew.

Just through the trees behind Jake Beckley's grave is a breathtaking view of the Mississippi River.

Cal Hubbard
Oakwood Cemetery, Milan

Only one man has ever been elected to the Baseball *and* Football Halls of Fame, and that is Cal Hubbard.

Bottomley's grave includes his distinctive nickname.

Between 1924 and 1929, he was an RBI machine for the St. Louis Cardinals. In that time, he never had fewer than 110 RBIs and twice led the league in the statistic. He led the National League in two-thirds of the Triple Crown stats in 1928, pacing the circuit in home runs and RBIs. He took home the MVP Award that year and helped the Cardinals reach the World Series, where they were bulldozed by the Yankees in four games. Lou Gehrig and Babe Ruth hit a combined .593 for the Series, with seven home runs. There was no chance for the Cardinals to compete. Bottomley batted .348 in 1931, his last season of excellence. He was traded by the Cards following the 1932 season and spent five more years between the Reds and the Browns. "Sunny" Jim still holds a share of the record for most RBIs (his favorite stat) in a single game, with 12, a feat he accomplished on September 16, 1924.

Cool Papa Bell
St. Peter's Cemetery, St. Louis

The first grave I visited on the other side of the state continued my exploration of the Negro Leagues. While St. Louis certainly doesn't have the black baseball legacy that Kansas City does, it can boast of being the final resting place of one of the largest names writ in the book of Negro Leagues history.

Besides the Baseball and Football incarnations, Cal Hubbard has been inducted into six other Halls of Fame.

He joined the National Football League New York Giants in 1927 and built a nine-year career that was hailed by some as that of the greatest tackle of all time. Hubbard was able to retire from football early because he had already been building a second career as a baseball umpire, working his way through the ranks of the minors during the off-season. He joined the major leagues in 1936. He was so mild-mannered that few players argued with the massive Hubbard. His on-field career ended tragically when, while on a hunting trip with fellow Hall of Fame umpire Al Barlick, he suffered an eye injury that ruined his depth perception. His career was rescued when AL President Will Harridge hired him to serve as the assistant to Tom Connolly, supervisor to AL umpires. Hubbard later took over the head job in 1954 when Connolly retired, a position he held for another 16 years.

Jim Bottomley
I.O.O.F. Community Cemetery, Sullivan

Another of the oft-questioned early 1970s Frisch inductees, Jim Bottomley's period of excellence was admittedly short.

The two sides of Cool Papa Bell's marker are a resume set in stone.

Satchel Paige once said that Cool Papa Bell was so fast that he could shut off the light and be in bed before it got dark. It is possible there is some truth to that story, as the old-timey hotels that Bell and teammate Paige stayed in often had push-button light switches, which had a slight delay between when one depressed the button and when the electricity was cut off to the light source. Even if this story is apocryphal, there is little doubt that Bell was one of the fastest men to play the game.

His monument is impressive, nearing ten feet tall and four feet wide. It is covered in quotes by Bell himself as well as his family. It mentions his 28-year career, his reported lifetime batting average of .419, the fact that he was timed circling the bases at 11 seconds, and his marriage of 62 years. The back reads like a resume of his notable accomplishments as well as his most endearing personality traits. The stone was dedicated during a special ceremony on July 20, 1996. Guest speakers included Edward Stack, President of the

Hall of Fame, and former teammates Cowan "Bubba" Hyde and Ted "Double Duty" Radcliffe. The Governor of Missouri proclaimed the day James "Cool Papa" Bell Day throughout the state.

George Sisler
Old Meeting House Presbyterian Church Cemetery, Frontenac

When Ichiro Suzuki broke the 84-year-old record for most hits in a single season in 2004, he brought back to the public consciousness the name of the man whose achievement he surpassed, George Sisler. In a 15-year career, Sisler had more than 200 hits six times, including his record 257 in 1920 and another 246 in 1922. He twice hit over .400 and retired with a career batting average of .340, tied with Lou Gehrig for 16th all-time. After his retirement from playing, Sisler became the Commissioner of the National Semi-Professional Baseball Congress and stayed active as a scout and advisor. Sisler rests in the old burying ground of the Presbyterian Meeting House, originally founded to bury the St. Louis settlers who first came from Kentucky, Tennessee, Virginia, and New England. A weathered sign in the cemetery mentions the large number of former slaves who are also buried there, originally in unmarked graves but now under a collective stone that was placed in 1983.

Sisler died two days after his 80th birthday; his wife, Kathleen, died on her 96th.

Medwick hated his nickname, instead preferring to be called "Muscles."

Joe Medwick
St. Lucas Cemetery, Sunset Hills

"Ducky" Medwick had a 17-year career with a lifetime batting average of .324. Only three times did he bat lower than .300 in a season. A 10-time All-Star, in 1937 Medwick won the batting Triple Crown as well as the MVP Award. Still, it took 20 years for him to be elected to the Hall of Fame. This is commonly attributed to a tumultuous relationship with the press. Certainly, there seemed to be a greater appreciation of his career accomplishments after his death than there ever was during his life. He died in 1975 during spring training at the Cardinals' camp in St. Petersburg. His headstone features his name and dates, as well those of his wife, Isabelle. Medwick has an additional footstone that highlights his baseball exploits.

Stan Musial
Bellerive Gardens, Creve Coeur

Perhaps no other person is as synonymous with St. Louis baseball as Stan Musial. He is nothing short of a legend, and well-deservedly. He led the National League in hitting seven times and won three World Series. He collected three MVP Awards and came in second in MVP voting four more times. He hit better than .300 for the first 16 years of his career and then one final time in 1962, at the age of 41.

Musial was alive when The Hall Ball started, but he passed in January of 2013. Stew Thornley had posted a photo of Musial's grave, an indoor crypt in the mausoleum. The picture was pulled back far enough that I had a clear view of the room. We easily found the building and, using the patterns on the floor as a guide, the corner that was featured in the picture. Musial wasn't there. I searched the whole mausoleum, but Stan the Man was nowhere to be found. I was flabbergasted. Musial must have been moved. The office had closed. I had no clue where to look.

Bellerive is not small, totaling close to 45 acres. I would have to come back another day, which would throw off my (as usual) tight schedule. On a whim, as we were pulling away from the mausoleum, Anna suggested I pull into a section on the immediate right called "Garden of Rose Hill." In a tenth of a mile, we saw the name Musial engraved on a sizable outdoor crypt.

The grave of Stan Musial, found by the divine intervention of Anna.

Anna had found him. Immediately. It could have taken us hours. Anna was my talisman throughout this project. As I have mentioned before, she found the gravestone that started it all. She found the ball. She has inspired this from the very beginning. By that point I had lost count of how many hours she had spent wandering through cemeteries, trying to find a stone with me. I make sure that every time I am interviewed about the project, I mention Anna. The Hall Ball is hers as well as mine.

Finding Cristóbal

Cristóbal Torriente is often referred to as the "Cuban Babe Ruth," largely on the strength of a single performance during a series of exhibition games played in Cuba against the Bambino himself, along with a group of major league stars, in November of 1920. One of those contests featured Torriente clubbing three home runs, cementing his legacy despite the fact that the opposing pitcher was an out-of-place first baseman, fellow future Hall of Famer George Kelly. Tainted as that moniker-earning feat may be, there is little doubt that the giant of a man was one of the most prolific hitters in the history of professional Cuban baseball. Three years before Ruth traveled to Cuba, *Baseball Magazine* called Torriente "one of the greatest batsmen in the world." His dark skin and kinky hair guaranteed that despite all his talent, he would never play in the major leagues, even though multiple Cubans had already preceded him.

As mentioned in the chapter on Cuba, there was something of a mystery surrounding the burial place of Cristóbal Torriente. When I initially contacted Cubaball organizer Kit Krieger to explain what my needs were while I was there, he pointed out that he had been told that Torriente was not actually entombed in the Monument to Baseballists. He had been informed by Cuban sportswriter Sigfredo Barros that there was no record at the cemetery of Torriente's body being buried there.

The belief that Torriente is buried in Havana is largely due to a story from John Holway's book, *Blackball Stars*. In the book, Torriente's former teammate, Rogelio Crespo, recounts the tale of Torriente being disinterred from his burial site in New York City, draped in a Cuban flag, and brought back home to be given a hero's welcome. The action was overseen by none other than Colonel Jaime Mariné y Montes, aide de camp to dictator Fulgencio Batista and officially Cuba's Minister of Sport.

When I spoke with Barros, he emphatically denied that ever happened. According to him, none of the still-living old-timers who were boys when the body was transferred could recall any pomp and circumstance with his repatriation, and there was not one shred of documentation in the office of the *Cementerio de Cristóbal Colón* to indicate that Torriente's body was ever, in fact, brought to the cemetery. As far as they knew, Torriente was still in New York City, where he died.

When I returned home from Cuba, I contacted the New York City Department of Records and obtained a copy of Torriente's death certificate. From that I learned that he died at Riverside Hospital in the Bronx. Located on tiny North Brother Island, completely removed from the mainland of New York City, Riverside was a sanitarium for infectious disease. Its most famous resident, who was there concurrently with Torriente and who died just seven months after he did, was Mary Mallon, infamously known as "Typhoid Mary." The hospital was closed down in the 1960s, and the dilapidated buildings still remain today, inaccessible to most New Yorkers as the City has cut off access to the island completely.

The death certificate of Cristóbal Torriente.

Torriente's death certificate details that he had originally checked into the hospital in July 1937, suffering from pulmonary tuberculosis, and that he died on April 11 of the following year. The certificate explains that his body was to be claimed by his friend and fellow Cuban ballplayer, Ramiro Ramírez, and was being prepared by A. R. Hernandez, a Harlem-based undertaker. The mystery deepens when one looks at the bottom of the page. Next to "Place of Burial," it is clear that his original destination was City Cemetery. But that was crossed out and replaced with Calvary Cemetery.

The public burial ground on Hart Island is more commonly known as City Cemetery. Not far from where Torriente died on North Brother Island, it is a potter's field in the eastern Bronx cluster of Pelham Islands. The island has served multiple purposes since it was first purchased from the local Native population in 1654. It has been the location of a city prison, a sanitarium, a reformatory, a Civil War prison camp and, during the Cold War, a missile base. It was after the Civil War that the City first started using it for burials of the indigent and unclaimed. It was here that

Torriente was originally destined to spend eternity. That was when the Archdiocese of New York intervened.

There is only one Calvary Cemetery in the five boroughs, and it is located in Queens, just on the other side of the Queensborough Bridge. It has already been mentioned in these pages, as Hall of Famers Wee Willie Keeler and Mickey Welch are buried there. My first call to the cemetery left me stymied, as officials claimed to have no record for Torriente whatsoever. After pursuing a series of other failed leads, I called again a few months later. This time the person on the other end of the phone was able to confirm that Torriente was indeed buried there.

The initial confusion came from a number of errors in his cemetery record. His name is listed as "Christopher," his birthplace is noted as Puerto Rico, and the actual burial date differs from the date listed on the death certificate. Despite these inaccuracies, enough of the facts lined up that it was clear that this was the same man I was looking for. In April of 1938, Cristóbal Torriente was buried at Calvary. While able to confirm his burial, cemetery officials remained unable to find any evidence that the body was ever exhumed.

According to their records, Torriente is buried in Section 39, a large expanse owned by the Archdiocese that they use for charity burials such as Torriente's. Most of the graves are communal, with multiple burials in each plot, and his is no exception. As a result, it would take nothing less than a government action to open up the ground, identify and remove him from the tangle of other burials, and then have his body shipped internationally. It was possible to argue that the records at *Cristóbal Colón* did not weather the Revolution and were lost. Calvary, however, claimed to have accurate books dating back 150 years, and they could find no mention whatsoever of his exhumation taking place, an action that would likely have produced no small amount of paperwork.

I had become convinced that Torriente was buried in Queens. The story of his disin-

terment and heroic journey home was mere propaganda. After all, propaganda was perhaps Batista's greatest weapon. Once I felt secure in that belief, I decided that I did not need to rush taking the picture. I was hoping I might be able to get a marker placed before I finished the project. I reached out to Jeremy Krock, and the two of us began to get to work on the cemetery. Again, because it is communal, it is more complicated to get a stone placed there. None of the thousands of burials in Section 39 have stones. We knew it was unlikely they were going to allow an isolated one for an old ballplayer.

It was during this period that I received an email that forever changed the path of The Hall Ball. It was from Corey Kilgannon, a reporter with the *New York Times*. He had received a letter from Tony Milito (good ol' Tony) the previous year, extolling the tale of The Hall Ball. At the time, Kilgannon had filed it in his "to be considered later" folder. With the approaching post-season, he had decided that it was time to reach out to me. He wanted to know if I had anything local going on with the ball and if he and a photographer might be able to join.

I told him the tale of Torriente, and I could tell right away that he had found his lede. On a chilly, late-September morning, we went to Calvary. I had asked the cemetery to mark the location with one of the flimsy, plastic, temporary crosses they use to identify unmarked locations. Of course, they used the name they have on record, "Christopher." As I squatted down to take the photo for the project, the photographer from the *Times* squatted behind me, taking another photo that would ultimately be published in the paper. Every time I look at that published photo, the "meta-ness" of the "picture in a picture" strikes me as surreal.

The attention The Hall Ball received after the *Times* article was tremendous. I had people reaching out to me from all corners, all of them expressing their support. I had always been prepared for some sort of backlash about the project.

Torriente's grave at Calvary Cemetery in Queens.

People are funny about death and cemeteries. I was certain someone would think me a ghoul, or at least a little creepy. Now that the ball was receiving large-scale attention, the odds of this occurring certainly increased. Instead, the encouragement was universal.

I was hoping that the *Times* story would inspire the folks at Calvary to assist Jeremy and me in placing a monument near the section where Torriente was buried, if not directly on his grave. They had done something similar for Lorenzo Da Ponte, librettist for Mozart, whose own burial was a bit of a mystery. Da Ponte sports an impressive stone filled with the details of his accomplished life. It is on the edge of his section, lining the road, and technically does not rest on any grave. Krock and I have made multiple requests to Calvary, but as of this writing, they have gone largely unanswered.

* * *

A little more than a year after the *Times* article was published, I received an email from a Cuban filmmaker named Yasel Porto. Yasel was well-known in his homeland as the host of three television shows, including one called *Beisbol de Siempre*. He is a member of the selection committee of the newly revived Cuban Baseball Hall of Fame, and he is working on a nine-part film about Cuba's role in American baseball. Part of the story he is telling in his film is that of Torriente. He had read the interview in the *Times*, and his research for the film turned up something that he urgently wished to share with me. Something that could not be more surprising.

He had discovered Torriente's body. At *Colón*. In fact, because of the ossuary practice of burial, he had held what he believed to be the man's very bones. Porto contacted me because he wanted me to be a part of what we all hoped would be the final resolution to this mystery. He had enlisted a forensic expert, who was conducting tests on the remains. He was firmly convinced that he had found the Cuban Babe Ruth, and he asked me to return to Cuba to share his findings. How could I refuse?

In Havana I met with Porto, as well as Reynaldo Cruz Diaz, a young photographer who was rapidly rising in the ranks of Cuba's vibrant baseball journalism scene. Cruz Diaz and I had met on my first trip, and he was a huge help in finding me housing this time around. Reynaldo is one of a small handful of Cubans who are members of SABR, and he had managed to secure visas to the United States for Induction Weekend the previous two summers, no simple feat in the still complicated political situation between our two countries. We had connected each time, and I considered him a friend.

On my first night back in Cuba, *Beisbol de Siempre* hosted an event celebrating the career of superstar Carlos Tabares, who had retired the year before. In a bizarre twist that proves not only just how small the island of Cuba remains, but also how deeply baseball runs in Cubans' veins, before the event Tabares's mother revealed to our band that she was the granddaughter of Torriente's niece. Sadly, it was not a close enough relation for either Cuban or American science to be able to do a DNA match from the skeleton that Porto believed to be Torriente's. The line was not direct enough to be conclusive. Our search for a more direct connection had been fruitless.

We pursued other scientific avenues as well. The skeleton they had discovered was covered in soil, an unusual trait for a Cuban body, which is typically interred above ground. Working on the presumption that Crespo's story was true and that Torriente was initially buried in Queens, I had brought a soil sample from the area around the alleged grave. Aware of the fact that I was standing in broad daylight with a shovel, digging in the middle of a cemetery, I had collected only a relatively shallow sample. Sadly, that meant it was from too close to the surface to match the earth crusted onto the recently discovered body.

Baseball historian and former Cuban spy, Ismael Sene.

The most compelling of the scientific evidence came from the work of Dr. Dodany Machado, an expert in forensic facial reconstruction. I had the opportunity to meet Machado at the home of Ismael Sene. In addition to being one of Cuba's most respected baseball historians, Sene also served in Cuban foreign intelligence, known as MINREX, in Eastern Europe for 23 years. While we waited for Machado and the others to arrive, Sene entertained me with his collection of baseballs signed by Mickey Mantle and Willie Mays, as well as pictures he took in 1955 and 1956 of Yankee Stadium, the Polo Grounds, and Comiskey Park. There were also pictures of a younger version of himself smiling broadly as he stood next to a fur coat-clad Fidel Castro, who was charming a group of admiring young women. In another, he and Raul Castro were firmly gripping each other's hands while serious-looking mustachioed men stood nearby.

Later, after I returned home, I saw a 2017 interview with Sene on the National Geographic channel. While wearing the same Cincinnati Reds t-shirt he wore the day he met with me, he told interviewer Michael Ware, "I am a Cuban who has dedicated thirty-five years of my life … to try to do whatever I can to harm the United States. And in the last two-and-a-half years I do whatever I can to improve the relations between both countries." I cannot help but think that his enthusiasm for assisting Yasel and myself in our hunt for the truth was a small sample of his desire to bridge the two countries. When questioned, Sene echoed Barros's lack of memory regarding any sort of celebration with the return of Torriente's body. He could not even remember a story in the newspapers, and by 1938 young Sene was old enough, and a big enough baseball fan, that the elder version firmly believed he would recall an event that important.

When Machado arrived with Yasel and Reynaldo, we discussed his research. He pulled out a medical textbook written in English and opened to a section on the ulna, and a malady called "woodcutter's lesion." The "lesion" is really a spur on the olecranon, the bone that forms the most pointed part of the elbow. According to the text, it is a common affliction of "woodcutting, blacksmithing and baseball playing." Our skeleton had such an injury.

He also showed me a detailed computer reconstruction in which the face of Torriente was overlaid on top of the skull they had discovered. To emphasize his point, he reached into his bag and pulled out the skull, itself, and placed it in my hands. It was an intense moment, and I was awed. Machado's driver jokingly commented on my reaction, asking if I was frightened about holding a man's head in my hands. I explained that my reaction was not motivated by fear, but reverence. I had visited hundreds of dead ballplayers by this point, but this was something else entirely. I pondered the moment while Machado continued to explain the reconstruction. The expanse of the skull's nasal cavity, the distance between the eyes and the slight lift on the left side of the mouth did seem to be a precise fit when placed next to Torriente's photo.

As with much of the other evidence that had been collected, it was compelling, but not exactly irrefutable. Forensic facial reconstruction is considered to be a questionable science, and many courts will not even allow it to be submitted as evidence. I had hoped we would find something incontrovertible, but ultimately, the smoking gun was never located. By the time I left Cuba, I had come to believe in my gut that he had somehow, despite the records of Calvary, been brought home. But I could not in good conscience say that I was 100 percent certain.

Before I left, Porto and Sene accompanied me to *Colón* Cemetery, where I once again visited the 1942 Monument to Baseballists, the one featuring the crumbling *pelotero*. On my previous visit, I had admired this monument, but I had not photographed the ball there because I had been led to believe that Torriente had been interred in the 1951 incarnation. It turned out to be this earlier one that was housing his remains. I staged the ball and took the shot.

The alleged skull of Torriente.

Torriente's grave at *Colón* Cemetery, the 1942 Monument to Baseballists.

The Molina family plot, burial site of José Méndez.

Uncertain what I believed, I decided the project was going to include both the photo of the unmarked spot in Calvary and the formerly glorious tribute to Cuba's greatest heroes.

I still wasn't done. Porto's research into Torriente had revealed another surprising fact. José Méndez, whom I had thought had no questions in regards to his burial, was *also* not in the 1951 Monument. Porto had learned that virtually no baseball players were buried there. He believed that Méndez was entombed nearby, in the family plot of Méndez's friend, Augustín "Tinti" Molina, who was himself a catcher, first baseman, and manager in both the Cuban and Negro Leagues. Porto had been working on getting his remains removed from the crypt and placed in the Monument with Torriente's, but as of my visit, Méndez was still buried with his old friend.

When I left Cuba, I had more questions about Torriente, and Méndez than I did when I arrived. Despite that fact, I had been able to dig even deeper not only into Cuba's baseball history, but by meeting Porto and Sene, as well as reconnecting with Cruz Diaz, into Cuba's baseball present. These were the men, young and old, who were keeping the story alive for the current generation of Cuban fans, who are witnessing many of their greatest stars flee to foreign lands before joining the major leagues. To me, their passion for the stories of yesterday and their influence on the legacy of today is more than admirable, it's humbling. I was fascinated by Cuban baseball after my first visit. This return journey had taken that fascination and worked it even deeper into my bones, as lasting as the spur on a woodcutter's elbow.

Two Locals and a Louisiana Yankee
◆ ARKANSAS ◆

The *Little Rock Weekly Gazette* published an article from *Porter's Spirit of the Times* on October 29, 1859, called "Base-Ball Comforts." Clearly, by that time the people of Arkansas were familiar with the game. It took another eight years, including some time after the Civil War was over, for the sport to catch on with enough enthusiasm for clubs to be formed. In 1867, the Galaxy Club, Pulaski Club, and Guidon Club, all of Little Rock, as well as the Club of Washington and the Club of Pine Bluff, established their charters. Nearly 30 more clubs formed in the state by the time the first major league game was played in 1871. They featured such colorful names as the Lugenbeel Club of Fort Smith, the Stonewall Club of Jacksonport, the Modoc Club of Augusta, the Robert E. Lee Club of Russelville, and two different clubs sponsored by the Ku Klux Klan, one in Van Buren and one in Fort Smith.

While Arkansas has never had a major league team, it was a founding location in the development of Spring Training. Al Spalding's White Stockings spent their first spring in Hot Springs in 1886. The namesake waters and the mountainous terrain, perfect hiking for getting flabby winter legs into shape, inspired Spalding and his manager, Cap Anson, to bring their troops there prior to the start of the season. Coincidentally or not, the White Stockings won the pennant that year. Noting Spalding's success, other clubs followed suit, and within 10 years the Pittsburgh Alleghenys, Cleveland Spiders, Cincinnati Reds, and St. Louis Browns were all spending time in Hot Springs. Major League Baseball continued to train there until the final team, the Red Sox, left following the 1923 spring. Independent clubs, as well as Negro Leagues teams like the Kansas City Monarchs and the Newark Eagles, maintained a spring presence in Hot Springs until the 1950s.

Travis Jackson
Waldo Cemetery, Waldo

A total of six Hall of Famers were born in Arkansas, including Lou Brock, Dizzy Dean, Brooks Robinson, and Arky Vaughan, as well as two of the three men who are buried there. The first, Travis Jackson, was born, died, and was buried in Waldo. However, it was the diamond in northern Manhattan where this country boy became famous. Jackson spent 15 years as the shortstop of John McGraw's Giants. He was a consistent, occasionally brilliant hitter who appeared in four World Series, though his lifetime post-season batting average of .149 hints as to why the Giants won only one of those contest. A lifetime .291 hitter, Jackson's true contributions usually came on the infield, where he was one of the most talented fielding shortstops of his day.

Jackson's induction paved the way for infielders like Pee Wee Reese and Phil Rizzuto to have a chance.

Famous for training Yogi Berra, Bill Dickey also spent a spring in 1963 coaching the Mets' young catchers, as a favor to Casey Stengel.

Bill Dickey

Roselawn Memorial Park, Little Rock

Bill Dickey was born in Bastrop, Louisiana, but the family relocated to Kensett, Arkansas, when he was a boy. A promising high school player, he spent three and a half years bounc-

ing around the minors before being signed by the New York Yankees. Making his debut in 1928, Dickey created a direct legacy that could be found behind the plate of Yankee Stadium until 1963, 17 years after he played his final game. Despite being a catcher, a position that is so physically demanding that it is rare for a top-tier hitter to don the "tools of ignorance," Dickey retired with a lifetime batting average of .313 and hit over 200 home runs. He appeared in eight World Series, winning seven of them.

Dickey could be combative, once breaking Carl Reynolds's jaw in a brawl. He was also one of the savviest catchers in baseball. His career was already on the downslope when he left the Yankees in 1944 to serve in the Navy at the height of World War II. The Yankees brought him back after the war, in 1946, for a single season. He even managed the team for a time that year. He managed again the following year, this time for the Southern Association Little Rock Travelers, but after a miserable season he willingly accepted the Yankees' offer to, ostensibly, be the first base coach in 1948.

The Yankees actually brought him back for a higher purpose. They knew they had a diamond in the rough in young Lawrence Peter Berra, but he needed the kind of seasoning that a veteran like Dickey could provide. Berra later said, "I owe everything I did in baseball to Bill Dickey." Today, Dickey's gravestone sports the easily recognizable logo of an Uncle Sam top hat with a baseball bat forming the backbone of the letter "k," a Yankee buried in the South.

George Kell

Swifton Cemetery, Swifton

The final Hall of Famer buried in the state, George Kell, spent his entire life in Swifton. It makes sense that a man who saw so many employers in his professional baseball career would want to stay put during the off-season.

George Kell was once rescued from his burning home by a firefighter.

He saw playing time with the Philadelphia Athletics, Detroit Tigers, Boston Red Sox, Chicago White Sox, and, ultimately, the Baltimore Orioles. Kell once opined that baseball was "no game for a family man" because he was shuffled along so often in his career. While five teams in 15 years may not seem like many now, it certainly was during a time when top-tier stars such as Kell usually stayed put. Between 1946 and 1953, Kell consistently hit above .300, including a league-leading .343 in 1949. If possible, his 1950 was even better, when he led the league in hits and doubles and managed a .484 slugging percentage, despite hitting only eight home runs all season.

He played his last game at third base in 1958, for the Orioles, before being replaced by a youngster the team had been developing for some time named Brooks Robinson. In a strange twist of fate, 25 years later, both Kell and Robinson were part of the Hall of Fame class of 1983. It very likely marks the only time in Hall of Fame history that a player and his replacement were inducted at the same time. Kell extended his career in the game by becoming an announcer for the Detroit Tigers after Mel Ott, their previous broadcaster, died in 1958. He continued to call games until 1997, occasionally taking time off to be the family man that life as a player never afforded him.

Blessed Mobile

✦ ALABAMA ✦

A fun nugget of trivia for a theater guy such as myself is that the earliest amateur club in Alabama to be recorded, so far, was the Dramatic Club of Mobile. The team, which was large enough in 1866 to field two nines in order to have intra-squad play, was made up of members of the Mobile theater community. By 1868, the Dramatics were members of the National Association of Base Ball Players. That year they played the Montgomery Club for the state championship which, according to the May 7 edition of the *Hartford Courant*, they won.

Currently four teams that are a part of the Southern League (double-A) are based in Alabama, including the Birmingham Barons, the Huntsville Stars, the Mobile Bay Bears, and the Montgomery Biscuits. Alabama has a rich history of breeding future major leaguers. Over 330 men from the state have spent time in the big leagues. The state has also witnessed the birth of 12 Hall of Famers, an unprecedented number for such a small populace. Even more remarkably, four of them are from Mobile: Henry Aaron, Willie McCovey, Satchel Paige, and Ozzie Smith. For a city with just 192,000 souls, ranking it 125th in the country, that statistical anomaly cannot be ignored.

Joe Sewell

Tuscaloosa Memorial Park, Tuscaloosa

Only one of those 12 native sons stayed in Alabama to be buried. Joe Sewell made his major league debut in 1920, breaking in with the Cleveland Indians after Ray Chap-

man was killed by a beaning by Carl Mays. The Indians' first replacement for Chapman, a lifetime .196 hitter by the name of Harry Lunte, struggled. Sewell stepped in and was so successful the Indians asked permission from their World Series opponents that year, the Brooklyn Dodgers, to keep him on the post-season roster, despite his late-season addition being technically past the prescribed deadline. The Dodgers, not wishing to seem insensitive in light of Chapman's death, acquiesced. Sewell did not hurt the Dodgers too badly, batting a paltry .174 for the Series, but the Indians still managed to win despite the loss of their star shortstop.

Joe Sewell's final resting place, in Tuscaloosa. The University of Alabama Crimson Tide baseball team plays at Sewell-Thomas Stadium, affectionately called "The Joe."

Sewell spent 11 years with Cleveland and three more at the end of his career with the Yankees. He finished with a lifetime batting average of .312. Most amazingly, in a career that featured 8,333 plate appearances, Sewell only struck out 114 times, fewer than many modern players do in a single season. In 1929 he went 115 straight games without a strikeout. In 1925 he had 608 at bats and struck out a total of four times. Never before or since has a player had such a reliable eye. After he retired, he returned to his alma mater, the University of Alabama, and coached their baseball team for seven years. He owned a hardware and sporting goods store during his later years. Sewell passed away in 1990 in the most blessed of all baseball cities, Mobile.

A Pair of Pitchers
◆ MISSISSIPPI ◆

The connection between early amateur baseball teams and their local fire companies has been well documented, especially within the city of New York. That symbiosis existed in the far-flung reaches too, as a notice in the *New Orleans Daily Crescent* of July 13, 1860, proves. Creole Fire Company No. 9 took an excursion from their hometown of New Orleans to Biloxi, Mississippi, where they ate, drank, went to the public baths and, of course, played baseball. It is interesting to note that it was a fire company from New Orleans that played the first verifiable game of "base-ball" in the state of Mississippi. NOLA is a city with an extensive early history of the game that exceeds the preconceived notions of pre-war South game play, and will be looked at in greater detail in the next chapter.

Just over 200 major leaguers were born in Mississippi, but none of them have made the Hall of Fame. A few had substantial careers, including Don Blasingame, who played 12 seasons for five different teams and led the league in at-bats in 1957; Ellis Burks, who had a wonderful 1996 season in which he led the National League in runs and slugging percentage and finished third in MVP voting; Chet Lemon, who starred with the Chicago White Sox and the Detroit Tigers and was a three-time All-Star, and, most notably, Dave Parker. Parker was a seven-time All-Star, twice led the league in batting, twice in doubles, once in RBIs and, in 1978, won the MVP. He appeared in three World Series and won two of them, with the Pirates in 1979 and the Athletics in 1989.

Bill Foster
Carbondale Cemetery, Claiborne Co.

Of the two Hall of Famers who are buried in Mississippi, one was born in Texas and the other in Arkansas. The first is Bill Foster. A brilliant Negro Leagues pitcher whose name is unknown to many modern fans, he is most commonly mentioned in conjunction with the legendary Rube Foster, his half-brother. The two brothers battled with each other, including over baseball, and they were never close, but Bill certainly must have learned something from his older sibling. He mastered the skill of throwing an assortment of pitches and making them all look the same to the batter's eye when they came out of his hand. There is little doubt that a pitcher as great as Rube had some influence on his equally effective kin.

Twenty-four years after Foster retired from professional baseball, he took a job as the dean of men and baseball coach at Alcorn State College, in Lorman, Mississippi. Foster himself was a student at Alcorn before he began pitching in 1923 for the Memphis Red Sox. The cemetery itself is not located in Lorman, or even in an incorporated town. It is instead solely designated as being a part of Claiborne Co. I tracked through the soft, deep mud, each step sinking further into the earth as I went, and found the grave of Foster.

Before moving back to Mississippi, Foster was an insurance salesman in North Carolina.

The stone highlights the fact that he was elected to the Alcorn State University Hall of Fame in 2003, 25 years after his death. It makes no mention of his election to that other Hall of Fame in 1996.

Dizzy Dean
Bond Cemetery, Bond

In a sport that prides itself on its history of colorful characters, there may be none more offbeat than the one they called Dizzy. Jay Hanna Dean was born in Lucas, Arkansas, the fourth of five children. His mother died when he was just seven, and his father remarried a woman with three children of her own. Tending to a family that large often forced the sharecropping parents to move frequently to where the work was, leaving Dean with little formal education. It was that lack of schooling that helped give rise to a man whose grammar was creative enough to once inspire a collective of school teachers to file a formal complaint against him, when he was a broadcaster at the end of his career.

Dean's headstone has his birth name, while his footstone promotes his election into the Hall and uses his better-known nickname.

Despite the laconic and countrified persona, Dean was a master of his craft. His pitching career was relatively brief, just 12 years, and in only five of them did he pitch a full season, making his election to the Hall all that much more remarkable. He was a four-time All-Star who led the league in strikeouts four times and complete games three times. He won 30 games in 1934 as an important part of the Cardinals' rotation that beat Detroit in the World Series. Dean took home MVP honors in '34 and finished in second place in that award's voting the following two seasons. After an injury in 1937 reduced his playing time, he was traded to the Chicago Cubs before the 1938 season. He never recovered his former brilliance and was effectively done by 1941 after a single inning. The pain in his arm had become too much to bear. He did make one more appearance, in 1947, while a broadcaster for the St. Louis Browns and vocal critic of the team's pitching, when the club decided to bring him back for the final game of the season, juicing ticket sales and giving Dean one last chance for glory. He pitched four scoreless innings.

His grave is relatively plain for a man who was known for his tremendous self-confidence. There is a footstone that highlights his play with the St. Louis Cardinals and mentions his election to the Hall, but it is simple compared to some. The most touching features, and perhaps the greatest testament to his legacy, are the two baseballs that appear to be permanently attached to the footstone. They are official balls from the Dizzy Dean World Series, a Mississippi-based league for 6–16-year-olds that prides itself on the fact that it is "not for coaches, parents, or spectators. [It is] for the youth that play the game." The league emphasizes the fun part of the game and does not allow the "pressure and stress" that they feel has permeated the modern version of Little League and other youth travel baseball. If they were looking for someone to pay tribute to who epitomizes that essence of "no stress," they could not have done better than Dizzy Dean.

Let the Good Times Roll

◆ LOUISIANA ◆

Of all the Southern states, none has more references in the Pre-Pro Database than Louisiana. The first entry at Protoball for the state is 1857, though it is a vague reference to German and Irish immigrants playing sports at community picnics. For certain, by 1860 the Orleans Base Ball Club was in full swing. Both the 1857 and 1860 dates, and the fact that they were based in New Orleans, are significant when it comes to discussing the importance of the Civil War to the spread of baseball. Contrary to the myth that baseball only took hold in the south when northern prisoners played it in war camps, it is certain that the game was already flourishing. Nowhere is this more verifiably clear than in New Orleans.

There has never been a major league team in Louisiana, but there are currently three minor league teams. Both the Alexandria Aces and the LaFayette Bullfrogs play in the independent Texas-Louisiana League. The New Orleans Baby Cakes, known as the Zephyrs prior to 2017, are a Pacific Coast League affiliate of the Marlins. They have also been connected to the New York Mets, the Washington Nationals, the Houston Astros, and the Milwaukee Brewers, all since their exodus from Denver to New Orleans in 1993 to make room for the Colorado Rockies.

Ted Lyons
Big Woods Cemetery, Edgerly

The first Hall of Famer I needed to visit was on the other side of the state from NOLA.

Ted Lyons's stone is a style that is typically installed as a ground flush marker. His was installed upright.

Ted Lyons is buried in Edgerly, just over the Texas border in the southern portion of the region. For the first seven years of his career, Lyons was a reliable workhorse who won 21 or more games three times. A sore shoulder in 1931 cut his workload down to a third of the innings of the previous year and, although he did recover, he was never the same. In 1935 his manager, Jimmy Dykes, started pitching Lyons on six days' rest, earning him the nickname "Sunday Teddy." The results of this experiment were not immediate, as his 1936 ERA ballooned to 5.14, but he ultimately used the extra rest to recapture some of his previous form. He even won an ERA title in 1942, the final full season of his 21-year career.

Lyons turned out to be a stressful photo for me to take because I did something I have never done in all the years I have been traveling. I accidentally booked my rental car for the wrong airport. I flew into Houston, which has two airports. I reserved my car at William P. Hobby, and I flew into George Bush Intercontinental. The car company did not have any available vehicles at Bush, and they were unwilling to issue a refund. I had to take a cab to Hobby, losing a valuable hour of daylight. I made it to the grave with seconds to spare. Keen-eyed observers will see that the photo is a little dimmer, the print on the ball a hair grainier. I took the first photo at approximately five minutes past sundown. By the time I was done shooting, 10 minutes later, it was too dark for any of the photos to be readable. Crisis narrowly averted.

Mel Ott

Metairie Cemetery, New Orleans

Mel Ott was born on the southern side of the Mississippi in Gretna, the parish seat of Jefferson Parish, separated from the French Quarter of New Orleans only by the famous river. A prodigy, Ott was playing for semi-pro teams, earning an adult salary, as a 14-year-old boy. It was playing for one of those semi-pro teams that brought him to the attention of John McGraw. That was how the country boy from N'awlins became one of the greatest hitters in the history of New York City. Ott played for the Giants for 22 years. In that time, he twice led the league in runs scored, six times led the league in home runs,

six times led the league in walks, and retired with a lifetime BA/OBP of .304/.414. The Giants made the World Series three times in his career, winning it all in 1933. Ott batted .389 in the Series that year, clubbing two home runs with four RBIs as the Giants beat the Senators in five games. He died on November 21, 1958, from injuries sustained during an automobile accident on a foggy night in Mississippi.

Unlike my mad dash to get the photo of Lyons, the visit to New Orleans was the polar opposite of stressful. Scheduling myself to have a few days in town and needing only one grave, I was able to fully appreciate the sights of this historic and joyous city. Because I also visited three other states on this trip, I began in Edgerly and then circled through Arkansas, Alabama, and Mississippi before coming back into Louisiana on the eastern edge, making NOLA the last stop on the penultimate Hall Ball trip. I was joined for that final weekend by Anna and Amelia Michael. Anna and I did not meet Amelia until almost five years into the project, but since then we have become closer to her than any other person on the planet. She had also become my de facto business partner, helping me navigate the final stages of The Hall Ball. The three of us danced and sang and drank and ate and reveled in the approaching completion of the project. There was only one more journey to take, and it was the longest of them all.

The Symbolic Ones

By the completion of the project, 19 members of the Hall of Fame had been cremated, and the body of one, Roberto Clemente, had never been discovered. I had briefly toyed with the idea of reaching out to the individual families of those who had been cremated to see if they would give me access to the remains of their loved ones, but decided that was potentially pushing the boundaries of good taste a little too far. Instead, I formulated a plan for a series of symbolic photos to represent each of the respective men. For some, it was where their ashes were spread. For others, I needed to be even more creative. Photographing these gentlemen for the project required thinking outside the box.

Mickey Cochrane and Bill Veeck

On the shores of Lake Michigan, the coast of Chicago, Illinois

Mickey Cochrane was a catcher for the Philadelphia Athletics and Detroit Tigers from 1925 to 1937. His lifetime .320 batting average is the highest of any backstop in the history of the game, and in 1931 he inspired 19-year-old Mutt Mantle to name his son after him. Bill Veeck was likely the most imaginative individual ever to run a baseball team. Some of baseball's most indelible moments and icons we owe to him; he hired 3'7" Eddie Gaedel to pinch-hit in 1951, he created the exploding scoreboard, he hired 42-year-old Satchel Paige to make his major league debut, as well as 54-year-old Minnie Miñoso so that

the Cuban legend could become the first player to appear in a game in five different decades. He approved the disastrous Disco Demolition night in 1979, and he planted the ivy that today defines the outfield wall of Wrigley, way back in 1937. He did much of this while standing atop a prosthetic leg in which he had installed an ashtray. There will never be another like Veeck, and baseball is the poorer for it.

The photograph for Bill Veeck and Mickey Cochrane is the only "two-fer" in the project.

202

Both Cochrane and Veeck had their ashes spread in Lake Michigan. Though popular wisdom claims that Veeck's remains were interred at nearby Oak Woods, the cemetery has no record of his burial, and Stew Thornley has confirmed the reality with Veeck's son, Mike. The younger Veeck is a successful team owner himself, holding a stake in five different independent league teams, including the St. Paul Saints, which he co-owns with actor Bill Murray.

Tom Yawkey
Yawkey Wildlife Center, Winyah Bay, South Carolina

The first documented game in the history of South Carolina is also one of the most interesting games in the history of baseball. It took place in Hilton Head on Christmas Day, 1862, during the height of the Civil War. Members of the 165th Volunteer Infantry from New York took on a squad made up of members of the 47th and 48th New York Infantry Regiments. The soldiers were all from New York City and Brooklyn, the epicenters of the burgeoning baseball mania that was put on hold by the war, and likely played by the most current rules of the nascent game. Over 10,000 Union soldiers and Confederate prisoners watched, one of the largest crowds ever to see a match. One of those soldiers on the field of play was Sgt. Abraham G. Mills, who 40 years later headed the commission that erroneously credited Abner Doubleday as the creator of the game.

Tucked in a hidden southeast corner of South Carolina is the difficult to locate Winyah Bay. There, we found the Tom Yawkey Wildlife Center. Over the 43 years he owned the Boston Red Sox, Yawkey managed to turn a club that never won a World Series under his reign into a storied and beloved franchise. This despite the fact that he willfully hurt his club by refusing to join the rest of his fellow owners and accept integration. The Sox were the last team to integrate, in 1959.

The unlikely backdrop of Tom Yawkey's photograph makes it a personal favorite.

If there is any justice in the situation, it is that Yawkey was also extremely generous/reckless with his money, and he likely could have fielded better, cheaper teams if he hadn't been so blind.

Yawkey was a conservationist, and when he died in 1976 he left three islands that he owned off the coast of Winyah Bay to the state of South Carolina. Once a hunting ground for Yawkey confidants like Ty Cobb and Ted Williams, it is now a restricted wildlife preserve. Guests can visit, but only two days a week between September and May. Reservations must be made far in advance. When Yawkey died, he was cremated and his ashes were spread over the bay. The photo of the ball, resting on the weathered post next to the dock where one catches the ferry over to the preserve, is one of my favorites. The egret, perfectly poised in the water, and the small boat going by in the distance help frame a shot that symbolizes just how unpredictable the project could be.

One other tale emerged from the trip to photograph Yawkey. En route to Winyah Bay, immediately after taking the picture of Ty Cobb in Royston, Anna and I went to Greenville, South Carolina. It was a convenient stopping point in that day's driving, and it offered us an opportunity to go to Fluor Field and see the Greenville Drive, class-A affiliate of, interestingly enough, the Boston Red Sox.

It also gave me a chance to visit the grave of Shoeless Joe Jackson.

Jackson was the only banned member of the 1919 Black Sox who was destined for the Hall of Fame, though Eddie Cicotte could also have made a case. Jackson's potential future inclusion in the Hall will be debated in perpetuity with people falling on both sides of the aisle. One thing is certain. In his hometown, Jackson is beloved. A museum has been made from Jackson's old house, which was moved to right across the road from Fluor Field. His grave, at Woodlawn Memorial Park, may have been littered with more mementos than any I visited on the quest, with the exception of Babe Ruth's. There were dozens of baseballs, a bat and, of course, a pair of shoes.

Dick Williams
Doubleday Field, Cooperstown, New York

Despite its role as the folkloric birthplace of baseball (and it being the location of Abner Doubleday's grandfather's grave) there are actually no Hall of Famers *buried* in Cooperstown. However, in 2012 the family of Dick Williams, abiding by the two-time World Series champion manager's wishes, became the first to make the historic town the final resting place of a Hall enshrinee.

In a low-key memorial, the ashes of Williams were spread on Doubleday Field. The photo is from the perspective of the dugout steps where, just a few months before his death, Williams managed both Phil Niekro's Knucksies and Ozzie Smith's Wizards during the Hall's annual Father's Day Classic.

Ron Santo
Wrigley Field, Chicago, Illinois

It may have taken the Cubs 108 years to win a championship, but they far surpass their South Side rivals when it comes to beloved former players. Perhaps no player ever returned that love with such enthusiasm, creating quite as passionate a marriage, as Ron Santo. Making a big enough impression during his freshman year of 1960 to finish fourth in Rookie of the Year voting, Santo manned the hot corner of Wrigley Field for 14 years before spending one final year with the White Sox in 1974. Santo hit 20 or more home runs 11 times in his career. While his batting average broke .300 only four times, he was also a four-time league leader in drawing bases on balls, allowing him to also pace the circuit in on-base percentage in 1964 and 1966.

In the backdrop of Dick Williams's Doubleday Field-inspired photograph is the distinctive St. Mary's Church, originally built in 1867.

No amount of pleading could get me closer to Ron Santo's position at Wrigley Field than the track in front of the third-base dugout.

Almost 15 years after Santo played his final game, he started providing color commentary for Cubs radio broadcasts on WGN, further cementing his legacy with the club. He spent the next 20 years in the booth, waiting for the call from Cooperstown that never came. The announcement of his election, as a part of the class of 2012, happened on December 5, 2011, one year and two days after he succumbed to complications from bladder cancer and diabetes. In August of that year, on a day which featured the unveiling of a statue of Santo in front of Wrigley Field, the family held a private ceremony in which Santo's ashes were spread around third base in the iconic park. The photo was taken from the track running along the third base line, the closest a civilian could get to the sacred green of baseball's second-oldest stadium.

Early Wynn
Pitcher's mound at Progressive Field, Cleveland, Ohio

When I originally traveled to Cleveland for the project, I had no idea where the ashes of Early Wynn were. I subsequently learned that they had been spread around the pitcher's mound at Progressive Field (which was known as Jacobs Field at the time his remains were placed there), necessitating a second trip. After taking the very thorough public tour of the park in August of 2014, I approached the head groundskeeper, Brandon Koehnke. On that travel day for the Indians, he and his team were working on the field, and he was hesitant to let me get the photo. By that point the dirt had been freshly raked and the sprinklers had been activated. Ultimately he relented, though he insisted that he place the ball on the mound and that I not step on the dirt when I shot the picture. While it is mildly regrettable that you can barely see the writing on the ball, this photo marks the first time in my life I ever stepped between the lines of a major league field. It is without a doubt one of my favorite shots from the whole project.

Roberto Clemente
Piñones Beach, San Juan, Puerto Rico

Most fans know that Roberto Clemente died in a plane crash while bringing relief supplies to the victims of an earthquake in Nicaragua on New Year's Eve, 1972. His body was never recovered, despite the efforts of teammate Manny Sanguillen, who personally spent three days swimming off the coast of Isla Verde in search of his lost friend. Within weeks of his death, the normal five-year waiting period was waived, and Clemente was elected to the Hall of Fame, the soonest anyone has ever been enshrined after playing his final game.

Few know, however, about the subsequent court case. Submitted by Clemente's wife, Vera Zabala Clemente, and the families of the other victims, a court initially found the FAA at fault for the crash for allowing an understaffed, overweight, recently damaged airplane to take off that fateful night. The United States appealed the decision and ultimately won in a higher court. A later request to be heard by the U.S. Supreme Court was denied. For Vera, who had watched her husband fight for the respect to simply be called by his given name instead of Americanized derivatives such as "Bobby" or "Bob," it must have been a final insult.

Today Clemente is still a presence in Puerto Rico. An image of him surrounded by a Puerto Rican flag was for sale at the airport. He has a beautiful, though weathered, stadium named after him in his home town of Carolina, east of San Juan (as well as another in Nicaragua). The Puerto Rican stars of today, including Yadier Molina and Carlos Beltran, continue to speak of him with reverence. Despite this, Puerto Rico is not the baseball capital it once was, relinquishing that claim to the neighboring Dominican Republic. As a result, Clemente's legacy at home has a fragile feel to it.

The photo for Clemente was shot between my trip to Cuba and the final visit to Florida. It was taken on the beach at Isla Verde, near the location where the wreckage from the crash washed ashore in the dark days that followed his death.

Al Spalding
Point Loma Nazarene University, Point Loma, California

Al Spalding's legacy is still visible to this day as his sporting goods empire continues to thrive. He began as a talented pitcher for the National Association Boston Red Stockings before spending two seasons with the newly minted National League Chicago White Stockings in 1876–1877. He served as the Chicago manager during those two seasons, winning the pennant in 1876. He became one of the most powerful magnates in the game, if not the mightiest ever. It was he who created the commission that eventually tapped Doubleday as the sport's inventor. John Thorn, in his book *Baseball in the Garden of Eden*, points out that this was in no small part due to both Doubleday and Spalding being members of the same obscure religious order known as the Theosophists. The home base of this order was on Spalding's estate in Point Loma, California. After the Theosophists left following World War I, the site served as the campus of multiple colleges, as well as the home base for a bootlegging operation. The current college, Nazarene University, moved in after 1973. When Spalding died in 1915, he had his ashes spread on the grounds.

The house you see in the picture was Spalding's. As curious as it looks from the outside, with its purple glass dome (meant to channel personal energies) and spiral staircase to the roof, the interior hand-carved woodwork of Reginald Machell, resident master sculptor of the Theosophists, is another story altogether. A mixture of the divine and the obsessive, many of the door frames are an elaborate representation of interwoven tree-like branches that ultimately meet at the apex, where they are topped with various images, including musical instruments and nymphs.

Bob Lemon
Palmcrest Grand Residence, Long Beach, California

Like many players of his era, Bob Lemon missed three valuable years of playing time serving in the U.S. Navy from 1943 to 1945. Originally an infielder, while stationed in Hawaii he was converted to a pitcher. His first two years back, he split his time between the outfield and the mound, mainly coming out of the bullpen with 20 starts in 69 appearances with the Cleveland Indians. It was not until 1948 that he became a full-time starter. Despite this series of delays, Lemon still won 207 games, notching more than 20 victories in a season seven times in his career.

The energy-harnessing home of Albert Goodwill Spalding.

Bob Lemon had the second-highest number of home runs by a pitcher, with 35, tied with Warren Spahn and trailing only Wes Ferrell.

He died while living at the Palmcrest Grand Residence in Long Beach, California. I had hoped to see the room where he had lived. Unfortunately, the residence only keeps records for 10 years, and none of the current staff worked there in 2000, the year he died.

Roy Campanella and Don Drysdale

Forest Lawn Hollywood Hills, Los Angeles, California *and* Forest Lawn Glendale, Los Angeles, California

When Roy Campanella died in 1993, the three-time MVP's ashes were briefly interred at Forest Lawn Cemetery of Hollywood Hills. Also the burial place of Campy's first manager in the big leagues, fellow Hall of Famer Leo Durocher, the groundbreaking catcher did not stay long. At last report, his ashes are currently in the possession of his daughter.

Considering the biography of the half–Italian, half-black child born in Philadelphia, the giant mosaic called "The Birth of Liberty" seemed a fitting place for the photo assigned to this reluctant trailblazer.

The mural constitutes the entire 162-foot long north face of Forest Lawn's Hall of Liberty, a 1,000-seat auditorium. Featuring various scenes from the Revolutionary War, including some set in Campanella's birthplace, it also contains the inscription, writ large above, "God Gave Us Liberty. People Who Forsake God Lose Their Liberty.—The Founder."

Despite a severely damaged spine, suffered during an automobile accident at age 36, which left him wheelchair-bound for the remainder of his life, Campanella lived another 35 years. In that time, he remained active with the Dodgers, working with their public relations and scouting networks, as well as serving as an adviser during Spring Training.

"The Birth of Liberty" is the largest historical mosaic in the country and features scenes from Philadelphia, where Campanella was born.

I had to pretend I was family to get the people at Forest Lawn to show me where Drysdale's niche once was.

The photo of Don Drysdale was taken the same day as Campanella's at the niche where his remains were housed for nine years until they were collected in 2002. The stories of their ends constitute one of the oddest chains of coincidence in baseball history. The two played together on the Dodgers, briefly. Drysdale's first season was 1956, and Campanella's final one was 1957. Like Campanella,

Don Drysdale also had his ashes interred at a cemetery before they were collected by his family. As with Campanella, that cemetery was called Forest Lawn, part of a network of 10 Los Angeles-area cemeteries. Additionally, the cemetery that served as a temporary home for Drysdale's remains also holds a Hall of Fame manager, Casey Stengel. Finally, in a twist of fate that devastated Dodgers fans across two generations, the two legends died only a week apart.

The two men came from different backgrounds and played the game in different ways. Campanella was a star in Brooklyn via the gritty streets of Philadelphia. Drysdale was a local hero in the glamorous world of Los Angeles. Campanella was beloved by teammates and opponents alike for his jovial approach to the game. Drysdale was known to prefer to hit a batter rather than waste four pitches on an intentional walk. They were men of disparate times and places and styles, but the last chapters of their stories read as one.

Sparky Anderson
Sparky Anderson Field, Thousand Oaks, California

Sparky Anderson's photo was taken at the ball field that bears his name on the campus of California Lutheran University in Thousand Oaks, California. Anderson was a local and a huge booster of the college. The field was inaugurated in 2006, with 500 fans on hand to celebrate its dedication. We arrived at the exact moment the team was leaving for a game on the road, but were fortunate enough to find coach Adam Leavitt, who allowed us through the gate. After a quick search, Anna quickly discovered Sparky's seat. The legendary manager always sat in the same front row seat on the third base line when he attended games. A plaque was placed on it after his death. The bright yellow background makes this another favorite Hall Ball photo.

Leavitt went on to tell me his Sparky Anderson story. New to the squad in 2009,

Leavitt had an opportunity to talk to the venerable icon. Believing he was complimenting Sparky's record, which included five pennants and three world championships with two different teams, he stated that he felt that Anderson's career was superior to that of Bobby Cox. Anderson unloaded on Leavitt for insulting his friend Cox and stormed out of the room. The young coach was left stunned, confused as to what he had done wrong. Soon enough, Anderson returned to apologize for his outburst. What Leavitt didn't realize at the time was that the 75-year-old manager was already deep in the throes of dementia, which claimed his life a year later.

Kirby Puckett
Target Field, Minneapolis, Minnesota

Kirby Puckett's photo was the result of an odd opportunity. While booking my return trip from the West Coast journey, one of my flight options included an overnight layover in Minneapolis.

Taken at around midnight, Kirby Puckett's photo was shot later than any other I can remember in the course of the project.

I was undecided at the time as to what I was going to do about Puckett and thought I'd use the air travel serendipity to my advantage. The flight landed at 10:00 p.m., and the connecting plane left at 7:00 a.m., so the choices were somewhat limited. That's when I discovered Bill Mack's sculpture of Puckett that stands outside the gates of Target Field, the Minnesota Twins' home since 2010. Capturing the most iconic moment of Puckett's career, his fist pump after he hit the 11th-inning Game 6 home run in the 1991 World Series, he looks ferocious in bronze. Special thanks to SABR-mate Robert Tholkes for giving me a cozy bed to sleep in on this fortunate side trip on the odyssey.

Phil Rizzuto
Phil Rizzuto Field at Hillside High School, Hillside, New Jersey

A mainstay at shortstop for the dynastic Yankees squads of the 1940s and '50s, Fiero "Phil" Rizzuto appeared in nine World Series, winning seven of them. A lifetime .273 hitter, his election into the Hall is one that is considered suspect by many. However, his lifetime dWAR of 22.9, his 1950 MVP Award, and his five All-Star Game appearances certainly give his resume some weight. Born in Brooklyn, he and his wife Cora moved to Hillside, New Jersey, in 1950, where he lived for the rest of his life.

Rizzuto died on the 12th anniversary of Mickey Mantle's passing.

In February 2011, four years after Rizzuto died, the Hillside Board of Education named their high school athletic field after the famous local. Not solely a baseball diamond, Rizzuto Field also features the school's running track and football field. The photo is taken from the shortstop position, with the scoreboard bearing his name in the background.

Larry Doby
Larry Doby Field at East Side Park, Paterson, New Jersey

The name of Jackie Robinson is known by all, even those who do not consider themselves baseball fans. Larry Doby, who was the first African American to integrate the American League and the second black player in the majors overall, has suffered the fate of many who come second. Thus his name does not carry the same historical significance.

The statue of Larry Doby at Eastside Park was designed by Phil Sgobba.

It is a shame because, while not as flashy as Robinson (Doby had only 47 stolen bases in his career compared to Robinson's 197), his offensive statistics often outshined his counterpart's. Doby twice led the league in home runs, once in RBIs, once in slugging, and once in OPS, and he was a seven-time All-Star. Robinson himself appeared in only six Midsummer Classics. Born in Camden, South Carolina, Doby moved to New Jersey when he was 12 years old. He lived in the Paterson area the rest of his life. The ballfield in Eastside Park was named after him in 1998, and the statue you see in the photo was installed in 2002. After his 1998 election to Cooperstown, Doby was elected to the Eastside High School Hall of Fame the following year.

Joe Gordon
The National Baseball Hall of Fame and Museum, Cooperstown, New York

Joe Gordon was one of the humblest of ballplayers, and when he died in 1978 he requested that he have no funeral and his body be cremated. For sure, his stats are some of the most pedestrian of anyone in the Hall. Yet despite his lack of eye-catching season totals, he finished in the top 10 in MVP voting five times in his career, successfully winning the honor in 1942. He was elected to the Hall of Fame in 2008, 30 years after his death.

His daughter, Judith, gave his acceptance speech, in the text of which she stated, "We [his family] consider Cooperstown and the National Baseball Hall of Fame to be his final resting place." Inspired by her words, I chose to pose the ball in front of the Hall itself. It is the sole photo in the project that featured the place where I hoped it would ultimately reside.

Robin Roberts
Robin Roberts Field, Springfield, Illinois

Robin Roberts was a workhorse for the Philadelphia Phillies, topping the league in innings pitched five times and throwing more than 250 innings 10 times. While the bulk of his success came in the early and mid–1950s, he pitched for 19 years and won 286 ballgames with the Phillies as well as the Baltimore Orioles, the Houston Astros, and the Chicago Cubs before retiring in 1966. He was one of the leading figures in bringing Marvin Miller in as the head of the Players' Association, and after retirement he became a coach at the University of South Florida in Tampa. His original photo for the project was taken at Christ our Redeemer Church in Temple Terrace, Florida, where Roberts's funeral took place in 2010. However, while pursuing the symbolic photo of Al Barlick, I unexpectedly drove past Robin Roberts Field in his hometown of Springfield, Illinois.

My optimistic photograph for Joe Gordon.

This photograph for Robin Roberts was not planned, and was a happy accident that occurred en route to another picture.

I considered it a much more fitting tribute, and the resulting photo is the one you see here.

Al Barlick

Abandoned Peabody Coal Mine, Springfield, Illinois

The romantic image of the hidden gem rising from the coal mines of middle America to become a ballplayer in the major leagues is a truism when it comes to Al Barlick, except that he made his name as an umpire and not as a player. He had a 28-year career in the majors and called some the most memorable games in history, including serving as the first base arbiter on April 15, 1947, when Jackie Robinson played his first game in Brooklyn. He was behind the plate for six no-hitters and served on the crew of seven World Series. The first game he ever called, however, was as a member of the company team for the Peabody No. 59 coal mine, where he worked alongside his father. The ball is photographed at the last remaining physical structure from the mine, a shaft which is located one tenth of a mile off Old Route 36 in Springfield.

Barlick was known for having a booming voice, which carried his calls throughout the stadium.

Weaver was once quoted as saying that his epitaph should read, "The sorest loser that ever lived."

Earl Weaver

Memorial Field at the Y, Baltimore, Maryland

Memorial Field at the Y, located in Baltimore, Maryland, is a community-accessible baseball field with an all-weather surface that stands on the very footprint of Memorial Stadium, where Earl Weaver won four pennants and one World Series as the skipper of the Orioles. While history may best remember his rages at umpires, which led to him being ejected 94 times over the course of his career, Weaver knew how to win. He has the eighth-highest winning percentage for managers with more than 10 years on their resume. He died at sea, aboard the ship *Silhouette*, as part of a fan cruise sponsored by the Orioles.

Monte Irvin

Hinchliffe Stadium, Paterson, New Jersey

Monte Irvin's best years came as a member of Effa Manley's Newark Eagles. Although statistics are incomplete, he consistently ranked among the league leaders during his tenure from 1938 to 1948 (minus three years he served in the Army during the war). His first tryout for the Negro Leagues took place at Hinchliffe Stadium, in Paterson, New Jersey, not far from where he grew up after his family moved north from his birth state of Alabama.

The taking of the photograph of Monte Irvin was witnessed by over six million people, the average viewership of *CBS Evening News*.

The death of Doug Harvey was a decisive turning point in the project.

As a member of the Eagles, he played many games at Hinchliffe against the New York Cubans and the New York Black Yankees, both of whom called the stadium home. Hinchliffe is in the register of the National Trust for Historic Preservation and is one of the final remaining stadium facades from the Negro Leagues. When I took this photo, I was accompanied by Brook Silva-Braga, reporter for *CBS Evening News*. You can see his hand in the photo. The story of The Hall Ball had already been told in the *New York Times*, but with Silva-Braga's feature that aired on April 2, 2017, it had legitimately become national news.

Doug Harvey

Tony Gwynn Stadium, San Diego State University, San Diego, California

Umpire Doug Harvey's presence was so commanding that it earned him the nickname "God." It was a moniker that was well-deserved, after a lifetime of passion dedicated to his craft. Harvey knew as a child that he wanted to emulate his father, Harold W. Harvey, who was himself a baseball arbiter. The younger Harvey briefly played both baseball and football at San Diego State before injury ended his athletic career. Undaunted, he already had other plans in mind.

After six years working in the independent and minor leagues, Harvey joined the ranks of the National League in 1962, as part of Al Barlick's crew. Over the next 31 years, he became the most respected umpire of his generation. He oversaw 4,673 regular season games, fifth most all-time. He umpired in five World Series and six All-Star Games. He also officiated in nine National League Championship Series, the all-time record.

Harvey was sick during the final years of his life. I had received contact information for Harvey from Peter Golenbock, his biographer, who was a friend of The Hall Ball. But I never used it. I was first trying to arrange an opportunity to photograph Tom Seaver, in an attempt to coordinate a trip to California where both Harvey and Seaver lived. I was never successful, and on January 13, 2018, Harvey died at the age of 87.

According to the church where Harvey's funeral was held, he was cremated. I decided to visit Tony Gwynn Stadium at San Diego State University and stage a symbolic photo at the campus where the happenstance of a broken leg helped a young man focus on the dreams of his childhood. Accompanied by Meredith Brennan, who had supported my earlier visit to Arizona to photograph Ted Williams and Jocko Conlan, we scaled the infield walls to get onto the deserted diamond. I took multiple shots of various set-ups of the ball, including one with Harvey's name on a banner listing notable graduates. I ultimately decided to use the one you see because of the expanse of the field, the staging of the stool with the college name and, of course, having the name of the great Tony Gwynn in the background. The two men are tragically linked. Both battled oral cancers due to their usage of chewing tobacco. Harvey spent the final mobile years of his life doing volunteer work to teach youth to avoid the dangerous substance.

Harvey become an unexpected, decisive turning point for me. With his death, all I needed to complete the project were seven living Hall of Famers, not counting the newly minted Class of 2018. I was closer than ever. But there was something unsettling about the idea of the project moving forward because of the death of Harvey. He opened up a moral quandary for me that I never anticipated. I realized I had to make a decision about the ultimate fate of The Hall Ball much sooner than I expected. The thought left me breathless.

Paradise
◆ HAWAII ◆

Alexander Cartwright
Oahu Cemetery, Honolulu

The first time baseball appeared in the newspapers of Hawaii seems to be July of 1858, with a description in the *Pacific Coast Commercial Advertiser* of a Restoration Day festival game of "base ball." Even more significantly, recent research by Bruce Allardice reasonably proves that the first interracial game of baseball occurred on August 24, 1867. For many years that crown had been worn by Philadelphia, which hosted a contest between the Philadelphia Olympics and the all-black Pythians in 1869. Philly can still claim the mantle for the first interracial game in the United States. Hawaii was an independent nation at the time, still 92 years shy of statehood.

There is much speculation as to when baseball truly came to Hawaii. The greater portion of that speculation surrounds the man I was there to photograph, Alexander Cartwright, early member of the New York Knickerbockers, the most documented baseball team from the 1840s. His was also the final grave I needed to visit for that portion of the project to be complete.

Hawaii has never had a major league team because it is too remote, though there was an attempt to create a winter league that served as a bridge towards incorporating major league play with the Japanese Nippon League. The Hawaii Winter Baseball League began in 1993, and after a couple of false starts, folded for good in 2008. There was also a Pacific Coast League team called the Hawaii Islanders. It changed affiliations eight times in its 27-year lifespan as teams struggled to make the small market and distant location work. They played their last game in 1987.

There is a rabid desire for baseball there, with the islands' allegiances split between the Dodgers and the Giants. I learned this from Dan Cooke, weatherman for *Hawaii News Now-Sunrise*. It was 6:30 in the morning on my first full day in Hawaii, and I was standing just offstage, waiting for my turn to go on the air and talk to the people of Oahu about The Hall Ball. Anna, our children Finn and Violet, as well as Amelia and her kid Sage, all accompanied me. My oversized family was quite a sight. As they giddily waited for me, Cooke, reporter Steve Uyehara, and I chatted about local fandom.

The story of The Hall Ball had appeared on the *CBS Evening News* just two weeks before I went to Hawaii. The end of the segment mentioned that I was going to the Aloha State next, so I received a modest bump in media requests while I was there. It included a blurb for a newspaper, a radio interview with ESPN Maui, and two TV interviews, one of which was for *Hawaii News Now*. I happened to have chosen Cartwright's birthday for my visit, so I received an additional request to be a guest speaker for the Friends of Alexander Cartwright, who do an annual celebration at his grave.

Cartwright's grave has been a pilgrimage for ballplayers for decades. Babe Ruth even once paid him a visit.

Cartwright's route to Hawaii was a curious one. In 1849 he left New York City, where he was a contributing member of the Knickerbockers during their initial years of play, to pursue his fortunes chasing gold in California. Within the first year after the trek, he moved to Hawaii and never left. The ironic reason this son of a sea captain remained in Paradise can be found in an April 1865 letter to his former Knickerbockers teammate, Charles DeBost. "I am so fearfully sea sick when I go on the water, it deters me from traveling."

He became an important figure in Hawaii, advising the King and Queen. He played an integral part in updating Hawaii's nascent fire prevention techniques. Cartwright, like so many Knickerbockers, was a volunteer fireman, and he brought his skills with him to the place where he spent the last 42 years of his life. He is revered there like few other white men.

The plaque for Alexander Cartwright in the Hall of Fame has the following text: "Father of Modern Baseball. Set bases 90 feet apart. Established 9 innings as a game and 9 players as team. Organized the Knickerbocker Baseball Club of New York in 1845. Carried baseball to Pacific Coast and Hawaii in pioneer days." The request to speak at his

birthday celebration put me in an awkward place because virtually every word of that is historically incorrect. Those words came to be his legacy because in the scrum between Henry Chadwick and Albert Spalding to tap the sport's founder, the unlikely victor for the minds of "serious historians," those who knew enough not to believe the bunk about Doubleday, was Cartwright.

We now know that the man most responsible for the rules mentioned on Cartwright's plaque was Doc Adams, though even he did not *invent* baseball. No one did. Baseball is not an invention but an evolution.

I had become friendly with Adams's great-granddaughter Marjorie. We both hoped that he would be elected into the Hall as part of the class of 2016, and become a part of *The Hall Ball*. He fell two votes shy. Since that election, new documents have come to light. In April 2016, the "Laws of Baseball," literally written in Adams's hand, were auctioned off for the unprecedented sum of $3.3 million, the most ever paid for an item connected to baseball. Those documents prove that many of the rules that we think of as definitive, including those mentioned on Cartwright's plaque, were devised by Adams. He stands a good chance of being elected the next time the appropriate Veterans Committee looks at his case, in 2020.

As far as speaking to the Friends of Cartwright, I believe I struck an appropriate tone regarding Alexander's place in the pantheon. I respect the role he has played, even if none of the "facts" are right. So much of the history of baseball, at least as far as it pertains to the greater public, is myth. As a historian, I believe it is my duty to correct these misconceptions. I also think it is my job to remember and pass on those myths. If we look at the two side by side, we can not only see the true progression of our great game, but we can see how it captured the spectrum of public imagination like no other sport.

It was important to me that Cartwright be the final grave I visited. I had planned it that way for some time. It wasn't a hard decision to make. Hawaii was certainly the most expensive and far-flung trip, so saving it for last always seemed appropriate. I also appreciated the symbolism. Beyond my affinity for baseball in the 19th Century, Cartwright was, after all, the first-born member of the Hall, preceding Father Chadwick by four years. He is, within the current narrative of the plaques in the Hall gallery, where the story of baseball begins. Though I still had a few living players to go, I loved that he was where that portion of my story ended.

So Much for Symbolism

I was able to enjoy the completion of that symbolic moment, when I snapped the picture of Alexander Cartwright's grave, for roughly two months. Then I got an email from Stew Thornley telling me that all my carefully crafted and scheduled plans were for naught. He had found Lee MacPhail.

Lee MacPhail
St. James the Less Episcopal Church, Scarsdale, NY

MacPhail was one of the most influential executives in baseball history. Part of the only father/son combination in the Hall of Fame, he got his first baseball job right after serving in World War II. Larry MacPhail, his father, placed him in charge of the Kansas City Blues, a Yankees farm squad, before ultimately bringing him up to the parent club. Lee's tenure with the Yankees would outlast his father's, who was fired by the team after a public outburst following the 1947 World Series.

Lee stayed with the Yankees until 1958, when he became the general manager of the Baltimore Orioles, helping to build the team that swept the Dodgers in the World Series in 1966. MacPhail was working in the Commissioner's Office by then, assisting ill-prepared Commissioner William Eckert. MacPhail was named President of the American league in 1974, and he held that office until 1983. One of the most memorable moments from his tenure was the famous "pine tar" game, in which gamesmanship on the part of Yan-kees manager Billy Martin resulted in George Brett initially losing a go-ahead home run. MacPhail later ruled the home run valid, earning him the ire of his former employers. When he retired from baseball in 1985, he was one of the most respected and admired figures in the game.

Just prior to my Hawaii trip, Stew and I touched base, lamenting over the still-unknown fate of Lee MacPhail. Information about what happened to MacPhail after his death was scarce. There was no funeral, just a small memorial. After the initial obituaries, there was no media follow-up. Stew had previously spoken to MacPhail's son, Andy, and learned that he was "buried in Scarsdale," but he wasn't able to find out a specific location. Both Stew and I called the few cemeteries we could locate in Scarsdale and the nearby neighborhoods of Harts-dale and White Plains. Neither of us got anywhere.

The grave of Lee MacPhail, spoiler of symbolism.

MacPhail died in 2012, so I had spent close to five years doing intermittent searches for new leads. After calling all the cemeteries I could find in the area where the man's son claimed he was buried, to no success, I concluded that what the younger MacPhail had meant, in his brief initial exchange with Stew, was that the memorial that had been mentioned in the obituary had taken place in Scarsdale. I made the deductive leap that since our cemetery search had been fruitless, MacPhail had been cremated and was to be considered one of the Symbolic Ones.

To that end I went to 280 Park Avenue which, during MacPhail's tenure as the President of the American League from 1974 to 1983, served as the home office for the league. I attempted to get security at the building to show me which offices belonged to the American League, which is no longer housed there, but they were unwilling to let me go up the elevators. Instead, I took a picture of the ball with the façade of the building in the background.

While taking the picture, I had one of the more bizarre experiences in the life of the project. I was standing on the street, arm outstretched so I could frame the picture, when I heard a voice say, "Hey, you're the guy with the baseball." It was just after the CBS story, and he recognized me. He eagerly asked for a picture of me and the ball, which he couldn't wait to share with his wife. I have lived in New York City for almost 20 years and never, in all that time, has someone I did not already know recognized me. Of course, I had never been national news before. After he walked away, the remaining feeling was a mixture of pride and nausea.

After I took that shot, I considered MacPhail done. It was important to me that I take the picture before I went to Hawaii because I really did want Cartwright to be the last. Alas, it wasn't meant to be. In June, Stew bumped into Andy MacPhail again, this time at a Mets-Phillies game during SABR's annual convention. He used the opportunity to probe MacPhail for a few more details. That's when he learned that Lee was in the colum-

barium at St. James the Less, a small Episcopalian church.

I was a little chagrined. It was foolish that I hadn't also looked up all the churches in Scarsdale and not just what I thought were all the cemeteries. By not connecting that obvious detail, my seven-year plan for Cartwright to be the final grave was ruined.

It took me until September to get to MacPhail. The whole family was with me, all of us traveling back home from a weekend trip. We had been in Boston because the 19th Century Baseball Grave Marker Project had just dedicated a new stone for Andy Leonard, outfielder for the famed Cincinnati Red Stockings, the 1869 club that legitimized professionalism in the sport. If I couldn't end the graves portion of the project with the symbolism I truly wanted, at least I could take the final photo in conjunction with the ancillary mission that was born from the Hall Ball.

There is one feature in the MacPhail photo that makes it unlike any other picture that appears in the Hall Ball series. My oldest child, Finn, has no interest in baseball. The kids humored me for a few years, but as they grew they made it clear they were bored by their old man's game. I have no interest in forcing my passions onto my kids, so Finn accompanied me on very few of the Hall Ball trips. The kids were on this one because they were visiting a friend from camp while we were at the Leonard dedication ceremony. Finn knew this was the last one, however, so they offered to hold the ball so I could shoot it at the upright columbarium. It pleases me to no end that one of their hands, complete with bright pink nail polish, is the one that will forever be connected in my mind with this Hall of Fame son of a Hall of Famer.

* * *

Just two weeks after the Leonard dedication, the 19th Century Grave Marker Project had another celebration, this time for Hall of Famer Pud Galvin. I had originally shot Galvin's photo in August of 2011, and I detail that story in the chapter on Pennsylvania. Since he was impoverished at the time of his death, his ground-flush marker is on a family plot, bearing only his first two initials and his last name. Two vertical cracks run through it, assuring that its lifespan is limited.

When I took over the 19th Century Marker Project, I targeted Galvin early on while I was deciding which players to assist. He was a Hall of Famer, and he deserved more than what he's had for the last 115 years. Galvin had a substantial number of family members still alive, and it wasn't hard to connect with one of them. His great-great-granddaughter, Amanda Nespoli Minardi, was my liaison throughout the installation. She and the rest of her family were enthusiastically grateful to me for reaching out and happily agreed to let me place a new stone.

With the help of Pirates historian Craig Britcher, as well as Galvin biographer Chip Martin and SABR Forbes Field Chapter president George Skornickle, we wrote an epitaph that we felt appropriately summed up his career. I got permission from artist Dick Perez to use one of his drawings of Galvin which we had affixed to the stone. The updated photo of Galvin's stone is included here.

The updated stone for Pud Galvin.

In September of 2017, over 20 family members arrived from all over the country, and on an unseasonably warm day, we dedicated our new monument. Also on hand was Pittsburgh Pirates President Frank Coonelly, who addressed the gathered crowd. He invited a number of the Galvins, along with myself and Skornickle, to that night's game. The family was introduced on the field prior to the start, and then we all watched the contest from his personal suite at PNC Park. I had the pleasure of spending virtually the entire game next to Mr. Coonelly, with our conversation topics ranging from The Hall Ball, to protective netting in the stands, to the cost of college for our children. It was a memorable evening topped with an 11–6 Pirates win.

I had decided I would also visit the grave of Rufus "Sonnyman" Jackson while I was there. Jackson was a co-owner of the Homestead Grays, and I had written his biography for the SABR publication *Bittersweet Goodbye*, which tells the stories of the participants of the 1948 Negro League World Series. While researching him, I had become fascinated with the charismatic entrepreneur/criminal. I wanted to pay my respects before I left town.

He is buried at Homestead Cemetery, the same place as his business partner, Hall of Famer Cum Posey. Homestead is an unusual cemetery in that a large percentage of the graves are located within the sides of a steep hillside, making it difficult even to access some of the locations. When I was there in 2011 to photograph Posey, it was well-maintained and respectable, despite being in one of the poorer areas of Pittsburgh. There is a Civil War monument there, built in 1891 and "Erected to the Memory of the Country's Defenders." The ethnic background of those buried there is varied, from Swedish to German to Native American. Black and white lie side by side on the 35 acres of Homestead.

It is also the final resting place of three men who died during the "Battle of Homestead." On July 6, 1892, a labor strike by employees of Carnegie Steel turned deadly when Pinkerton Detectives, hired by Andrew Carnegie and Henry Clay Frick, clashed with striking workers. Seven people died. Three of them, John Morris, Joseph Sotack, and Silas Wain, rest at Homestead.

Having trouble sleeping after the celebratory dedication festivities, I began a little research to see if anyone else was buried at Homestead that I would want to visit. The Homestead Grays were one of the most successful and historically noteworthy teams in Negro Leagues history. There was a decent chance that one or two of those who donned the uniform stayed in the area after their playing days were over. Rather than finding a list of other notables at the cemetery, I discovered something far more unsettling.

In July of 2015, roughly four years after I last visited Homestead, the cemetery filed for bankruptcy. According to court documents, the unsettled debt totaled less than $10,000 on a property that was valued at $504,000. Despite this seemingly surmountable amount on a piece of land with such value, according to the lawyer who represented the cemetery, the cost of perpetual care was too much for them to manage. Homestead stopped taking new orders for burials and simultaneously left people who had pre-purchased plots to their own devices when it came time to bury their loved ones. For a short time, a chain was strung across the entrance to the cemetery for fear of potential lawsuits that would have no direct defendant, since there was no longer a board to answer any claims. People were forbidden from even entering the cemetery to visit. The chain was later removed after sufficient public outrage.

For the next two years, Homestead was maintained by a group of volunteers, collectively called Help Homestead Cemetery. They did their best to care for the 35 acres, including its imposing hillsides that your average push mower would struggle to handle. Then, in August 2017, the group disbanded, citing too few volunteers and too much work to landscape the site.

The identical graves of Homestead Grays owner Rufus Jackson and his wife, Helen Mae.

Now, gravesites are maintained solely by the loved ones who come to visit. The rest of the cemetery has been given over to mother nature. A number of the graves have already been swallowed by the tall grass and encroaching soil. If there is no resolution soon, much of the cemetery will be impossible to traverse during the height of summer.

The symbolism was not lost on me. On a weekend in which we celebrated the long-overdue stone of one Hall of Famer, another (Posey) is at risk of being absorbed by the earth. I had taken on the role of head of the 19th Century Baseball Grave Marker Project because I believed in its mission. It is not easy to encapsulate the story of a life in eight square feet of granite, but it's the best system we have come up with to assuage the grief of those left behind and to assure future family and historians of a corporeal link to the past. It may be an endless task. For every grave I help to mark, another one in need seems to emerge.

It took some hunting, but I eventually found the gravesite of Jackson. He's buried in one of the flatter sections of the cemetery, and his grave was recently mowed. His stone is understated, especially considering that at the time of his death he had a decent amount of wealth. His wife, Helen Mae, lived another 41 years after Jackson died. She is buried by his side with an identically designed marker.

The Living Members

◆ IV ◆

In 2017, I decided to spend an entire week in Cooperstown, a luxury I had never experienced. I rented an old farm house about 30 minutes outside of town, and I indulged my artistic spirit, tapping away at the keyboard of my computer until late in the night with no sounds to distract me beyond the summer breeze and the crickets. I wrote about 20 percent of the book you are reading over those seven days.

Much of that time was spent in the A. Bartlett Giamatti Research Center at the Hall of Fame. With the generous assistance of library director Jim Gates and his faithful staff and interns, I submerged myself in the player files that the Hall keeps. They were invaluable not only for anecdotal tales, but for giving me a sense of who some of these men were as people, in details shared by the scribes of their times.

I took four photos over that Induction Weekend, and all were shot under first-time circumstances for me. This was largely because I had such a luxuriant amount of time while I was in town. I photographed both Iván Rodriguez and John Schuerholz on Saturday morning, during the annual golf tournament. Hall of Famers and their guests participate in a light-hearted round of golf at the Leatherstocking Golf Course at the Otesaga Resort, where the members stay. I had learned from Cubabalista Lisa Farbstein, who is a master at autograph hunting, that if I parked off to the side of adjoining Glimmerglen Rd., I could get access to some of the players when they played through the 10th hole.

That year, Rodriguez brought his friend, Hall of Fame golfer Chi-Chi Rodríguez. Chi-Chi paused his game to tell us all a ridiculous joke. ("Did you hear about that new documentary about constipation? It hasn't come out, yet.") I was able to get Iván with some assistance from a little boy who was standing next to me. Rodriguez was about to drive by in his golf cart when the high-pitched cries of five-year-old Jackson Bell caused him to pull over. After he signed for the enthusiastic, young autograph seeker, I was able to get the affable catcher to hold the ball from his cart before he pulled away.

Without the assistance of Jackson Bell, I likely would have missed my chance to photograph Rodriguez.

221

Jeff Bagwell stayed after the Q & A to sign autographs for quite some time.

John Schuerholz turned on a winning smile as soon as I asked for the photograph.

Bud Selig and Jeff Bagwell were both photographed on the Monday morning of Induction Weekend. After the tremendous emotional highs of the Sunday induction, along with a weekend filled with tens of thousands of fans spilling through the streets of the tiny town for the big ceremony, the informal Q & A the Hall conducts with the new inductees on Monday morning was a peaceful respite. Most of the crowd had left, and the thousand or so that remained gathered at Doubleday Field to hear the newest members talk a little bit about their experiences. The panel was hosted by broadcasting legend Peter Gammons.

My first time attending the roundtable, I was thrilled to be able to get the photo of Selig before the event, as he entered Doubleday. If one looks closely, one can see Chi-Chi Rodriguez in the background of his picture. The shot of Bagwell was taken after the event, from the bleacher seats. That is why Bagwell, who was still standing on the field, has the appearance of being so far below the camera's point of perspective. It is the only one in the project shot from such an angle.

A zoomed-in view of Selig's right lens would show yours truly taking the picture. It was the only one in the project in which I am obviously visible.

*   *   *

As mentioned, while waiting on the golf course for the Rodriguez and Schuerholz photos, I met Jackson Bell. An adorable and persuasive tyke, he was also one of the most dedicated autograph collectors I had ever met. He knew exactly what he wanted and was a motivating force in his family's vacation planning. His father, Mark, was with him on the course that day. Mark and I discussed the amazingly focused nature of his son's obsession, as well as the pitfalls of trying to connect with living members of the Hall of Fame.

Mark was not much of a baseball fan. He preferred basketball. But he admired his son's dedication, and his own mildly obsessive nature thrived in helping Jackson try to meet all of his heroes. The chilly morning air was warmed by getting to meet this father and son, who are more alike than likely either of them realizes.

While waiting for the golf tournament to start, I explained the project to Mark, letting him know which living Hall of Famers I still needed. He informed me that he and Jackson were planning on driving to Waukesha, Wisconsin, the week following Induction to get the autograph of Henry Aaron. The man many consider to be the legitimate home run king did not participate in Hall of Fame weekend autograph events, but he was doing a signing in the sizable suburb located 30 minutes west of Milwaukee.

I was faced with a difficult decision. I had given the ball to Tony Milito to get the photos of Red Schoendienst and Bill Mazeroski. The difference was that Tony had been an advocate for the Ball for some time and had shared so much of himself for the advancement of the project. I had just met Mark and Jackson. Could I really trust them to take the ball and assure its safe return? While my optimistic nature wouldn't allow me to believe that Mark would do something so horrible as to steal the ball, it was always possible that he could lose it. I had absolutely no real information about these new acquaintances upon which to base an informed choice.

I trusted my gut and at the end of the weekend, I gave them the ball. I reached out to Mark later in the week, in an effort to show him some examples of previous photos so that he would have some idea of how to stage the picture. He did not respond that night. I began to be filled with no small amount of terror. Had I made a terrible mistake? I reached out to him again the following night, and he almost immediately replied, apologizing for not responding sooner. He had been in a bible study class when I had the texted the night before and had neglected to follow up. I breathed a sigh of relief.

A few days later, Mark sent me the photo you see. At first he tried to prank me, saying that he wasn't successful. His honest nature made him confess almost immediately. It was such an important picture for the project. Aaron isn't just a Hall of Famer. He is in a pantheon so rare that I had begun to doubt I would ever be able to get the photograph. Perhaps more so than any other member that I did not shoot myself, I wish I had met Aaron.

Henry Aaron image courtesy of Mark Bell.

Yet I cannot regret giving the ball to the Bells. After all, I never got a chance to connect with Aaron, myself. There would not be a Hall Ball photo without trusting that the baseball gods would send my creation home. From nearly the beginning, I knew the Ball was going to be a communal effort. Mark and Jackson expanded the circle of angels that made the final product possible.

The Veterans Committee tasked with electing the class of 2018 definitely appreciated the work of the 1980s Detroit Tigers. Jack Morris and Alan Trammell, both long overlooked by Hall voters, were teammates in Motor City from 1977 to 1990. Their election gave Tigers fans something to cheer about during a season in which their team finished 34 games below .500. Despite healthy Detroit representation in the Hall, Morris and Trammell marked the first time two Tigers were elected in the same year.

My interactions with the two of them, famously opposite in temperament, were vastly different experiences. Morris was signing for JP in White Plains, barely a month after his election. So close to the end of the project, I had begun to lose patience with all the waiting.

Alan Trammell has long been considered one of baseball's "good guys," and my interaction only confirmed that assessment.

Rather than hiding in the back while Morris finished on the floor, I jumped in line with the autograph seekers. When it was my turn, I approached him and gave the rap. He first looked at the JP rep who was assisting him, obviously perplexed by my unusual story. He then hesitantly picked up the ball and gave me something between a smile and a grimace. I snapped the photo, thanked him, and walked away. As I was departing, I heard him say, "What the hell was that?"

The Trammell picture was taken just two weeks later in Hasbrouck Heights, New Jersey. Again, I just jumped into the line, no longer willing to wait. The interaction itself was as different from the Morris one as the men themselves. Trammell was warm and inviting, and his smile was genuine. As with the interactions with members like Ernie Banks and Pedro Martinez, Trammell gave off a vibe of kindness that was difficult to miss.

The photograph of George Brett was the result of over a year of communication between me and Brett's brother, Bobby. I knew

Jack Morris agreed to the photograph, though he clearly did not know what to make of my effort.

that Bobby handled George's public appearances, and prior to the 2016 Induction, I reached out to him to see if it was possible for George to carve out 30 seconds of his time to let me take a picture in Cooperstown. Bobby explained that George tends to shy away from the fans during Induction Weekend, but if I was willing to come to Arizona for Spring Training, he believed he could make George available to me. I told him I would make every effort to do so and would reach out when I could confirm dates and times.

Life, and the responsibilities of maintaining a full-time job, made it impossible for me to attend Spring Training in 2017. I wrote Bobby and explained my predicament, and once again pled for a chance to shoot George during Induction festivities. Again, Bobby said that he would make George aware of my request, but that it would be much better received at Spring Training. I did not shoot the Kansas City Royals third baseman that July either.

The trip to take the photograph of George Brett was the farthest I traveled for a picture of a living Hall of Famer.

Finally, in 2018, my schedule cleared enough that I was able to travel to Arizona. I once again reached out to Bobby and he let me know that yes, he was still willing to coordinate a meeting with me and George. I arrived early at Scottsdale Stadium, where the Royals were challenging the Giants in one of the final pre-season tilts before regular season play began. I immediately spotted George by the batting cage and patiently waited for him to finish instructing the remaining members of the Royals' spring roster. As he was approaching the dugout, I shouted his name, but he did not appear to hear me. I frantically remembered to call out, "Bobby mentioned me!" George immediately changed course and allowed me to snap off a few shots of him holding the ball.

Later, Bobby himself arrived at the game and invited me to join him. He was accompanied by a nine-year veteran of the National Football League, Jim Obradovich. The tight end, who played for the Giants, 49ers, and Buccaneers, was a childhood friend of the Brett boys. While both Bobby and Obradovich were kind and gracious hosts, I did not participate in the conversation that day as much as I observed it. There was an ease between these two men of sport who had known each other from their youngest days. I simply enjoyed the game from the vantage of a fan in the front row, soaking up the nourishing Arizona sun in the middle of what was, back at home, a frozen March. Sadly for Giants fans, the most memorable moment of that preseason tilt was when a liner ricocheted off of Giants ace Madison Bumgarner, fracturing his left hand and causing him to miss the first two months of the 2018 season.

Trevor Hoffman was appearing at a show in Chantilly, Virginia, sponsored by Steiner Sports. I had just returned from my trip to Arizona to photograph Brett and wasn't able to get away again so quickly, so I called Steiner and spoke to Justin Petrie. My initial contact with Steiner, Brendan Herlihy, was no longer with the company, so I had to convince Petrie that the project and my request were genuine. Thankfully, he agreed to take the picture for me.

I brought the ball to the Steiner offices in New Rochelle and left it with them. Although the Mark Bell experiment had been a success, it still filled me with no small amount of anxiety to leave the ball with yet another person. Steiner is one of the most reputable companies out there, so my logical mind knew it was safe. But this close to the end, logic gave way to paranoia often in the week Petrie had the ball. I had nothing to fear. He sent me the picture via email the day after he took it and told me I could swing by the office to pick the ball up anytime. I still remember the protracted exhale.

The final three living Hall of Famers were photographed during Induction Weekend, 2018. After getting Jack Morris, Alan Trammell, and Trevor Hoffman, I still needed the remaining members of the Class of 2018, Jim Thome, Vladimir Guerrero, and Chipper Jones. I spent the majority of the long weekend walking around Cooperstown with eyes peeled, in a state of readiness that I admit to no longer enjoying. When the project began, there was a thrill that came from the fact that at any possible moment, I could bump into a Hall of Famer I still needed.

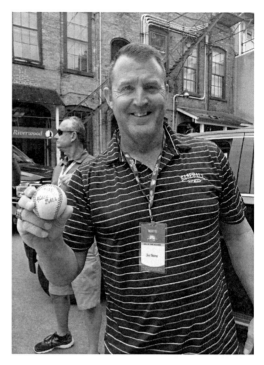

Like Alan Trammell, Jim Thome has long been considered a kind soul, and his encouragement of the quest was much appreciated.

Trevor Hoffman image courtesy of Justin Petrie.

After the warmth of Thome, the cool chill exuded by Guerrero was palpable.

That had become much less likely. The ones I still needed weren't going to be found just hanging out on Main Street. Instead of a treasure hunter, I had started to feel like a stalker.

I had no success the first few days, so I went to the roundtable discussion at Doubleday Field on Monday morning, where the year before I had been able to photograph Bud Selig and Jeff Bagwell. This year, however, security dropped off the inductees in a fenced-off section of Doubleday, instead of in the middle of the crowd as they had the previous year. None of the players came up to the stands after the interview was over, as Bagwell had done. The roundtable ended and the players were driven away, and I still hadn't photographed any of them.

I quickly ran across the street to the Tunnicliff, where all three of them were going to be signing. Anna jumped in line to buy the autograph tickets, just in case, and I went behind the building where I knew the players would be dropped off. The first car to arrive carried Jim Thome. When he got out of the vehicle, one of his assistants did what he could to rush Thome through the few of us who had made our way to the back, but I kept pace and gave my pitch. Thome stopped and took the ball. When he heard that I intended to donate the finished product to the Hall of Fame, his eyes lit up and he gave me a warm smile, followed by a genuine, "That is an amazing thing you're doing, man. Congrats," before he was pushed in the building by his diligent handlers.

I ran around the front and canceled the ticket for Thome, but there had been no sign of Jones or Guerrero, so we pulled the trigger on those and waited in line with the crowd. It was there that I ran into Jackson and Mark Bell, who were once again on their annual autograph-seeking pilgrimage. Knowing that I didn't actually want the autographs that came with the tickets I paid for, Mark offered to pay for half of the Jones ticket if I took Jackson inside with me (they already had Guerrero). I readily agreed.

First call was for Guerrero. MAB had structured things differently this year, selling more "photo-only" tickets, so I had purchased one of them. When inside, I asked their official photographer if, instead of using the photo he was going to take, I was allowed to take a photo of my own. I explained the project and he agreed. I handed the ball to Guerrero, who gave a very small smile, as though the action were causing him a small measure of pain. I did not give him the story. There was a line of people, and I had already broken protocol by taking my own pic. I thanked him and made my way back outside to the Bells.

Eventually, we were called inside for Jones's autograph. As we were making our way through the line, I could not stop thinking that this was the last time I would be doing this. For eight years, I had waited in countless lines and dozens of backroom corners, hoping for an opportunity to cross another one off the list. This was it. One last line and I would be done. I want to say I felt relief, but I only felt anxiety. What if Jones signed Jackson's ball but refused to let me take the picture? It was always possible.

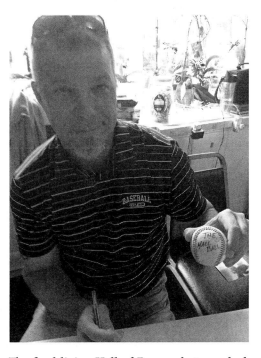

The final living Hall of Famer photographed, Chipper Jones.

The small oval to the left of the stitches is the interrupted "C" in Chipper Jones's signature.

We approached Jones, and Jackson immediately kicked his own natural adorableness into high gear. Jones happily signed his ball, and then Jackson stepped away to let me approach the man I personally witnessed demolish my Mets through the 1990s and early 2000s. I held the ball out to him, and before I could get the first word out of my mouth, he did the thing that I had always feared but had somehow managed to avoid. He started to sign it.

Seventy-six Hall of Famers held the ball before Chipper Jones did that day, and with almost each of them I made a point of beginning the rap with, "I am not looking for a signature today, sir," in an effort to keep them from signing it. Jones never gave me a chance. It is one of the great punchlines of the ball that it was the very last Hall of Famer who held it who managed to mark it. He had already penned a curled "C" before I, probably too forcefully, blurted out, "No!" He stopped and gave me a questioning stare, and I quickly explained the project and that I was just looking for a photo. With a quizzical look that I had become rather accustomed to, he held the ball up, I took the photo, and like that, I was done. The last living Hall of Famer had been photographed.

The ball was complete.

The White Whales, the Hall of Fame, and the Baseball Reliquary

An astute and knowledgeable reader will notice a slight flaw in my claim that the ball was complete. Chipper Jones marked the 317th member of the Hall I photographed, and with the election of the 2018 class the actual total of Hall of Famers stood at 323. So what of the other six? The answer lies in the moral quandary I mentioned earlier when discussing the picture of Doug Harvey.

I knew from the beginning that the process was going to take long enough that there would be Hall of Famers who were alive when I started who would pass before I could reach them. The very first one, Sparky Anderson, died just three months after I began. I decided very early on that I would not spend much time lamenting these as lost opportunities because of the inevitability. It was, so to speak, a risk of this particular quest. Including Harvey, 10 Hall of Famers passed away after the project began but before I could take their photos while they were alive: Anderson (died November 2010), Bob Feller (December 2010), Harmon Killebrew (May 2011), Dick Williams (July 2011), Gary Carter (February 2012), Lee MacPhail (November 2012), Earl Weaver and Stan Musial (who both died on January 19, 2013), Monte Irvin (January 2016) and Harvey (January 2018).

There was something different about the death of Harvey, however, that made me question how I wanted the project to end. When the other nine players died, I was still very much mid-process. There were still graves I needed to visit. However, by 2018

that portion of the project was complete. All that remained were living players.

The remaining six, whom I had begun to think of as my "White Whales," were: Ken Griffey, Jr., Sandy Koufax, Willie Mays, Willie McCovey, Nolan Ryan, and Tom Seaver. I had, over the years, attempted to reach out to these remaining players in multiple ways. I contacted both the Reds and the Mariners about Mr. Griffey, to no avail. I exchanged numerous emails with no fewer than four people in the San Francisco Giants organization to try and reach Messrs. Mays and McCovey. After numerous promises that my request would be forwarded to the correct people, I never received a final reply. I camped out at Astros Spring Training when I knew Mr. Ryan was in town, and I sent repeated emails to Astros rep Gene Dias. Again, no luck. I even received a very kind letter from Nancy Seaver explaining that her husband had essentially stopped making baseball-related appearances and was not interested in meeting with me.

The only one that I did not perhaps put my "all" into was Mr. Koufax. A friend of mine, who is influential in SABR, knew someone who ate lunch with Koufax, and he tried to connect us. Another SABR acquaintance, a writer who is friends with Koufax biographer Jane Leavy, reached out to see if she could be of assistance. Neither personal connection turned out to be fruitful. I even contacted the New York Mets because I knew of Koufax's close friendship with team owner Fred

Wilpon. For a time, you were more likely to find Koufax at the spring camp for the Mets than the Dodgers, so I explored that path. I never heard back. The one thing I did not do was contact the Dodgers. This was, in part, because I knew that Koufax's relationship with the Dodgers was strained at times. It was also because at that point in the process, it was very clear to me that reaching out to the teams was not useful. Not a single one of the photographs of The Hall Ball is a result of assistance from one of the clubs.

The initial inspiration for the project was to honor all the players in the Hall, both the famous and the more obscure, the still vibrant and the long deceased, in a way that had never been done before. I never saw my visits to the graves as anything but a respectful celebration of extraordinary lives. However, as I considered how fruitless my efforts to reach those final living players had been, I began to see a possible dark side to the project.

I could, quite simply, wait them out. Griffey is only three years older than I am, but of the remaining gentlemen, the youngest is Nolan Ryan, at 71. I was 46. Since I had no luck connecting with them while they were alive, I could wait for them to pass and visit their graves. But that thought, of waiting, filled me with horror. For the first time, the aspect of visiting the graves did not feel respectful. The idea of them being "White Whales" became an eerily accurate symbol to me. I had no interest in being Ahab, following my obsession past all bounds of sanity and decency.

I could have, of course, just kept plugging along, writing the Giants and Astros every few months to see if the right person finally read my email and I struck gold. But that could take years, and with each new year a fresh crop of Hall of Famers would be crowned while my list would continue to grow. As I mentioned, the trips to Cooperstown for Induction Weekend had started to make me feel like one of those troubled men I saw far too often, lurking outside of Nicoletta's Italian cafe on Main St. in hopes of getting Reggie Jackson to sign the 10 bats and 50

baseballs they brought with them. It was just no fun anymore. I needed the project to end or not only would I be Ahab, but also a contemporary Sisyphus, rolling a beat-up baseball up the same hill every July.

All of these swirling thoughts led to the decision that the class of 2018 would be the final one for The Hall Ball. After Induction, I would spend the next few months making a last-ditch effort to reach those remaining players. But no matter where I stood, I was going to donate the ball at the completion of the season, after the World Series but before the Veterans Committee announced their picks for the class of 2019 in December. I knew that this was not necessarily staying true to the initial vision of the ball, which included ALL the players. However, the relief that flooded through me when I accepted this conclusion was all the evidence I needed that I was making the right choice. Besides, 317 out of 323 is a 98.1 percent success rate, and there is not a single statistic in baseball in which 98.1 percent success would be seen as anything but Hall of Fame–worthy.

There was always the chance that once the Hall of Fame accepted the ball, they might be willing to take those final pictures. They had made it clear throughout the process that they could not help me because this was an independent project. But once the ball was in their possession, it would be the property of the Hall of Fame, independent no more. It was always possible that they would even continue to update it. In my fantasies, I saw them photographing the new classes when the members went on the celebratory tour of the Hall that each new inductee takes. Should they decide that they were going to leave the ball "as-is," well, I would be fine with that, too. All that mattered to me was the sure feeling that I had done my best and that the ball was going to be displayed so that others could appreciate what I had done.

I reached out to Sue MacKay, whom I had originally touched base with seven years earlier on the day I took the picture of Yogi Berra, my first living Hall of Famer. She thanked me and asked if I had any photos of the ball. I sent her a link to the website where all 317 photos could be viewed. A few days later I asked her if she wanted me to send a brief description of the project for her to give to the Hall's Acquisitions Committee. I never assumed someone had heard of the ball, and I wanted to be sure they each understood the depth and breadth of the project. She said that would be helpful, and she again asked me if I had any photos. I once again sent her the link to the site as well as attaching some of the more eye-catching pictures. She again thanked me and said she would get back to me.

It would be foolish to pretend that I did not spend every second of the day the committee was meeting awaiting to hear the ball's fate. I had lived with this idea for over eight years. I traveled thousands of miles, spent tens of thousands of dollars, enjoyed the 15 minutes that the *New York Times* and *CBS Evening News* provided, and told the story of the project to hundreds, if not thousands, of people I had met over the course of this quest. Some were ordinary fans, waiting in line at a baseball card show. Some were influential individuals like John Thorn and Hall of Fame President Jeff Idelson. The ball had taken me far and wide and opened many doors for me along the way. On that day, the conclusion of this epic quest was finally about to be written.

Ms. MacKay did not contact me that day. By late morning of the following day, I had waited long enough, so I wrote her. It took about 45 minutes to receive the response.

"Good morning Ralph, The Acquisitions Committee met yesterday afternoon and decided to graciously decline your kind donation offer of the Hall Ball."

There was more, but it wasn't until later that I actually read that part. I couldn't get past that first sentence.

They didn't want it.

Miraculously, this news did not devastate me. Sure, I had always had faith that they would accept the ball. I believed I had made them a very special gift, and who would possibly decline something that had been created with such love and devotion? However, I cannot say that I was surprised. As I had explained numerous times in the past, whenever anyone asked if the Hall of Fame was assisting me, the Hall had made it very clear throughout that this was my project, not theirs. It would be a lie to say that their ambivalence towards it was shocking. Disappointing? Without a doubt. But not shocking.

I wrote Ms. MacKay and asked if the failure to take the last six pictures was a determining factor. She informed me that played no role in their decision. Instead, she explained their reasoning thusly:

> The group felt that it is the Hall's duty to preserve history and not make history, which is why we did not participate in the process. As you mentioned, the photos are a key component to the project and it is too large of a story to tell on the exhibition floor. Your book is the perfect place to recount your travels with the accompanying photographs. It is your personal journey that readers can savor in print, and the book is a permanent way to document and convey your experience. We would be pleased to place the book in the Hall's permanent collection.

On the surface, her explanations all make a kind of sense. I could even choose to not scratch too deeply below that surface and take some pride in the idea that I "made history." That was, in a way, what I was attempting to do. Plus, they invited me to submit a copy of this very book you are reading to their permanent collection, which is an honor.

It was impossible, however, for me not to explore those reasons more deeply. The Hall hadn't made the ball, *I* had, so I was slightly confused about the logic of her first reason. The second one, that it is "too large a story," also struck me as odd. Ms. MacKay and I had, during that first visit in 2011, discussed that the project would best be viewed on a simple tablet device. Because of the enormity of it, it would be unthinkable that the Hall would print every photograph and take up museum wall space to display them. They don't have the real estate. But a single baseball, an iPad, and a sign explaining what it is don't seem to need more than a few square feet, at least to me.

The final reason, that of it being a personal story, also seemed less than entirely legitimate. On display at the Hall, for some time now, is a t-shirt created by Brian Bolten, a fan who visited all 30 stadiums in a single road trip in 2000. An impressive accomplishment, for sure, but one in which I see little difference in regards to the nature of the donation. A fan went on a quest and gave the Hall a memento. Beyond the fact that in my case the memento *was* the quest (and that I visited 10 times the number of locations), the personal nature of the story is a similar one.

I spent a week turning over all of this in my mind before I was even ready to tell anyone what had happened. When I did, I chose to do it via a blog, on the website. I let everyone know what occurred and asked for advice on how I should proceed. A few people encouraged me to keep trying to get the last six. They could not imagine stopping when I was this close. Most offered words of sympathy. Some voiced their own personal thoughts on the Hall of Fame, and how their refusal evidenced what kind of museum it wanted to be.

Perhaps that was what was at the heart of their decision and my miscalculation, that being the very nature of the museum itself. Yes, there was a similarity between the stadium t-shirt and The Hall Ball, but they are also vastly different. Bolten's stadium tour is the kind of adventure most fans could envision. It is a quest that has, frankly, been repeated ad nauseum. But who in their right mind would travel to over 200 cities, towns, hamlets, and "census-designated places" to visit a bunch of granite markers? Likely fewer than five people have ever made such a journey. It is, admittedly, an esoteric passion.

The Hall is designed around appealing to all that is heroic and legendary. Its members are the greatest of all those who ever took the field, and the images of them that fill the museum are of when they were young and strong. They are pictures from a time when they could climb walls, fly through the air,

run with the swiftness of thoroughbreds, throw with the strength and speed of a bullet, and hit a baseball farther than any other humans alive. In the pictures for The Hall Ball those same men are largely either bent with age or reduced to dust. My project likely would not make people think of a time when they themselves were children, but instead of certain inevitabilities that face us all. To me, that is a beautiful thing. If I didn't think so, I wouldn't have created it in the first place. I can see now, though, how it did not fit with the nostalgic glow with which the Hall imbues the artifacts in the museum.

As if all of my thoughts weren't enough of a jumble, Willie McCovey died two weeks after the Hall of Fame's rejection of the project. McCovey had been battling multiple ongoing health issues, including the lasting effects from a 2014 infection so severe that doctors had to restart his heart three times. Stunned that the list of living players was suddenly reduced to five, I did not know if I should take McCovey's death as a sign that I had made the right choice in ending the project, or if I should push on a little longer. I ultimately recalled the sensation of relief at the thought of being finished and decided to stick with that feeling.

Another recurring idea, from the folks who shared their thoughts as to the ball's future, was that perhaps it could find a different home. Predictably, it was largely my historian friends who expressed this idea. I had already considered that, but I was skeptical that another museum would want it. It was crafted with a very singular host in mind, and I believed that any other museum would consider it an imperfect fit.

I began to do some digging, just to see what was out there. My first stop was to the website of The Baseball Reliquary. I had been following their quirky posts on Facebook for some time, and I was always struck by how unlike the Hall of Fame they seemed to be. Founded by Terry Cannon in 1996, and funded in part by the Los Angeles County Arts Commission, the Reliquary is currently housed at Whittier College in Pasadena, California. In addition to an extensive library and reading room, which they call their Institute of Baseball Studies, they also sponsor events and even have their own hall of fame, entitled the Shrine of the Eternals.

Unlike the Hall, which largely bases worthiness on statistical output, the Shrine is dedicated to those individuals who have had an impact on the game both inside and outside the lines. Shrine members include World War II spy and 1920s and 30s backup catcher, Moe Berg; Dr. Frank Jobe, the creator of the now ubiquitous "Tommy John" surgery; Dummy Hoy, a player mentioned previously in these pages whose stats could actually qualify him for the Hall, a remarkable feat considering he was deaf for the entirety of his professional career; and Ila Borders, a woman whose list of gender stereotype–defying baseball firsts is worthy of a book in and of itself. 2001 inductee Jim Bouton referred to the Shrine of Eternals as "the people's Hall of Fame."

They also have a collection of odd artifacts, for sure. That is because, as their website points out, their mission is to foster "an appreciation of American art and culture through the context of baseball history and to exploring the national pastime's unparalleled creative possibilities." When creative possibilities are explored, you end up with things like the hair curlers worn by Dock Ellis, an athletic supporter worn by 3'7" Eddie Gaedel in his lone major league at-bat, and a half-eaten hot dog that was partially consumed by Babe Ruth. The more I learned about their collections, the more I realized that despite the ball being inspired by the Hall, the Reliquary was actually a perfect fit for my creation.

I reached out to Cannon via Facebook. Although we had been social media "friends" for some time, I had never spoken with him. I sent him a message, introducing myself and asking if he had ever heard of The Hall Ball. This is the response I received:

> Hi, Ralph, yes I am quite familiar with The Hall Ball, and was very surprised that the HOF declined to accept it as part of its permanent collection. Down the road, if you get to a point where you might consider another venue as a possible repository for The Hall Ball, please consider the Baseball Reliquary, and its sister organization the Institute for Baseball Studies at Whittier College, as a possibility. Although we are nearly 3,000 miles from Cooperstown, our organization's grassroots dedication to, and passion for, baseball match the nature of your project very nicely. And no matter what you decide to do in the future, I would like to discuss the possibility of your loaning the ball to the Reliquary for a major exhibition we are planning next July in Pasadena, to accompany our 21st annual Shrine of the Eternals Induction Day. The exhibition will celebrate the Art of the Baseball, and will feature baseballs that have been autographed, altered, handpainted, etc. I'd love to feature The Hall Ball as a centerpiece of the exhibition, with accompanying text and photos describing the history of the project. Let me know what you think.

Just like that, The Hall Ball had a home.

I cannot describe the rush of emotions that overcame me on receiving this message. I had reached out to Cannon to make a pitch for the Reliquary to take the ball and instead, he pitched me. He actually wanted it. And if I chose to give it to him, it would be housed with a number of other unusual examples of baseball history. My little misfit toy had found the island where it could comfortably live with the other misfits, and it was on my very first post–Hall attempt to find it a home.

It shouldn't have mattered to me, I know. I did not need proof that the project was worthy of people's attention. I already had that. But it was a hard blow when the Hall rejected it, and I spent days wondering if the whole thing had just been a foolish enterprise. Cannon's message, so effusively enthusiastic about the ball and his desire to make it part of his collection, was exactly the salve I needed. The July exhibition also gave me an opportunity to be on the West Coast, where I would be able to take a day to make the long drive to Colma. There I would visit Cypress Lawn Memorial Park and the modest grave of Willie McCovey, making him the last photo of the project.

The pictured version of McCovey's grave was a temporary marker that was still in place when I visited him in July 2019. A permanent one was installed two months later, in September.

The Reliquary also gave me a worthy ending to this book. You see, it's not just the ball that I am completing, after eight years of travel and toil. It's also this work you hold in your hands. For almost as long as there has been a Hall Ball, there has been the idea of writing about the adventure. The stories took many forms, and the version you are finishing right now is the final incarnation of what was a vastly different book back at the beginning. It is not an exaggeration to say that I am almost as proud of it as I am of the ball.

I hope you have enjoyed the story. I also hope you have learned a few things along the way. I know I did. That, more than anything, may be the greatest gift of this journey. When it began, I was interested in the history of baseball. Now, it's what I want to do with my life. I will always love the theater. It is too formative in who I am for me to completely escape it, but the adventure that was this ball and this book created something new in me. It sparked a fire, and now my free hours are filled with learning the stories of those individuals, famous and obscure, whose lives tell the story of our great game.

It began with a weathered, water-soaked baseball fished from Willow Brook on a warm summer afternoon. It led me to the four corners of America and beyond. It led me to a whole new future.

I hope your dreams lead you to yours.

A Eulogy: April 17, 2017

The following is the text of the speech I gave to the Friends of Alexander Cartwright when they invited me to discuss The Hall Ball at their annual celebration honoring Cartwright on the anniversary of his birth. I include it here because when I wrote it, I was very much thinking of it as a eulogy for the project. It is, if I may say so myself, a perfect summation of what the experience has meant to me.

*   *   *

When I decided to take a photograph of a single baseball with every member of the Baseball Hall of Fame, living and deceased, I could not have possibly imagined this moment. Here I am, standing in paradise, with a group of people listening to me tell the story of what brought me to this place, on this day of celebration, while those people who love me most stand close by. I just thought it would be a fun thing to collect. I had no idea that this project was going to change my life in such a fundamental way.

I loved baseball as a kid. I played Little League. I collected baseball cards. I grew up in upstate New York, so I was a Yankees fan, like my father, until 1984. Then two things happened. The Mets started to get good and I hit puberty which, to me, meant rebelling against everything my father stood for. I remained a fanatic until 1994, when I graduated from college to pursue a career in theater and, simultaneously, the infamous players' strike happened. I stopped paying attention to the old game.

I moved to the city in 1998, and I started working for Calvin Klein, as the manager of their mail room. I was still having trouble get-ting that theater career to take off. One day, the owner of the company gave me tickets to his box at Yankee Stadium. That warm July night, the day after David Cone had pitched a perfect game on Yogi Berra Day, I sat only 10 feet from the field. The smell of the grass, a luxury in New York City, was intoxicating. The sheer sense memory thunderbolt of all those hours spent at Shea Stadium, and the fields of the Hudson Valley Little League, was a transformative experience. My love of the game was rekindled.

That very night I started studying the history of baseball. I watched Ken Burns' epic documentary on constant repeat. I read every book the New York Public Library had to offer. By the summer of 2010, I considered myself to have a pretty solid background in the story of baseball and how it came to be the sport it is today. For example, I knew that it was not invented by Abner Doubleday and that we owed a much greater debt to Alexander Cartwright's New York Knickerbockers.

But what The Hall Ball has taught me is that the amount of what I knew about baseball at that point in my life was the barest drop in the great depths of its rich history. So much of what we think we know about baseball is myth and legend. The true story of how it came to be the game we play today is unknown to most people.

This summer the Hall of Fame will induct five more members, bringing the current total to 317. Even the most ardent fan would be hard-pressed to name 100 of them. And the Hall is just a microcosm. A total of 18,951 men have played major league baseball as of this writing, and more join the list every day. Countless thousands more men and women have played professional ball in the Negro Leagues, the All-American Girls Professional Baseball League, and in Japan, Venezuela, Cuba, and over 20 nations across the globe.

There is so much out there to know. How does one person begin to even comprehend the vast sum of it all? For me, that answer was The Hall Ball. I didn't know that in August 2010. But that is what it has become. A crash course in the history of baseball.

Since then I have become a member of SABR, the Society for American Baseball Research, and been active in its efforts. I have become the head of a committee called the 19th Century Baseball Grave Marker Project, dedicated to placing stones at the previously unmarked graves of the game's pioneers. We placed our first last fall, for James Whyte Davis, who joined the Knickerbockers the year after Alexander Cartwright left to seek his fortunes West.

I have had the honor of holding the game books of the Knickerbockers, 170-year-old documents, in my hands. As a contributor to the Protoball Database, a web-based effort to chronicle every instance of the game before it became a professional enterprise in 1870, I have been transposing the Knick game books into digital format so that future historians can understand how the game evolved from a loose collection of guidelines to the 172-page document that constitutes the current Major League Baseball Rulebook.

I have befriended some of the greatest historians in the game, whose stores of knowledge keep the true story of our game's history alive. They are the keepers of truth, and I consider it an honor that I get to learn at their sides, just as I consider it an honor that I am standing before you today.

And I owe it all to The Hall Ball.

The journey that brought me here started in Staten Island, just six miles from my home at the time, with a visit to the then-unmarked grave of Sol White, the great Negro League player, manager, executive and historian.

Since then I have traveled over 20,000 miles. I have been to over 30 states and almost 200 cities and towns. I went to Puerto Rico and Cuba. I am on this very day standing in a place that has always had the unreal quality of nirvana to me.

I have stood by the graves of giants, like Babe Ruth and Lou Gehrig, and seen first-hand how a stone can tell the story of a man. Ruth's marker is gigantic, as tall as two men, almost as wide, a stone carving of Jesus with his arms wrapped around a little boy in a baseball uniform adorning the front. Gehrig's is in a different cemetery that shares a border with the one where Ruth lies for all eternity. His stone is modest, discreet, adorned with only a small copper door within which the ashes of the Iron Horse and his beloved wife Eleanor are placed. The gravestones, in their stark difference, are perfect symbols of these men.

I have paid homage to some of the lesser-known names of the game. Men like Jack Chesbro, whose league-leading 41 wins in 1904 remains a record to this day, but whose story is rarely told today. His marker is not one of the finely carved geometric works like you see around you now, but instead is a giant boulder that looks as though it just rolled out of the Berkshire Mountains, the foothills of which serve as Chesbro's final resting place. Or men like Arky Vaughan, who was raised a country boy in Arkansas and then moved to the remotest part of northeastern California after his days of being one of the best run scorers of the 1930s and '40s were over. He moved there for the fishing, and that's where he died, just four years after he played his last game. He fell out of his fishing boat and drowned. Today, his grave is the most isolated of the Hall of Famers, located six hours from San Francisco to the south and six hours from Boise, Idaho, to the north.

I have visited the cemetery in Los Angeles where two of the game's most influential owners both lie. Walter O'Malley became a villain to the people of Brooklyn and a savior to the people of Los Angeles (and Hawaii) when he initiated the great migration west and brought the Dodgers to California. Buried just a few hundred yards away is Effa Manley, the sole woman in the Hall of Fame. Co-owner of the Newark Eagles, with her husband Abe, it was she that was the real driving force behind the team, a shining example of the fact that a woman can love the game with just as much passion as a man.

I've been to the cemetery in Baltimore which has the distinction of being the burial ground of the most Hall of Famers. Ned Hanlon, who led the National League incarnation of the Baltimore Orioles in the 1890s, and his three protégés, Joe Kelley, Wilber Robinson, and the legendary John McGraw, are buried in nearby plots of New Cathedral Cemetery. These four men, each raised in the northeast, formed connections amongst each other and the city they came to call home. Now, after lifetimes spent pursuing the craft of baseball, they lie there together, forever.

I have stood in places meant to symbolize those who chose not to be buried after they died. I went to Springfield, Illinois, to find the last remaining physical structure of the Peabody No. 59 coal mine, a shaft a tenth of the mile off the road in the middle of the woods. It was at that mine where Al Barlick started his career when he umpired his first game for the company team. I have stood on the beach of San Juan, Puerto Rico, where some of the wreckage of the plane carrying the legendary Roberto Clemente washed ashore after it crashed on New Year's Eve in 1972. I stood in front of the mound of Progressive Field in Cleveland where Early Wynn's ashes were spread, and I stood near the third base line of Wrigley Field where Ron Santo had his cremated remains forever interred within the Friendly Confines. I have gone to the cryonics facility in Scottsdale, Arizona, where, contrary to urban legend, the entire body of Ted Williams lies in a frozen state.

I have looked at enough graves to know that at this point in history, as the stars of the 1940s and '50s are quickly leaving this earth, the inscriptions on their stones are more likely to mention their military career than their baseball exploits. This is especially true if they starred in the Negro Leagues, and likely needed the assistance of the U.S. government to provide a stone after they passed.

I have seen the graves of two men who have come to symbolize the story of the Negro Leagues. Josh Gibson, who died penniless, intoxicated, and raving mad, has a simple, small stone which contains his name, the years of his birth and death and the words, "legendary baseball player." Meanwhile, in Kansas City, there is the mammoth three-tiered structure that is the marker for Gibson's sometimes battery mate, sometimes opponent, Satchel Paige. Paige lived to 76 years of age and, despite his spendthrift ways, made enough money from his time as the biggest draw in black baseball to die in comfort. He passed during a blackout in Kansas City, on June 8, 1982, the day my wife was born.

I have seen the final resting place of two men whom history has labeled the game's vilest racists, and discovered that there is always more to the story. When I visited Royston, Georgia, I saw a small town with a state-of-the-art medical system funded by a legacy that was left by the business-savvy Ty Cobb. I learned soon after, when I read Charles Leerhsen's brilliant book, *A Terrible Beauty*, that most of what I had been taught about Cobb was a lie. The legend of the racist, hateful Cobb has been corrected by historical research. But before that book, my journey had already shown me a man whose wisdom and generosity still provides college scholarships to the poor youth of his community to this day.

Similarly, I drove down a hidden, overgrown road, whose "no trespassing" sign and closed gate I ignored because my satellite map had shown me that Rogers Hornsby was at the end of it. Hornsby, too, was known for a hateful streak. His body lies in a small cemetery that is on family land in the small town of Hornsby Bend, Texas. Adjacent to it is a Mexican cemetery, land donated by the

Hornsby family to the local Mexican church to assist its poor, immigrant members with a place to put their loved ones. There is always more than one side to the story.

I've seen the cemetery in Chicago that contains two individuals whose influence and truly racist natures actually contributed to the prevention of black men playing major league baseball between 1887 and 1947. Cap Anson, one of baseball's first superstars, once refused to allow his team to play against any club that featured a black player on their roster. Kenesaw Mountain Landis, as baseball's first commissioner, had it within his power to end the "Gentlemen's Agreement" that barred blacks from the majors. Instead, he insisted there was no such conspiracy. It took his death before Jackie Robinson was allowed to set foot on a major league diamond. In a poignant irony, Oak Woods Cemetery, where they both lie, is currently almost entirely staffed by African Americans.

I have gone through the heavily Amish land of Peoli, Ohio, to find the legendary Cy Young, and I have stood 100 yards from where Lincoln delivered the Gettysburg Address to take a picture of the grave of the much lesser known Eddie Plank, in Pennsylvania. I have visited the grave of Old Hoss Radborn, in a cemetery in Bloomington, Illinois, where, in a bizarre twist of fate, the father of Abner Doubleday is also buried in an unmarked grave. I have visited Henry Chadwick in Brooklyn, whose grave resembles a baseball diamond, with stone bases marking the four corners of the plot.

I have visited Paul Waner in Bradenton, Florida, and Lloyd Waner in Oklahoma City. Harry Wright in Bala Cynwyd, Pennsylvania, and George Wright in Brookline, Massachusetts. Three-Finger Brown in Terre Haute, Indiana, Ray Brown in Dayton, Ohio, and Willard Brown in Houston, Texas. Eddie Collins in Weston, Massachusetts, and Jimmy Collins in Lackawanna, New York. Rube Foster in Blue Island, Illinois, and his half-brother Bill in Claiborne Co., Mississippi. Walter Johnson in Rockville, Maryland, Ban Johnson in Spencer, Indiana, and Judy Johnson in Wilmington, Delaware. King Kelly in Mattapan, Massachusetts, and George Kelly in Colma, California.

I've met living members, over 65 of them so far. I've met Bobby Doerr, who played his first game in 1937, 10 years before my own father was born. And I've met Greg Maddux, whose rookie card was part of my own collection, with a career that began at the exact moment my youthful love of the game ran its hottest. I've met tender souls like Ernie Banks and Yogi Berra who have, since I photographed them, gone on to the other side. I've met hard men like Bob Gibson and Johnny Bench, whose pictures for the project felt more like work than fun.

I have traveled to Cuba, a country that for my entire life was a forbidden land. There, I found a culture that embraces baseball with a single-minded fervor that America has not experienced since before World War II. I saw games in five provinces of the strong-hitting, weak-pitching Cuban *Series Nacional*, their version of the major leagues. I visited the Monument to Baseballists in Havana, where over 50 Cuban heroes lie. I drove three hours outside of Havana to visit the tiny town of Cruces, where I got to share a Buccanaro *cerveza* with Martín Dihigo, Jr., before we drove to his father's grave and played a game of catch by the body of the only man to be elected into the Baseball Halls of Fame of five different countries.

Which brings me to today. As exotic as Cuba was, it was a mere 1,300 miles from my home. Today, I stand in a place that is 5,000 miles from where I live. I heard lots of stories about Hawaii as a kid, because my upstate New York, Italian-American uncle fell in love with a Hawaiian woman. Their wedding was a luau. Everyone wore leis and at one point the groomsmen came out in grass skirts. Hawaii was a mythical place that I always swore I would see someday. Today is that day because of this baseball.

For a theater guy such as myself, there is tremendous beauty to Alexander Cartwright being the last grave I needed to visit to complete my project. It is the alpha and the omega. Cartwright is the firstborn member of the Hall of Fame. He remains, to this day, the first person in the Hall to have ever picked up a bat. Recent research has proven that Cartwright is not responsible for those things with which he is credited on his plaque in the Hall. As a historian, it would be irresponsible of me to ignore that. But, as most of you know, Cartwright was more than that. As a member of the Knickerbockers, he likely umpired the first game they ever played. And though he did not author the modern rules, he was a member of the 1848 rules committee. His civic contributions to the state of Hawaii have made him beloved in his adopted home.

And he has, since his election into the Hall of Fame in 1938, served as the sole reminder to those who view the game through the lens of the Hall, that there was a time before it became America's Pastime. A time when we were just putting the pieces together to make something different from cricket, and rounders, and "one cat, two cat," and town ball, and all the other bat and ball games that came before baseball came to be. We owe Cartwright

and his family a debt for keeping that door open, for encouraging new research that lets us continue to find the true story behind the creation of baseball.

And thus it is a fitting place that this part of The Hall Ball comes to an end. With the man who represents baseball's beginning. Because the story of baseball carries on. More men will be elected to the Hall, and I have no idea if the ball will continue to join them. The Hall Ball itself is such a tiny piece of the story of the game. But it's my piece, and I am honored to be able to share it with you today.

Fin.

Index

Numbers in *bold italics* indicate pages with illustrations